Weaving In the
Women

Weaving In the Women

Women

Transforming the High School English Curriculum

Liz Whaley & Liz Dodge

BOYNTON/COOK PUBLISHERS
HEINEMANN
Portsmouth, NH

Boynton/Cook Publishers, Inc.
A subsidiary of Reed Elsevier Inc.
361 Hanover Street
Portsmouth, NH 03801-3912
Offices and agents throughout the world

The authors and publisher wish to thank those who granted permission to reprint previously published material:

Page vii: "The Parable of the Cave or: In Praise of Watercolors" by Mary Gordon. In *The Writer on Her Work*. Published by W. W. Norton. Reprinted by permission of Sterling Lord Literistic, Inc. Copyright © 1989 by Mary Gordon.

Page 1: Excerpt from "Käthe Kollwitz" by Muriel Rukeyser, from *Out of Silence*, 1992. TriQuarterly Books, Evanston, IL. Copyright © William L. Rukeyser. Reprinted by permission.

Page 251: Excerpt from "To Be of Use" from *Circles on the Water* by Marge Piercy. Copyright © 1982 by Marge Piercy. Reprinted by permission of Alfred A. Knopf, Inc.

Every effort has been made to contact the copyright holders for permission to reprint borrowed material. We regret any oversights that may have occurred and would be happy to rectify them in future printings of this work.

Library of Congress Cataloging-in-Publication data
Whaley, Liz.
    Weaving in the women : transforming the high school English curriculum / by Liz Whaley and Liz Dodge.
        p.   cm.
    Includes bibliographical references and index.
    ISBN 0-86709-327-7
    1. American literature—Women authors—Study and teaching (Secondary)   2. English literature—Women authors—Study and teaching (Secondary)   3. Women and literature—Study and teaching (Secondary)   I. Dodge, Liz.   II. Title.
PS42.W48   1993
810'.71'273—dc20   93-17827
                                                            CIP

Designed by Jenny Jensen Greenleaf.
Cover: Tapestry, Chimu, Peru. Courtesy of Anni Albers.
Printed on acid-free paper in the United States of America.
97 96 95   EB   2 3 4 5 6 7 8 9

To our mothers
Helen Egbert Gates (1902–1992)
Louise Riblet Leyon
and
For our grandchildren: those here—
Joshua Jennings Whaley
Ethan Delevan Whaley
Sarah Ashley Eldredge
Thomas David Eldredge
—and those to come

Theodore Roethke said that women poets were "stamping a tiny foot against God." I have been told by male but not by female critics that my work was "exquisite," "lovely," "like a watercolor." They, of course, were painting in oils. They were doing the important work. Watercolors are cheap and plentiful; oils are costly: their base must be bought. And the idea is that oil paintings will endure. But what will they endure against? Fire? Flood? Bombs? Earthquake? Their endurance is another illusion: one more foolish bet against nature, or against natural vulnerabilities, one more scheme, like fallout shelters, one more gesture of illusory safety.

There are people in the world who derive no small pleasure from the game of "major" and "minor." They think that no major work can be painted in watercolors. They think, too, that Hemingway writing about boys in the woods is major; Mansfield writing about girls in the house is minor. Exquisite, they will hasten to insist, but minor.

MARY GORDON
"The Parable of the Cave or: In Praise of Watercolors"

Contents

Acknowledgments

We could not possibly acknowledge all the people who have inspired us over the years: family members, friends, mentors, teachers, colleagues, students. We wish, instead, to thank those who read the manuscript of this book: Cathryn Adamsky, Deborah B. Estaver, Mary Fosher, Susan D. Franzosa, and Doris Pailes.

We also thank our editor, Dawn Boyer, for her tireless enthusiasm and vigorous support.

Foreword

Weaving In the Women is very exciting, and I am honored to be in on the historic moment of introducing it to high school teachers who are hungry for inspired examples, resources, reassurance, and permission for the imagination to play. The book comes from two high school English teachers who consistently, and with tremendous success, gender balance their reading lists and teaching methods, so that both boys and girls become genuinely engaged in reading, writing, and speaking about their perceptions and experiences.

For many years, other teachers have asked Liz Whaley and Liz Dodge to write about their English classes. Their down-to-earth talks at seminars and conferences reveal that they are very effective as teachers, that they use a great deal of women's literature in high school classes, and that they teach students to lead discussions themselves. Their book is here at last. It is tight, spare, brisk, and practical. It is also compendious, wise, and, as the students say, "awesome."

The book allows us to follow Dodge and Whaley's processes of thought as they choose works to assign for all periods of English and American literature. They describe dozens of ways in which they create student-centered classrooms. They discuss their ways of devising grading that is consistent with student-centered learning. They describe a women's studies course which they have taught for years. And they include invaluable, brief annotations on literary works by women from many centuries which they have used with success in grades 9–12.

The authors are prodigious readers. They love to read literature in English, in all genres, from all periods. They have read thousands of works by women, and have chosen works for class with care. They do not simply find a piece of writing which "works" in class and use it over and over. They experiment continually with new texts, sequences, and assignments. As teachers, they model the ongoing intellectual and personal development which they encourage in students.

Nearly ten years ago, in a faculty development seminar, I heard an English teacher from a well-known New Hampshire private school ask Liz Whaley, teaching in a New Hampshire public school, for help in rethinking American Literature II. The first school's reading list included six authors, all white; Whaley's included forty-four authors, drawn from nearly all of the main U.S. ethnic groups. Two women were on one list, nineteen on the other. The two lists overlapped in the case of three authors: Cather, Hemingway, and Faulkner.

The students in the first class were disaffected. Whaley's students were eager to come to class. I remember sensing the intellectual rigor and challenge in the way she was teaching. The other class reminded me of traditional English classes of my own (mostly public school) education, in which we "discussed" a few long works very slowly, the whole class going over the same page at the same time, answering the teacher's "questions" until we figured out how the teacher wanted us to see the book, which was, I surmised, the point of English class. This book explains what these two gifted teachers do to get away from that familiar model.

Dodge and Whaley write that "teacher-centered learning" makes students dependent upon adults, in that it ignores students' percep-tions, and does not let them generate topics for discussion. They write, "We don't want students to ask 'What do you want?' We don't want them to spend their creative energies second-guessing us. We do want them to be interested in communicating clearly to us and their classmates because they know we are interested in knowing what they have to say."

Some educators say you cannot start where the students are, that is, take students seriously, unless they are "gifted," or privileged, or interested to begin with. But Whaley and Dodge do simply start where the students are, in a high school whose students say very familiar things. "Are we going to read all stupid books this year?" "Why are all the stories so sad?" "What's [this woman] complaining about?" "We don't want to read about pregnancy; none of us wants to think about that now" (while, in fact, there may be one pregnant girl in the class).

Dodge and Whaley did not wait until the society itself had raised its awareness and understood the need for women's literature in all students' education. They saw the damage done by womanless curricula and decided, with the members of their department, to give all of the students a feminist, gender-balanced, and multicultural English curriculum now. In doing so, they created the engaged, interested students other teachers yearn for. They have developed manifold ways of having students choose works, analyze, share, compare, testify, evaluate, make ideas their own, and generate knowledge. They have found "What students discover, they own and treasure."

Weaving In the Women is a pedagogical and bibliographical treasure trove of feminist scholarship and also a very friendly teachers' guidebook. Readers who are new to the idea of teaching women's literature may take away memorable quotes, an awareness of large annotated bibliographies, original ideas for assignments, and a sense of invitation and permission for teaching about women without apology or defensiveness. Those who are experienced in teaching about women's literature will be supported in what they already do, and will appreciate hundreds of further resources, lists of videos, units, and projects, and insights from the authors' years of experience. Teachers in university-based Schools of Education will find rich resources of nonsexist, nonracist teacher-training of a very practical kind: lists of works which appealed to students in a given class; examples of examination questions which students appreciated. Some readers may also wish to mine the book for resources for adult reading groups and classes, such as the always heavily subscribed night courses which Liz Whaley has taught for eleven years in Durham, New Hampshire, under the title "Women's Literature for the Community."

Weaving In the Women is a great antidote to professional development in-service sessions which imply that high school English teachers are to blame for students' disengagement from reading and writing, or for sexism and racism in schools. The book is not about teachers-as-problems. It is about how two seasoned scholar-teachers have co-created rigorous, meaningful schooling for all students. And the book is also about their pleasure in having given empowering opportunities to students: "At the end of courses, even at the end of units, students strike out on their own, at our invitation and with our blessing, swimming away. Some flounder, out of shape or lazy, when the going gets a little deep; others paddle around shallows, not yet ready or willing to move out; and some 'swim off with sure strokes almost out of sight.' Part of the great fun of watching the strong swimmers is knowing what they sometimes do not yet know: they're using their own power, power they've accumulated for themselves because they've welcomed opportunity just about every time it has come along."

Dodge and Whaley do not ask other teachers to do what they do. They simply describe, in an informal, direct way what they have done. Their style is usually simple and straightforward: "You may be wondering why we're going into this detail about the way we conduct the class; it's because we want to show how we build up to having student groups conduct the class entirely on their own at the end of the semester." They are blunt about some of the authors they don't select. "We don't get involved with Margaret Fuller. She doesn't appeal to our high school students. Though her ideas are feminist, her writing is dull and labored. We tell students about her, however, and some of them enjoy reading a biography of her, for her life was colorful." They are candid on pitfalls of group work: "Students can come to class unprepared and jump into discussion after it gets going and they find an opening, especially if no writing has been assigned."

I find the book both unassuming and dazzling, as an example of feminist scholarship, pedagogy, and educational theory. I wish my own daughters, nieces, nephews, and I had had such teaching.

Dodge and Whaley want to make things better for the next generation; they have already done so, but knowing that these things take time and work, they dedicate the book to their grandchildren—"those here and those to come."

Peggy McIntosh
Associate Director, Wellesley College Center for Research on Women

Introduction
Why This Book?

Fiction, under our androcentric culture, has not given any true picture of woman's life, very little of human life, and a disproportioned section of man's life.

CHARLOTTE PERKINS GILMAN
"Masculine Literature"

What would happen if one woman told the truth
about her life?
The world would split open

MURIEL RUKEYSER
"Käthe Kollwitz"

Many of us in secondary school English education have been working in our own ways, often in isolated positions, to make the curriculum and the classroom more inclusive. Some of us have recognized the need for both boys and girls to be made aware of literature by female authors (Anglo-European American, African American, Latina, Asian American, and Native American) and have begun to implement changes. This book is for those of us who want more nuts-and-bolts material, strategies, and suggestions to help us continue to do what we have already started doing.

This book is also for those interested in, but not yet engaged in, designing an inclusive high school English program. To achieve that goal, we believe that not only must the canon be revised, but also the classroom must be transformed to insure that all voices are heard.

In addition, this book is for those who can't redesign their entire English program, but who are looking for ways to be more feminist in what they're doing so that they can teach the available books and anthologies from a feminist perspective.

What do we mean by feminist? by feminism? Here is our definition: Feminists believe that social, economic, and cultural barriers exist for women. Further, feminists work in both the public and the private sphere to break down those barriers. Finally, feminists look over their shoulders to see what they can do for the young people, especially the young women, coming after them.

We recognize and accept that many of us teach in very traditional schools with firmly entrenched tracking systems that include courses such as English 9, 10, 11, and 12. In many of our schools the curriculum is well established, with few if any electives. Nevertheless, we believe that all English teachers can and should work toward including more literature by and about women and toward a more feminist approach to teaching, empowering both young women and young men and opening up English to something more exciting and more interesting, ultimately leading students to take charge of their own learning.

Moreover, we believe that these concerns should extend to social studies teachers, and math and science educators, and others as well; and that, in the twenty-first century, education will have to become much more inclusive and multicultural. We think, therefore, that teachers in disciplines other than English will find helpful materials and ideas in this book.

We provide rationales and underlying assumptions, examples of revised curriculum units, specific ways to restructure classrooms, and at the end of every chapter appropriate lists of books, some annotated. These lists include works for use in classrooms and resource books for teachers. The lists are not exhaustive; they consist of works we know about and have used; they are places to begin, suggestions.

We do not seek to preach to the unconverted or dictate to the uninitiated. We are just two teachers who want to share our experiences in high school classrooms, telling our story, describing the activities we've tried (not all have worked), and reporting on some of the female authors we've included. We know that many of you read the same journals we do—*English Journal, Educational Leadership, Phi Delta Kappan, Feminist Studies*—and know about the work of such writers as Dale Spender, Carol Gilligan, and Elaine Showalter. We are not going to cite the research and enumerate all the scholars who have expounded the theory and provided the statistical studies that authenticate work in gender-balanced curricula and classrooms. That would be another book (and someone should write it). Our book reflects our experience with these materials. Our hope is that this book will contribute to the dialogue among high school teachers.

Where we teach, English courses consist primarily of untracked electives, without AP or honors classes. The department's rationale for electives includes its commitment to the school district's philosophy of individualized instruction: meeting the needs, talents, and interests of all students in any classroom through a variety of learning and evaluation activities. (We and our colleagues spend whole days discussing this notion of individualized instruction; what you have here is an oversimplification.) All students take a required year-long course their ninth-grade year and a required semester course, "Writing Workshop," sometime before they graduate; both are heterogeneously grouped. (Alternative courses and pathways exist for some students.) All of the other courses are semester electives. Although these electives are not tracked, they are designed to meet various skill and interest levels, including short reading and writing assignments, practical language skills, genres, and longer assignments. Students pass along their impressions and judgments so that over time courses earn and lose reputations for such things as their difficulty or usefulness after graduation. English teachers must approve students' selections, partly as a way to discuss the students' future plans, needs, and expectations for the courses they've chosen. Any student may take almost any course (though a few have prerequisites, such as a certain grade in Writing Workshop or a portfolio of original work for admission to Advanced Writing); almost every class has a wide range of students, from grades 10 through 12, from all levels of ability, and from the disaffected to the highly motivated.

Chapters 3, 10, and 11 deal with these widely heterogeneous classes. Chapters 4 through 9 deal with American and English literature courses, where students tend to be more ambitious and are usually planning to attend four-year colleges. Teachers are up-front about the fast pace and lengthy reading and writing assignments, but any student may take these courses. In addition, the school offers a seminar in literature for second semester seniors who have taken any two semesters of American and/or English literature and earned a grade of B+ or better in all English courses. It is an opportunity for them to fill in the gaps in their reading: they design the course, deciding what to read and write. Even though officially the curriculum is untracked, in practice, a few courses are less heterogeneous than others. Heterogeneity can work; self-selection may narrow the range in some courses; electives increase student motivation. All these factors set up an expectation for a variety of points of view in any one classroom.

Transforming our curriculum and pedagogy isn't easy. Those of us who are poking and prodding ourselves and our school systems know we measure our progress inch by inch. For example, three years after attending a summer institute on women in nineteenth-century America that modeled student-centered pedagogy, and a year or so after participating in our day-long workshop for secondary English teachers on bringing women into the curriculum and making pedagogical changes, a friend felt that she was ready to restructure her classroom. At the beginning of the fourth quarter, she moved her ninth graders into a circle and implemented a student-centered pedagogy. Much to her delight, the change produced results: her students remembered most of what they had learned that quarter for the final exam. (They did not remember much from the earlier quarters, nor had previous classes.) Almost two school years had elapsed before she was ready for these changes. We move at our own pace. Change may come slowly; that's okay.

Now for our stories.

I, Liz Whaley, graduated from Lexington High School in Massachusetts in the late 1940s at the top of my class, a very competitive young woman. I had won all sorts of prizes in English in whatever competitions in writing, reading, and even speaking that were available. (Now part of me decries competition and pushes for cooperative and collaborative learning as well as for less competition in sports. But that's another story.) I went on to a four-year prestigious woman's college where I studied with some wonderful female—as well as male—professors. I did not question the canon. I did not notice that I read very few works by women; I did not notice that women had not filled places of power around the world throughout history and that they still didn't. My parents had encouraged me and told me I could do anything I put my mind to.

When I graduated from Wellesley College in 1952, the last thing I wanted to do was teach. I had no interest in graduate school. I wanted to be on my own in New York City, and so I was, as an editorial secretary supporting herself while dreaming of writing the Great American Novel, and as an editorial assistant in a literary agency and later in two publishing houses. But I didn't get promoted to editor. When such a position opened up, a man was hired. At the time, I felt that my nonpromotion was due to my incompetence. Not until twenty-five years later, in the late 1970s, after eight or nine years of high school teaching did I look back and realize how I had been discriminated against professionally because I was a woman.

I didn't become a high school English teacher until I was thirty-eight. By then my children were in elementary school, I needed full-time work for financial reasons, and I thought I could be of use to the world as an educator. I had been a lifelong reader; I felt I should put my knowledge and skills to use. And so while completing my M.A. at the University of New Hampshire, I started teaching at a small public academy in Northwood, New Hampshire, where my husband and I were both the English department and the library staff. We had the autonomy to design some wonderful minicourses—everything from Mystery and Suspense and Literature of Abnormal Psychology to Black Literature and Science Fiction and Fantasy. I wasn't a feminist then, but I remember teaching Shirley Chisholm's

Unbought and Unbossed in an autobiography/biography course and my students writing to Chisholm inviting her to speak at our graduation (she couldn't make it, but wrote us a gracious note in declining).

Before coming to Oyster River High School in Durham, New Hampshire, I spent a year at Old Orchard Beach, Maine, where I taught four sections of junior English and one ninth-grade section. My principal, who had been the junior English teacher for many years, insisted I use a certain American literature anthology, but the selections from authors like Poe, Emerson, and Thoreau were simply too difficult for the two sections of General English 11 I had. At one point, I threw the book aside and concentrated on our class newspaper, the *Whaley Daily*. We had fun, and I acquainted the students with some politics in the process. For example, when Karen Silkwood's death in an auto accident made the front page of *The New York Times*, we followed the story, which became increasingly buried by the press.[1]

A turning point came in the late 1970s. Although reading Betty Friedan's *The Feminine Mystique* in 1963 and participating in civil rights demonstrations and protests against the Vietnam War in the late 1960s and early 1970s had heightened my consciousness, it wasn't until an English teachers' conference in 1977 in Hartford, Connecticut, that I took a giant step toward feminist teaching. There, at a workshop on women's literature, I walked into the room and heard a medley of music, everything from "A Pretty Girl Is Like a Melody" to "The Girl That I Marry" to "Paper Doll." When you hear songs like that one right after another and realize that the message to young women is be pretty, be sweet, be pink and white, be submissive and you will get your man—when you realize that, you're galvanized into action. At least I was. I read more and more, attended more workshops and launched my own high school women's literature course in the spring semester of 1978.

---

[1]A worker at the Kerr McGee plant in Kansas, Karen Silkwood had uncovered violations of safety regulations regarding plutonium rods and was going to blow the whistle on the company. She had involved a reporter from *The New York Times*, but the night she was on her way to meet him her car was run off the road and she was killed.

As an educator of high school students, I realized I must become a feminist educator. I must make my students aware that women have been left out, not only out of the curriculum, but also out of the institutions of power. Women, who make up more than half the world's population, have been excluded. In the last twenty-five years, many books about women in the curriculum have been published. Many women's studies courses have been started at colleges and universities across the country. Writing by women from early times through the 1950s has been recovered, brought out in new editions, and introduced by feminist scholars.

Since 1978 I have taught a one-semester course in women's literature for high school juniors and seniors at Oyster River High School. Some years sufficient subscriptions allow me to have a section of the course each semester. I have used consciousness-raising essays and films, historical feminist papers, and literature by women. At the same time I have infused a feminist perspective into all my courses, from Short Story to Senior Seminar in Literature, from Popular Literature to American Literature I and II. I have insisted that the American "melting pot" is a misnomer; we must think instead of an American *tapestry,* and we must bring in all the diverse strands.

In the beginning when I added women writers to my courses, I encountered some resistance, often from boys: "How come I never heard of this woman writer? Is she really good?" More often I noticed a certain silent conspiracy among the males, a turning to each other and a rolling of the eyes that meant, "Here she goes again, dragging in another female author." Also, since I have been teaching Women's Literature, I have at times been called a boy-hater and a girl-lover. Though it is untrue, boys have been known to say, "You can't get an A with Whaley unless you're female." If you add women authors to the curriculum, if you make sure girls get to speak in class, you are perceived as treating males poorly. It's hard to shake these misperceptions, but I have learned to live with them. Along the way, however, the resistance to reading women authors has vanished. I hardly ever hear that questioned now.

I have changed the way I teach. I gave up desks in rows years ago. I sit in a circle with the students. I try to get them to take charge of their own learning. I try to get them to come up with the questions to ask about the literature we're studying. I want them to make connections between what we've read earlier and now. I want them to make connections with their own lives, between past and present, between what they've been told and what they have learned for themselves.

Liz Whaley has just told you her story. Mine, Liz Dodge's, begins in Wellesley, Massachusetts. Growing up, I was a tomboy. My two brothers remember me spending most of my time playing sports or climbing trees. For years I found boys and men more interesting than girls and women: they seemed to be doing all the important work and having all the adventures. I've seen nearly every John Wayne movie twice, some three times! My reading was all by and about boys and men: Zane Grey, Dostoevsky, Emerson, Winnie the Pooh, T. S. Eliot. But it's never too late. "The worm will turn," my father always said. In my late forties I discovered the significance, sorrow, struggles, and power in the lives of women.

My commitment to teaching began in college, where I studied philosophy and became convinced that education could be, next to the home, a strong force in helping young people recognize and develop their free will, the power of their reason, and the reach of their hearts. After earning a B.A. in English Literature in 1958 at the University of New Hampshire, I began teaching from behind a lectern to students behind their rectangular desks arranged in a hollow square around the room in imitation of my favorite (and best) high school English teacher's classroom. Every night the custodians would rearrange the desks in rows until I was able to break through their amazement that I wanted them in a rectangle. Would you believe I once called my students Miss and Mister, also in imitation of my favorite high school English teacher? The difference between the two of us was that I was hiding and controlling while he was not: he invited his students to think for themselves and direct the course of the discussion. For example, when I was a senior, his first assignment in English was for groups of students to present each book of Plato's *Republic* to the class, fielding the questions and making sense of the passages. I was assigned to Book 1; I haven't worked so hard since. I still hear his

"Come, people, come; think, people, think" after he had read us an article from *The Atlantic Monthly* or opened the discussion of some section of *Crime and Punishment*. Only in the last seven years have I fully understood his student-empowering pedagogy.

In my first eleven years of teaching I was very good at getting students to think about the literature and draw the same conclusions as mine. It was easy enough to control the questions and ask them in the right order to get to the key ideas. In no way was the literature supposed to cut into anyone's real life. My preparation consisted of formulating and ordering questions: What is significant about the setting? Analyze the main characters. What is the conflict? Who/what wins? What is the author's main point? All of these as if right answers existed. Then, the last question, if we had time: What do you think about the story? I thought students were to discover what I knew or believed about the literature. We trundled through all the texts in this fashion, and all the texts were by men.

I was a long time coming around to a student-centered, gender-balanced classroom. After a twelve-year hiatus (I had taught for seven years, six in public high schools and one for the University of New Hampshire Extension Program at Pease Air Force Base) during which my three children were born and the youngest had grown to the age of eight, I returned to teaching in 1978 at Oyster River High School and found Liz Whaley challenging me: "Why are you teaching just men? Just *A Separate Peace, Julius Caesar,* and *Lord of the Flies*? What about the women?" I didn't knuckle under right away, as my excellent education hadn't mentioned women on any grand scale: I remembered only the Brontës, George Eliot, and Emily Dickinson. Besides, I didn't know any works by and about women. But I listened to Liz. The lectern disappeared, I started calling students by their first names, I added *To Kill a Mockingbird, The Bride Price,* a short story by Mary Wilkins Freeman, another by Sarah Orne Jewett. When Liz went off on sabbatical in 1985, I worked very hard at finding and learning about women and minority authors to teach her American Literature II classes. Since I could not pretend to be an expert on these unfamiliar authors and because I had become determined to adopt Liz's techniques, I found ways for students to raise the questions, work in groups to teach their classmates, and write responses to works. The linchpin fell into place in 1987 when I attended a National Endowment for the Humanities summer institute on nineteenth-century women in American culture, where Liz taught. Not only did I discover more American women authors, but the institute modeled a rigorous student-centered pedagogy. My conversion was complete.

Now I sit comfortably in the circle, I tolerate the silences, I start off class with, "What did you make of the reading last night?" or "Any general reactions?" I have no idea where the comments will take us, but oddly enough, we end up looking closely at the text, discovering key ideas, and finding out about each others' lives. I listen and learn along with the students. In addition to reading and rereading the assigned material, my preparation consists of dreaming up a different way to divide students for small-group work, or formulating tasks and open-ended questions with which to set students to exploring what they know, or devising situations wherein students can learn from each other and still examine the text. I count the number of women in any unit to insure a balance; I count the number of nonestablishment authors, too. Sometimes I notice that the young women in the class have more to say about stories by or about women, but I don't feel guilty that the young men have hunkered down some on those days: the young women have been dropped into silence for years. And rarely does anyone complain about reading another story about a woman.

Over the years of reading works by women (many of them for an evening class Liz facilitates), I find that the stories of people not in power appeal to me. They touch my life over and over in interesting ways. Of course, C. P. Snow's "corridors of power," the demolition of monsters, and the issues of a free economy continue to fascinate me, but I find equally fascinating women's private stories: feisty females rebelling against the law and customary practices, or wives divided unhappily between personal ambitions and society's roles for them. I find I want to read about women, *people like me.*

Enough about us. What do we want from our students? We want them to do their homework in every sense of the word and then to question our authority or anyone else's about why one particular text should be studied at the expense of another. We want them to appreciate the rich diversity and complexity and excitement and color of the many different kinds of American literature from early times until now. And this extends to British literature, world literature, and whatever other literature they read in their courses.

And then we want them to go into their science and social studies and foreign language and music and art courses and say, "Where are the women?" "Why aren't you teaching me about the women?"

The ripples have expanded in our high school in the last thirteen years. We have an English department of six committed to multiculturalism, nonsexist language, and gender balance. We have a nonsexist language policy for all course titles, publications, and documents issued from our school district. Of course, these have to be monitored carefully; not everyone is totally committed.

Those of us who have felt for the past twenty years that it is high time curriculum be transformed to include the experiences, achievements, and perspectives of women have watched with dismay the erosion over the past ten years of advancements that have been made. It is as if the patriarchy has stepped in and put its big foot down, claiming that feminism was all right for a while, but enough is enough: now is the time to get back to the basics of the stalwarts and standards and standbys of the DWEM philosophy: works of Dead White European Males. Not to mention the DWAMs, which are even more important and rampant in most high school curricula— Dead White American Males, everyone from Hawthorne and Irving to Mark Twain and Longfellow and on to Crane, Frost, and Steinbeck. We object, we object strongly, not to teaching the works of these authors, but to the policy of teaching theirs to the exclusion of others'.

The patriarchy humored us for a while; feminist scholarship proliferated in a varied array of disciplines, from anthropology to zoology. Women's studies courses, and then women's studies minors and majors bloomed at many colleges and universities. Feminist bookstores, feminist quarterlies and journals and book reviews flourished. But still, women have little public power and, while we recognize and acknowledge the supportive men who work with us on these issues, many of the "old boys" aren't changing much.

Of course, we want our students to know about Shakespeare, Dickens, Whitman, and Ralph Ellison. But it is just as important that they learn about Mary Wollstonecraft, Jane Austen, Amy Lowell, and Toni Cade Bambara. And to think that Hemingway, Faulkner, and Fitzgerald are the only giants of the 1920s and 1930s is irresponsible. Katherine Anne Porter, Eudora Welty, and Anzia Yezierska are equally important. To teach the Harlem Renaissance with only Countee Cullen, Claude McKay, and Langston Hughes and leave out Gwendolyn Bennett, Zora Neale Hurston, and Helene Johnson would be to miss half the pattern.

We need to put the pressure on. We need to encourage a generation of new young teachers and people preparing to be teachers (not to mention all of us working hard right now to transform our courses) to take seriously this notion of multiculturalism and diversity, at least to the extent that women's lives and works are represented in what we teach. The authors of this book have much experience in workshops and conferences for teachers along the lines of curriculum transformation and feminist, student-centered pedagogy.[2] People often ask us if we have anything in writing besides all our handouts. So here, in book form, are our ideas and strategies. We want to share the wealth; we want the ripples to grow wider and wider. We want to weave the women into the tapestry.

Works Cited

CHISHOLM, SHIRLEY. 1970. *Unbought and Unbossed.* Boston: Houghton Mifflin.

FRIEDAN, BETTY. 1963. *The Feminine Mystique.* New York: Norton.

---

[2] By *feminist pedagogy* we mean student-centered pedagogy, but with a special awareness of the young women in the classroom to insure that they get equal time, that we respond to all students in the same way, and that we require from all students the same things.

Useful Works for Teachers

BROWN, LYN MIKEL, and CAROL GILLIGAN. 1992. *Meeting at the Crossroads: Women's Psychology and Girls' Development.* Cambridge, MA: Harvard University Press. A study of girls at the Laurel School, tracing the increasing loss of assertiveness as girls reach adolescence.

GILLIGAN, CAROL. 1982. *In a Different Voice: Psychological Theory and Women's Development.* Cambridge, MA: Harvard University Press. Groundbreaking book studying girls in terms of their moral development and in contrast to Kohlberg's study of boys. In this study girls are seen to have different concerns growing up—they are more cooperative and sharing rather than seeking justice and wanting to win.

GILLIGAN, CAROL, NONA P. LYONS, and TRUDY J. HANMER, eds. 1990. *Making Connections: The Relational Worlds of Adolescent Girls at Emma Willard School.* Cambridge, MA: Harvard University Press. Essays based on research done at an exclusive girls' private school, each beginning with a question arising out of the research. Again girls' voices are brought into the study of adolescence and questions about the meaning of self, relationship, and morality. The book shows that girls at puberty are in danger of being silenced—losing their voices and losing connection with others.

GILLIGAN, CAROL, JANIE VICTORIA WARD, and MILL MCLEAN TAYLOR, eds. 1988. *Mapping the Moral Domain: A Contribution of Women's Thinking to Psychological Theory and Education.* Cambridge, MA: Harvard University Press. An expansion of the theoretical base of *In a Different Voice.* In fourteen articles, the authors apply their research methods to a variety of situations in which "the contrasting voices of justice and care clarify different ways in which women and men speak about relationships and lend different meanings to connection, dependence, autonomy, responsibility, loyalty, peer pressure, and violence."

GILMAN, CHARLOTTE PERKINS. 1970. "Masculine Literature." In *The Man-Made World; or, Our Androcentric Culture.* New York: Source Book Press. An early discussion of sexism in literature.

SHOWALTER, ELAINE. 1985a. *The Female Malady: Women, Madness, and English Culture, 1830–1980.* New York: Pantheon. Shows how cultural ideas about proper feminine behavior have shaped the definition and treatment of female insanity.

———, ed. 1985b. *The New Feminist Criticism: Essays on Women, Literature and Theory.* New York: Pantheon. The title says it all.

———, ed. 1989a. *Speaking of Gender.* New York: Routledge. Important essays by both males and females, elucidating the use of gender theory in literary criticism and interpretation.

———, ed. 1989b. Revised Introduction. *These Modern Women: Autobiographical Essays from the Twenties.* New York: Feminist Press. These essays were originally published anonymously in 1926–27 by *The Nation. The Nation* sought to find out women's views on a variety of topics, such as men, marriage, children, and work, from women active in public and professional life. Showalter identifies the authors and examines their lives. She gives us firsthand accounts of feminism in the 1920s and its relevance to contemporary times. Very instructive and illuminating: the media in the 1990s, as they did in the 1920s, proclaim women to be of the "Post-Feminist Generation."

———. 1990. *Sexual Anarchy: Gender and Culture at the Fin de Siecle.* New York: Viking. Makes telling comparisons between sexual behavior and societal censorship of the 1880s and 1890s and the end of the twentieth century.

SPENDER, DALE. 1980. *Man-Made Language.* London: Pandora. Dale Spender is an Australian feminist living and working in London. In this book she argues that since much of women's historical oppression has been structured through patriarchal language, women need to expose the limitations of male meanings and declare their own so that they can move toward autonomy and self-determination. The chapters have many subheads, including "Constructing Women's Silence," "Women's Talk: The Legitimate Fear," and "The Politics of Naming." Eminently readable, as Spender always is, free from academic jargon and cant.

———. 1982. *Women of Ideas and What Men Have Done to Them: From Aphra Behn to Adrienne Rich.* London: Routledge. Writing in a lively, humorous style, never boring or overly pedantic, Spender shows how men have taken whatever ideas of women they found useful and systematically removed others so that women every fifty years or so have had to reinvent the wheel. Includes chronological list of 150 women Spender has retrieved; good bibliography, excellent index.

————. 1986. *Mothers of the Novel: 100 Good Women Writers Before Jane Austen.* London: Routledge. Spender discovered a rich tradition of women writers before Austen; this book identifies, retrieves, annotates, and analyzes the works of many unknown women, reinforcing Spender's thesis that men let these works disappear from print. Since this book was published, many of these novels are back in print.

————. 1989. *The Writing or the Sex?: Or Why You Don't Have to Read Women's Writing to Know It's No Good.* New York: Pergamon. In questioning differences between men's and women's writing, Spender argues that the differences are not so much in the writing as in the response of patriarchal publishers and critics to it. Since men have had primary control in establishing values about literature, they determined early on that male writers were more important. Spender advocates a literary criticism that allows women to determine the values, or at least some of them.

ONE

Why Study Women?

Where is it leading us, the procession of educated men?

VIRGINIA WOOLF
Three Guineas

Since the world has been run by men for at least the last two thousand years, naturally males have seemed the superior gender, and their achievements have taken precedence over those of females. White whales have been given more importance in literature than gardening or childbirth (Donovan 1982, p. 28—a variation of her point). Why? If we look at Peggy McIntosh's "Interactive Phases of Curricular Re-Vision" (1983), we see that while men have designed the laws and waged the wars we have come to think of as "history," women have woven the fabric of supportive life so the men could do these great things. And women have all along been doing their thing: being nurturing and compassionate, being peace-makers, conversation extenders, helpers, child rearers. But at the same time they have been thinkers, philosophers, readers, writers, critics, knowers. They had little access to public power or authority, few forums. They weren't in any positions of power to object in 1746, Dale Spender in "Disappearing Tricks" (1980) tells us, when Mr. Kirkby in England "invented his Eighty-Eight Grammatical Rules; Twenty-One stated that the male gender included much more than the female" (p. 166). She goes on to say that in 1553 few women objected when a Mr. Wilson argued

17

that it was more " 'natural' to place the man before the woman (as, for example, in male and female, husband and wife, brother and sister) . . . as he was writing for an almost exclusively male population of educated people" (p. 166). There were no women in Parliament in 1850 when an Act of Parliament was passed "in which man was legally made to stand for woman" (p. 166).

It has taken many, many years for women to get what Virginia Woolf said they would need in order to gain fame and stature as artists and writers: five hundred pounds a year and a room of their own. We need to study women because otherwise we see only half a picture of the human race. Peggy McIntosh[1] has worked a long time on curriculum transformation and has identified five interactive phases teachers often go through as they complete this transformation (she uses history as an example in naming the phases, but the phase theory can apply to all disciplines):

Phase 1: Womanless and All-White History.
Phase 2: Exceptional Women and Persons of Color in
    History.
Phase 3: Women and People of Color as Problems,
    Anomalies, Absences, or Victims in History.
Phase 4: Women's Lives and the Lives of People of Color *as*
    History.
Phase 5: History Redefined and Reconstructed to Include
    Us All.

In Phase 1 we note the absence of women in the various disciplines. Phase 2, including exceptional women, seems at first glance an improvement over Phase 1, but it identifies the famous and "great"

[1]Peggy McIntosh was Program Director for a series of four regional seminars for faculty development programs in women's studies for secondary school teachers from 1983 to 1987. Liz Whaley participated in the first of these year-long seminars. Since 1987, McIntosh has been Co-director of the National SEED Project on Inclusive Curriculum: Seeking Educational Equity and Diversity. This project has established over 250 teacher-led seminars on gender balance and multiculturalism in K-12 curricula and teaching methods. McIntosh was also a core team member responsible for researching and writing sections of the American Association of University Women's 1992 report, *How Schools Shortchange Girls.*

women only—Emily Dickinson and Willa Cather, for example. But, as McIntosh says, "there were all the other women . . . whose lives remain completely invisible to us. That's the trouble with Phase 2. . . . It conveys to the student the impression that women don't really exist unless they are exceptional by men's standards" (p. 8).

In Phase 3 the canon is challenged. McIntosh says, "We ask who defined greatness in literature, and who is best served by the definitions?" She also says:

> Phase 3 curriculum work involves getting angry at the fact that [women] have been seen only as an absence, an anomaly or a problem . . . rather than as part of the world, part of whatever people have chosen to value. There is anger at the way women have been treated throughout history. We are angry that instead of being seen as part of the norm, we have been seen, if at all, as a "problem" for the scholar, the society, or the world of the powerful. People doing scholarship in Women's Studies get particularly angry at the fact that the terms of academic discourse and of research are loaded in such a way that we are likely to come out looking like "losers" or looking like pathological cases. . . . Phase 3 work makes us angry that women are seen either as deprived or as exceptional. I think that the anger in Phase 3 work is absolutely vital to us. Disillusionment is also a feature of Phase 3 realizations, for many teachers. It is traumatically shocking to white women teachers in particular to realize that we were not only trained but were as teachers unwittingly training others to overlook, reject, exploit, disregard, or be at war with most people in the world. One feels hoodwinked and also sick at heart at having been such a vehicle for racism, misogyny, upper class power and militarism. (p. 10)

In Phase 4 women are studied on their own terms. According to McIntosh, "One studies American literature of the 19th century not by asking, 'Did the women write anything good?' but 'What did the women write?' One asks not 'What great work by a woman can I include in my reading list?' but 'How have women used the written word?' In Phase 4 one asks, 'How have women of color in many cultures told their stories?' not 'Is there any good third world literature?' " (p. 17).

Phase 3 is issues-oriented and negative; Phase 4 is plural, positive, and respectful of many kinds of being and knowing. Interaction between 2, 3, and 4 will eventually take us to Phase 5, in which curriculum (or knowledge) gets "redefined, reconstructed to include us all." In this phase, power may be shared across previous lines of sex, race, class, and culture. McIntosh thinks this transformation may take one hundred years.

Twenty to twenty-five years ago the elite Ivy League male colleges and universities started admitting women. Young women who previously had clamored to be accepted at Wellesley, Smith, Vassar, Bryn Mawr, and Mount Holyoke were now insisting on their right to attend Yale, Princeton, Harvard, Dartmouth, and Williams. The prevailing attitude seemed to be: Wow, isn't this wonderful for the women? Aren't they lucky? No one, or very few, asked the more important question: What can these young women do for the all-male bastions? Gradually over the last twenty years this second question has come to be recognized as equally important. Most of the all-male clubs have given way to equal membership, to admitting women. Alumni, of course, have not all gone along graciously with the changes. Upon hearing that Yale undergraduates were going to admit women to the august Skull and Bones Society, some older alumni had the locks changed in the middle of the night to bar entrance. Ultimately, the undergraduates prevailed. Young women have insisted on equal access, and the young men who value their friendship have supported them.

At Dartmouth College in 1982, ten years after women had been admitted, Mary Donovan published the provocative article "Why Study Women?" in the October issue of the *Dartmouth Alumni Magazine*. In it she told of a tenured male Dartmouth professor who had asked her a few years earlier what she was writing about—"other than *women*, that is?" Donovan went on to say that the word *women* was spoken with "such a hiss of condescension that the professor's meaning was unmistakable: Women are trivial, inconsequential, beside the point" (p. 27). Dale Spender (1982) has shown how many women through the ages have questioned the patriarchy and the male assumption of superiority and privilege, and she has also documented the consistent male habit of repressing publications by women or letting them quickly go out of print. She wrote:

> Fundamental to patriarchy is the invisibility of women, the unreal nature of women's experience, the absence of women as a force to be reckoned with. When women become visible, when they assert the validity of that experience and refuse to be intimidated, patriarchal values are under threat. When we know that for centuries women have been saying that men and their power are a problem, when we are able to share our knowledge of today and combine it with that of the past, when we construct our own alternative meanings and traditions, we are no longer invisible, unreal, nonexistent. And when we assert that the reason for women's absence is not women, but men, that it is not that women have not contributed, but that men have "doctored the records," reality undergoes a remarkable change. (p. 11)

The result of all this repression of women's works by men is that women have had constantly to get women into print and keep them there. Spender and others have worked diligently to bring into print the works of women writers from as far back as the sixteenth century and earlier—to see that they are not erased entirely. In *Mothers of the Novel* (1986), Spender lists a hundred novels published before Jane Austen's. About these books and the women writing them Spender says:

> That the eighteenth century women should have written at all is in itself a contradiction. For women who had no rights, no individual existence or identity, the very act of writing—particularly for a public audience—was in essence an assertion of individuality and autonomy, and often an act of defiance. To write was to be; it was to create and to exist. It was to construct and control a world view without interference from the "masters." No woman writer was oblivious to this; all of them had qualms about the propriety of being a woman and a writer, and almost all felt obliged to defend themselves against attack. Which is why so many of them apologise for their audacity and presumption. I think it is also why so many of them "reformed" the male characters in their novels. (p. 3)

21

Women have always written, but not necessarily in traditionally accepted ways. In some cases, reading works by women from earlier eras has meant studying their letters. And that is a fine and necessary idea whose time has definitely come. In this age of high technology, five-minute sound bites, two-minute attention spans, complete indifference to communication by mail, and overemphasis on telecommunication, we need to read the letters of, for example, George Eliot, Elizabeth Barrett Browning, Louisa May Alcott, Virginia Woolf. In those letters, students can discover some of the most astute thinking of the times. To be sure, these are women who also published traditional literature; we can read that, too. But in their letters we get the pulse of the time, their daily activities, history, and women's acknowledgment of the poor state of women's rights.

In addition to letters, many excellent journals by women have been retrieved and published in well-edited and well-introduced versions. We have "The Journal of Madam Knight" by Sarah Kemble Knight from the 1700s; *Mollie,* the journal of Mollie Dorsey Sanford from the 1800s in the West; and *The Journals of Louisa May Alcott.* The latter provides readers with a look into the soul of the woman who was forced to write popular novels such as *Little Women* and *Little Men* to support her family. In her journals we see how completely Alcott was attuned to the literary leaders of her day—Emerson, Thoreau, Hawthorne. And we can read her uncensored thoughts which were not meant for publication. She had left instructions that the journals be destroyed after her death; however, knowledgeable people recognized their importance to scholars and Alcott lovers. She began her diary, or journal, when she was eleven, and used it well. (High school students enjoy reading entries, especially from her earlier years.)

Just as we are beginning to have available wonderful writing, both fictional and autobiographical, by Asian American women (Maxine Hong Kingston, Amy Tan, Gish Jen, Cynthia Kadohata, Jung Chang), so too we have writing by immigrants: Anzia Yezierska's *Bread Givers* and "Children of Loneliness," for example—her autobiographical fictional works about growing up on the Lower East Side in the first two decades of this century. And we have Native Americans.

From reading Zitkala-Ša's "The School Days of an Indian Girl" students can learn firsthand what it was like for an Indian child of eight to be taken to a white school to become educated, only to be assimilated and have her dignity stripped away: she was made to wear immodest clothes, give up her comfortable moccasins, and have her hair shorn.

Another discovery shows that Mark Twain wasn't the only humorist of his day. Marietta Holley (1836–1926), who was often compared with Mark Twain, created a character named Samantha who wrestled with the social issues of the day, particularly ones pertaining to women. Jane Curry has edited a collection of Holley's writings, *Samantha Rastles the Woman Question*; this book is a natural for studying along with Twain. Some of the chapter titles are "On the Tuckerin' Nature of Pedestals," "On Looking to Nature for Women's 'Spear'," and "On Soothin', Clingin' and Cooin'."

In short, feminist scholars have found many earlier works by women, and today women's works are available. Let's use them.

In the midst of the controversy over "political correctness," which has become so widespread (thanks largely to the media), we feel that we must hold on to multiculturalism and pluralism more than ever. We need constantly to question traditional white male standards of excellence in writing and literature; for example, every summer we find ourselves asking if we should keep teaching William Bradford and William Byrd in American literature courses. Are not Anne Bradstreet and Mary Rowlandson just as important? Sure, we want to hold on to James Fenimore Cooper, Washington Irving, Edgar Allan Poe, Ralph Waldo Emerson, Henry David Thoreau, Nathaniel Hawthorne, Herman Melville, Samuel Clemens, and all the other regulars appearing in most high school American literature textbooks. How much richer this list becomes, however, when interlaced with Benjamin Banneker, Phillis Wheatley, Linda Brent (Harriet Jacobs), Frederick Douglass, Lydia Maria Child, Mary Wilkins Freeman, Sarah Orne Jewett, and Frances Ellen Watkins Harper!

A steady stream of books and articles against multiculturalism and feminism has been appearing lately—by Allan Bloom, E. D. Hirsch, and Dinesh D'Souza, to name a few. Others, like Daniel Kegan of

Yale, James David Barber of Duke, and Lynne Cheney, past Director of the National Endowment for the Humanities, misinterpret pluralism as the lowering of standards. The National Association of Scholars is implementing the ideas of Bloom & Co. It's become trendy to belittle diversity—to insist that the purveyors of multiculturalism and gender balance on college campuses are out to do away entirely with Western Civilization—in fact, with any Eurocentric—courses. This assertion is patently unfounded; no one has set out to do away with the likes of Plato and Dante. We have called for a greater inclusiveness, that is all. But the critics seem to think the only way to true liberal education is to emphasize Western thinkers exclusively. Of what are these people afraid? Are they truly believers in the sanctity of free inquiry at the university? If we do not read and study about the many peoples and cultures, including the women, of the world, past and present, how can we ever hope to get along with each other? In fact, a 1985 review of over a hundred research studies concluded, "Pupils who are exposed to sex-equitable materials are more likely than others to 1) have gender-balanced knowledge of people in society, 2) develop more flexible attitudes and more accurate sex-role knowledge, and 3) imitate role behaviors contained in the materials. . . . The evidence is strong in support of using these materials to improve the learning experiences of both females and males" (Scott and Schau 1985, p. 228).

We also need to redefine standards of artistic merit. What are these standards and who defined them? The criteria perhaps need to be changed. In our efforts to find women to include in the curriculum, we don't need to ask: Who were the best women writers in the 1700s? We need to ask instead: What were the women in the eighteenth century doing? What did they write? Then, as we retrieve more and more of those writings, we can pick and choose which ones are the best to teach our young people. Art historians have asked the same questions about what women were doing, and as a result, quilts, for instance, have come to be considered respectable parts of our art legacy.

In her essay "Why Study Women?" Mary Donovan says that her question

24

raises fundamental questions about the concept, purposes, and content of a liberal-arts education. . . . When you study women you are forced ultimately to re-examine all you have been taught and to recast in a fresh perspective age-old questions: What is truth? What is morality? What is progress? What is civilization? What does it mean to be human? Moreover, when you study women, you also end up asking the fundamental question Virginia Woolf posed in *Three Guineas:* "Where is it leading us, the procession of educated men?" (p. 31)

And so, on with the necessary canon reformation. Bring in the women. Weave them in. Here's to diversity!

Works Cited

ALCOTT, LOUISA MAY. 1989. *The Journals of Louisa May Alcott.* Eds. Joel Myerson, Daniel Shealy, and Madeleine B. Stern. Boston: Little, Brown.

AMERICAN ASSOCIATION OF UNIVERSITY WOMEN. 1992. *How Schools Short-change Girls.* Washington, DC: American Association of University Women Educational Foundation.

BLOOM, ALLAN. 1988. *The Closing of the American Mind.* New York: Simon & Schuster.

DONOVAN, MARY. 1982. "Why Study Women?" *Dartmouth Alumni Magazine* (October).

D'SOUZA, DINESH. 1991. *Illiberal Education: The Politics of Race and Sex on Campus.* New York: Free Press.

HIRSCH, E. D., JR. 1988. *Cultural Literacy: What Every American Needs to Know.* New York: Vintage.

HOLLEY, MARIETTA. 1983. *Samantha Rastles the Woman Question.* Ed. Jane Curry. Urbana: University of Illinois Press.

KNIGHT, SARAH KEMBLE. 1990. "The Journal of Madam Knight." In William L. Andrews, ed., *Journeys in New Worlds: Early American Women's Narratives.* Madison: University of Wisconsin Press.

McIntosh, Peggy. 1983. "Interactive Phases of Curricular Re-Vision: A Feminist Perspective." Working Paper no. 124. Wellesley, MA: Wellesley College Center for Research on Women.

Sanford, Mollie Dorsey. 1976. *Mollie: The Journal of Mollie Dorsey Sanford in Nebraska and Colorado Territories, 1857–1866*. Ed. Donald F. Danaker. Lincoln, NE: Bison.

Scott, K., and C. Schau. 1985. "Sex Equity and Sex Bias in Instructional Materials." In S. Klein, ed., *Handbook for Achieving Sex Equity Through Education*. Baltimore: Johns Hopkins University Press.

Spender, Dale. 1980. "Disappearing Tricks." In Dale Spender and Elizabeth Sarah, eds., *Learning to Lose: Sexism and Education*. New York: The Women's Press.

———. 1982. *Women of Ideas and What Men Have Done to Them: From Aphra Behn to Adrienne Rich*. London: Routledge.

———. 1986. *Mothers of the Novel: 100 Good Women Writers Before Jane Austen*. London: Pandora.

Woolf, Virginia. 1938. *Three Guineas*. New York: Harcourt Brace Jovanovich.

Yezierska, Anzia. 1975. *Bread Givers*. New York: Persea.

———. 1981. "Children of Loneliness." In Nancy Hoffman, ed., *Woman's "True" Profession: Voices from the History of Teaching*. New York: Feminist Press.

Zitkala-Ša. 1985. "The School Days of an Indian Girl." In *American Indian Stories*. Lincoln: University of Nebraska Press.

Useful Works for Teachers

Chapman, Anne, ed. 1986. *Feminist Resources for Schools and Colleges: A Guide to Curricular Materials*. New York: Feminist Press. Detailed annotations of bibliographies, reference works, and periodicals. Section on interdisciplinary approaches. Pages 62 through 75 offer valuable annotated entries on all sorts of useful books for English teachers.

Lauter, Paul, ed. 1983. *Reconstructing American Literature: Courses, Syllabi, Issues*. New York: Feminist Press. A collection of syllabi for college courses that can easily be adapted for high school use. Survey courses, particular periods, and genre courses; inclusive.

McINTOSH, PEGGY. 1990. "Interactive Phases of Curricular and Personal Re-Vision with Regard to Race." Working Paper no. 219. Wellesley, MA: Wellesley College Center for Research on Women.

PEARLMAN, MICKEY, and KATHERINE USHER HENDERSON. 1990. *A Voice of One's Own: Conversations with America's Writing Women.* Boston: Houghton Mifflin. Discussions with many of the contemporary writers recommended in this book: Amy Tan, Louise Erdrich, Gloria Naylor, for example.

ROSE, PHYLLIS. 1985. *Writing of Women: Essays in a Renaissance.* Middletown, CT: Wesleyan University Press. The "Renaissance" refers to the last twenty or thirty years of proliferation of books by and about women. Rose wants women admitted to the canon. Book is divided into "Lives" (Willa Cather, Isak Dinesen, Christina Rossetti, among others) and "Works" (Virginia Woolf, Colette, Margaret Drabble, among others).

SPRETNAK, CHARLENE. 1978. *Lost Goddesses of Early Greece: A Collection of Pre-Hellenic Myths.* Boston: Beacon. Invaluable for integrating the female element into mythology courses. Illustrated, only 125 pages. Pronunciation guide. Read about how the Pandora myth got turned upside down—and cry!

STOCK, PHYLLIS. 1978. *Better than Rubies: A History of Women's Education.* New York: Capricorn. Covers the education and training of women from the Renaissance to the present. Describes how certain women (Christine de Pizan, Mary Wollstonecraft, Madame de Maintenon, Florence Nightingale, and Emma Willard) tried to break through the prevailing belief that women should be trained to be good wives and mothers. A fascinating walk through some of the doldrums of white women's education.

TWO

Modifying Pedagogy

The inability of silent women to find meaning in the words of others is reflected also in their relations with authorities. . . . Authorities bellow but do not explain.

MARY FIELD BELENKY et al.
Women's Ways of Knowing

As the authors of *Women's Ways of Knowing* have written, many aspects of traditional pedagogy have silenced female students. But classrooms are changing, and efforts to empower female students are empowering all students. Just as activities for gifted and talented students stimulate all students, so pedagogical adjustments to consciously bring in female students result in raising the level of participation and learning for all students.

If, as Emily Style (1988) has written, education is both a mirror and a window, students need to see themselves as well as to look out the window to a broader view. As a mirror, education helps students to identify themselves; as a window, it helps them discover the world. These images imply both the inclusion of women and minorities in the content and the sharpening of each individual student's vision. Therefore, we support reader-response approaches to literature, starting with where the students are. Through this approach, students find out how the literature they read speaks to them; and teachers and peers value their responses. As a result, students take themselves as learners and the literature seriously. What students see for themselves will be so much more indelible and valuable. If all the symbols in *The Scarlet Letter* do not get "learned" or "taught," so what? In the last analysis we learn only what we own, and we own only what is relevant and useful and meaningful to us at a particular moment in our lives. We must let students respond viscerally and emotionally at first to what they read; and they must speak up. Hence the classroom must be a place of trust and a place that is nonthreatening. We must encourage, we must insist that all the voices be heard—especially the quiet ones. We must not allow students to hang back, to wait to respond, to speak only when called on.

No. We must unsilence the silenced.

We all want our students to take charge of their own learning, but they need practice; and teachers need practice in letting them. Students must be required to lead the discussion on the poem, the story, the chapter, and the essay, to share their questions and insights with the other students in the circle. And, yes, we should sit in circles to establish at the outset that everyone has a part to play. Everyone can see all the others, hear them, and talk to them. Teachers should be in the circle, not up front, pontificating. We need to change the way we teach; we cannot just add women to the curriculum and stir.

But where to begin? We began by examining our assumptions about learning, our roles as the teacher, and the students' roles. The following three assumptions (Dyro 1987) underlie the pedagogy we advocate in this book:

1. Knowledge is of many kinds and is many-sided. Reality is not of one kind, not singular, not limited to the dominant culture's perception. Rather, it is complex; each of us experiences it differently. Any piece of literature touches each of its readers in a slightly different place, stirring up a variety of reactions. Students bring their own experiences, facts, and feelings to the literature, and each adds some dimension to the reading. No longer, then, does the teacher have, or need to have, *the* reading. Instead of looking for the universal meaning or theme (and we wonder

just what universal means as we wonder who can speak for us), the students and teacher explore how their different views shed light on the literature at hand. Of course, some interpretations and responses will be more helpful and compelling than others, but the point is, we do not have to reach a single truth. We become interested in how students arrive at their opinions. This "how" leads to the second assumption.

2. Total objectivity is false and unattainable. Just as all literature springs from some context, so every reader brings a context, a social, economic, political, personal context. This context makes us at least partially subjective; that is, we do not read and respond with just a cool, logical left brain. Since our experiences inform our attitudes and conclusions and since our experiences differ, we must value all views. We need to speak and listen if we are to see the richness of the reality the literature and our students' lives expose. Why pretend to be objective? Why not acknowledge the wrinkles and dips and curves in our thinking created by the weights of our experiences? Such acknowledgment supports the third underlying assumption.

3. Differing perceptions and conceptions of reality create differing and valid ways to make sense of the world. No one can deny the reality of your experience; your experience is your experience. Another's experience may be different; neither is inferior or silly or wrong. When it comes to interpreting a poem or discovering what a story is all about, the differing readings expand the work. Why not go around the class to hear all the views, begin a dialogue, examine the text to see what precipitated the reactions?

Here's an example of how these three assumptions are reflected in the classroom. After reading Anne Tyler's "Teenage Wasteland," ninth-grade students disagreed on why Donny, a fifteen-year-old boy, did poorly in school, got in trouble, and finally ran away from home. Some blamed the school, some blamed his mother's insecurities, some his tutor, some Donny himself, some his uninvolved father. All students found some evidence in the story for their opinion, and most referred to their parents or teachers or their own efforts as they explained their opinions. A few felt sorry for Donny, but they excused him less as other students pointed out that he made many decisions, lied, and "was just a weak person." None of the classes has ever been able to arrive at a consensus about even the most or least important factor in Donny's running away; student papers explaining why Donny runs away differ widely, from "Donny just needed to grow up" to "Donny felt betrayed." After all was said and done, the class agreed on one thing: Donny's life was a wasteland, complex and hurtful.

When the above three assumptions govern pedagogy, teachers create student-centered classrooms. In *Women's Ways of Knowing* (Belenky et al. 1986), the authors describe four general differences between teacher-centered and student-centered learning.

The first difference has to do with the teacher's approach: playing the believing game, not the doubting game; looking for what students know, not what they don't know; looking for what is accurate, not what is inaccurate. Instead of poking holes in students' thinking, teachers acknowledge the validity of their ideas (even as they urge them to reexamine the text) by asking, "How do you know that?" or "Can you tell me more?" In student-centered pedagogy, teachers do not look for a winner, but rather for ways all can win, if, indeed, they want to use the idea of winning at all. Moreover, they choose to agree, to join, to grant another's viewpoint more than to seek control or to have the last word. Teachers will not play devil's advocate; they believe that honesty and sincerity will prompt closer investigation of the literature and people's reasons for thinking and feeling about it as they do. For example, instead of asking students to argue for or against a statement of interpretation, why not ask them to explain to what extent they agree or disagree with it? Instead of the teacher's constructing an interpretation of a poem, why not invite students to describe what images came to mind as they read, what feelings they had, what single word they found the most interesting, or what issue or theme they thought the poem raised? One day, when these kinds of questions were asked before a group of students led the discussion of a poem, everyone in the class had some point of connection, some curiosity about what the teaching group would ask and say.

Collaborative learning exposes another contrast. For one thing, when students collaborate, they pool ideas to create and explore a position rather than attack or defend a position. With practice they learn to create a dialogue with other positions rather than reason against another position. After a while students want to understand and be understood more than they want to prove or disprove. Often groups report in narrative form, a more helpful form than argument; even the quiet ones feel comfortable describing what happened or what they felt. For example, during the 1991–92 school year, two ninth-grade classes studying grammar used formal collaborative learning. Students took on the usual roles of coordinator, recorder, observer, and encourager, changing roles for each new activity. They studied how their group worked well together and where they needed to improve as they moved through a series of exercises to discover the uses of the apostrophe. It worked, for not only did the groups involve all their members, but for the first time in years most of the students got A's and B's on the test rather than D's and F's.

The third area of contrast between teacher-centered and student-centered classrooms lies in ways to evaluate student learning. Instead of measuring interpretations against some absolute or conventional standards or the teacher's conclusions, teachers might ask what the students' goals were and how close they come to reaching them, or what was their purpose and whether it was accomplished. When students explain their responses to a story, they may begin with their feelings but usually end up analyzing what in the text evoked those feelings and why. We no longer believe that feelings cannot be trusted, that they cloud our thinking and should not be a part of our analyzing; on the contrary, perhaps caring about the subject may drive thinking deeper. Then reason can become a way to see other points of view in addition to being a tool for analysis. The first time our American Literature class read Amy Tan's *The Joy Luck Club*, we asked the students to write a response, not the usual analytical paper, to any aspect of the novel they found interesting. The responses included poems, poems plus detailed explanations of how parts of the novel generated the images, comparisons of student families to one or more of the Asian American families, and discussions of how being born in the year of the Tiger formed Ying-ying's character. These students decided what they had learned and how best they might show it.

The fourth and final difference is that student-centered learning welcomes diversity and options as part of expanding our knowledge and validating students' insights. Teacher-centered learning makes students dependent upon adults by dismissing or not even asking for their perceptions. We don't want our students to ask, "What do you want?" We don't want them to spend their creative energies second-guessing us. We do want them to be interested in communicating clearly to us and their classmates because they know we are interested in knowing what they have to say.

Clearly, as pedagogy shifts, teachers' roles change. Sitting in the circle, teachers are neither just other students nor just experts. Do they accept any idea from students? No. But recognizing that students will not experience the literature in the same way they do, teachers ask how and why students think the way they do. More important, they restate student opinions rather than judge them. They clarify disagreements, saying such things as, "I hear Ruth saying 'x' and Peter saying 'y.' " Then Kyle is apt to say "z" and perhaps Anita will say "w" or maybe "x, y, *and* z." Teachers put opinions into larger contexts such as history, current affairs, or student lives: "Would this be true today? Is it true in your experience?" All of these teacher comments build a more complex picture, a picture complex enough to integrate and accommodate differing experiences and perspectives. Along the way, students, we hope, will be modifying their ideas, discarding some, adopting others, walking around the subject to see it from another vantage point.

When teachers' roles change, so do the students'. Teachers know that when they start asking, "What in your experience or the text makes you react this way?" they are taking the students' voices seriously. As teachers leave the stage, students cease to be the audience, and they become key players, no longer targets but creators of

34

knowledge. As teachers focus less on students' deficiencies, students begin to take responsibility for learning, becoming active in the classroom, recognizing and using others' insights and struggles to clarify and enrich their own insights. As students become aware of what they need and want to know, teachers become resources and facilitators. As students start writing about what is important to them, they become more effective writers. As students confront differing and often conflicting conclusions, they become more critical thinkers, more aware of the politics of negotiation, more sensitive to the legitimacy of opposing points of view; some even look forward to discussions to see what will unfold.

Such classrooms do not spring up whole just because the bell rings to summon us all to work. Everyone works day by day to create them. In such classrooms, all kinds of kids feel at home and it's okay to change your mind and personalize issues. In such classrooms a dialogue is under way to find common ground. People take time to discuss the process, the status of the class, what's going on. People test their assumptions and turn to the silent ones, asking them what they think. Teachers complicate things rather than simplify them, and they learn along with their students because they haven't got all the answers figured out ahead of time. The discussions spring not out of the air whimsically, but from information and from what the text has to say and from facts in people's experiences. People investigate their sources and values. Teachers ask students to transfer what they've learned to new situations. Collaboration gets a workout. Teachers and students see dissent as healthy, ambiguity as inescapable. Teachers resist their need for closure. Nearly everyone participates, and students take some responsibility for each other, for the planning of activities, and for their successes and failures. Valuing their own experiences, students seek to include the differences rather than dilute, dismiss, or devour them to fit some generalization. Of course, some students fail here, too.

This chapter has been full of theory; one more piece needs to be explained. Teachers in education classes told us to start where the students are, but they never taught us just how to do that. Over time, in the classroom, we learned—learned to include opportunities for students to decide what's important to them, to explore student-chosen aspects of the literature, to have students study in depth works of their own choosing, and to evaluate students on works of their choice (taken from a specified list) so that at the end of a unit or course, they know some works well. We call this an island theory of learning because these works are like islands, islands to which other works, issues, and authors can be connected as they come along. Over time a webwork of bridges begins to bind the islands together until a whole land/seascape evolves.

How do we help students create these islands? It isn't enough for them just to read a story or poem for homework. It isn't enough for teachers to point out and explicate all the "meaningful" sections. Instead, for example (to return to the ninth-grade class), we ask the students reading Tyler's "Teenage Wasteland" to pick one passage they find the most interesting or important. The next day we go around the circle with the students explaining why they picked their passage and inviting discussion about it. Other students with the same passage jump in with their comments; students with related passages do, too. By the end of that period (or the next) every student has contributed and usually all the issues, characters, and "meaningful" parts of the piece have been probed. We teachers will often take a turn, especially if a favorite passage has not been mentioned. This activity generates more discussion and greater coverage if the class is heterogeneous. Also, the further away from students' experiences a work is, the more important it is to let them decide where to begin the discussion. In addition, when using this pick-a-passage scheme, questions come up about passages students have not selected, and the class as a whole can work at them (or students turn to the teacher for information). If nothing else, students, even the less able ones, go away at the end of class with one passage they can discuss in a paper or on a test; they have one solid connection to that work. Knowledge cannot be handed out like ice cream cones to be swallowed up by agreeable children; it must be discovered. What students discover, they own and treasure.

Enough about theories of pedagogy. In the following chapters, as we discuss works by women to weave into English classes, we will describe more strategies and activities.

Works Cited

BELENKY, MARY FIELD, BLYTHE MCVICKER CLINCHY, NANCY RULE GOLD-BERGER, and JILL MATTUCK TARULE. 1986. *Women's Ways of Knowing: The Development of Self, Voice, and Mind.* New York: Basic Books.

DYRO, PEGGY. 1987. "Teachers and Social Change." Paper presented at Humanities Conference, Wellesley College Club, Wellesley, MA, November 15.

STYLE, EMILY. 1988. "Curriculum As Window and Mirror." In *Listening for All Voices: Gender Balancing the School Curriculum,* pp. 6–12. Summit, NJ: Oak Knoll School.

TAN, AMY. 1989. *The Joy Luck Club.* New York: Ivy Books.

TYLER, ANNE. 1986. "Teenage Wasteland." In Susan Cahill, ed., *New Women and New Fiction: Short Stories Since the Sixties.* New York: Mentor.

Useful Works for Teachers

DUMOND, VAL. 1990. *The Elements of Nonsexist Usage: A Guide to Inclusive Spoken and Written English.* New York: Prentice Hall. This dandy little (practically pocket-sized) book gives reasons to avoid sexist language, shows how to recognize and eliminate underlying discriminatory language, offers ways to get around sexist writing, and gives a glossary of nonsexist do's and don'ts.

ELGIN, SUZETTE HADEN. 1984. *Native Tongue.* New York: Daw. A wonderful science fiction novel that begins in 2205 in a world where women's rights had been rolled back in 1991 with the passage of the Twenty-Fifth Amendment. The Twenty-Fourth Amendment had repealed women's right to vote, and the Twenty-Fifth declared women to be minors and seriously curtailed women's participation in public life or office. Centers on female perceptions and experience, which means ultimately envisioning a new reality.

FLYNN, ELIZABETH A., and PATROCINO P. SCHWEICKART. 1986. *Gender and Reading: Essays on Readers, Texts, and Contexts.* Baltimore: Johns Hopkins University Press. Explores the relationship between gender and reading in three sections entitled "Research and Theory," "Texts," and "Readers."

FRANK, FRANCINE WATTMAN, and PAULA A. TREICHLER. 1989. *Language, Gender, and Professional Writing: Theoretical Approaches and Guidelines for Nonsexist Usage.* New York: Commission on the Status of Women in the Profession, The Modern Language Association of America. Part 1, "Language and Sexual Equality," contains several fascinating chapters, including "English Handbooks 1979–85: Case Studies in Sexist and Nonsexist Usage." Part 2, "Guidelines for Nonsexist Usage," includes "Common Problems of Sexist Usage," and Part 3 includes an extensive (though unannotated) bibliography of works cited; the Suggestions for Further Reading, also extensive, is annotated.

FREIRE, PAULO. 1970. *The Pedagogy of the Oppressed.* New York: Continuum.

———. 1973. *Education for Critical Consciousness.* New York: Seabury Press.

———. 1987. "The Banking Concept of Education." In Donald Bartholomae and Anthony Petrosky, eds., *Ways of Reading.* New York: St. Martin's.

GREENE, MAXINE. 1986. "In Search of a Critical Pedagogy." *Harvard Educational Review* 56:4 (November). Greene argues for humane teaching to move young people "into their own interpretations of their lives and their lived worlds."

HALL, ROBERTA, and BERNICE SANDLER. 1982. *The Classroom Climate: A Chilly One for Women?* Washington DC: Association of American Colleges. Project on the Status and Education of Women. Statistics and anecdotes demonstrating the disadvantages for women in the classroom with suggestions, some by implication, for warming the chilly climate.

HOWE, FLORENCE. 1984. *Myths of Coeducation: Selected Essays, 1964–1983.* Bloomington: Indiana University Press. These essays chart Howe's evolution as a feminist teacher, scholar, and writer and also reveal the myths of coeducation—for example: that admitting women to men's education and treating women like men will resolve problems of sexual inequality. Howe says, "Not so." Some chapter titles: "Feminism, Fiction, and the Classroom," "Sex-Role Stereotypes Start Early," "Women's Studies and Social Change," and "The Power of Education: Change in the Eighties." Primarily about postsecondary education, it nevertheless has decided ramifications for secondary schools. Eminently readable: no jargon or high-flown academese.

LOTT, BERNICE. 1987. *Women's Lives: Themes and Variations in Gender Learning.* Monterey, CA: Brooks/Cole. A thorough examination of how gender is learned. Calls on scholarly research and popular resources; lengthy list of references; quotes statistics but also uses fiction and poetry. Especially recommended are first five chapters: childhood through adolescence.

LYONS, NONA P. 1987. "Ways of Knowing, Learning and Making Moral Choices." *Journal of Moral Education* 16:3 (October). Follows the tenets of Gilligan and identifies "epistemological perspectives in girls' thinking that link ideas of self, knowing and morality."

MAGGIO, ROSALIE. 1988. *The Nonsexist Word Finder Dictionary of Gender-Free Usage.* Boston: Beacon. Set up like a dictionary, but with delightful epigraphs at the beginning of each new letter. Valuable appendices, dealing with various problems that occur when one tries to use nonsexist language. One of the best is "Solving the Great Pronoun Problem: 14 ways to Avoid the Sexist Singular" by Marie Shear.

MAHER, FRANCES A. 1985. "Pedagogies for the Gender-Balanced Classroom." *Journal of Thought.* 20:3 (Fall). An extended discussion and application of some of the ideas explored in the article below.

———. 1987. "Inquiry Teaching and Feminist Pedagogy." *Social Education.* March. Explores the limitations of inquiry teaching when compared with feminist pedagogy, by which Maher means "a combination of teaching practices and curriculum content that explicitly relates students' viewpoints and experiences to the subject matter, yielding for each topic a sense of personal involvement and multiple, mutually illuminating perspective taking."

McCONNELL-GINET, SALLY, RUTH BORKER, and NELLY FURMAN, eds. 1980. *Women and Language in Literature and Society.* New York: Praeger. Much to choose from; two highly recommended pieces are "The Psychology of the Generic Masculine" by Wendy Martyna and "Don't 'Dear' Me!" by Nessa Wolfson and Joan Manes. Has both a name/title and a subject index.

MILLER, CASEY, and KATE SWIFT. 1991. *Words and Women.* New York: HarperCollins. An update of authors' 1976 *The Handbook of Nonsexist Writing.* Good companion piece to Maggio's *Dictionary.* Provocative chapters include "Who Is Man?", "The Great Male Plot," and

"Language and Liberation." Readable and full of facts, historical information, and current debates on nonsexist language straight from today's newspapers. The appendix reprints the authors' important and prophetic column from *The New York Times*, April 16, 1972: "One Small Step for Genkind."

MILLER, JEAN BAKER. 1986. 2nd Edition. *Toward a New Psychology of Women*. Boston: Beacon. A revolutionary book, recognizing and redefining the daily experiences of women. Shows how, as Adrienne Rich says, the personal is the political.

NODDINGS, NEL. 1984. *Caring: A Feminist Approach to Ethics and Moral Education*. Berkeley: University of California Press. Particularly useful are Chapters 1 through 4, where Noddings defines terms and describes the "care giver" and "care receiver" (think teacher and student), and Chapter 8 on moral education and the caring classroom in the caring school.

REICH, ALICE H. 1983. "Why I Teach." *The Chronicle of Higher Education*. October 19. Inspiring short piece by associate professor at Regis College. Reich wants students to care about making the world a better place; she wants them to be active learners. "What keeps me at it is not the exceptional student—one, in my definition, who shares and is able to articulate and act upon my vision of the world—but the possibility that every student will find a voice, a way of being in the world that changes it."

RIEF, LINDA. 1992. *Seeking Diversity: Language Arts with Adolescents*. Portsmouth, NH: Heinemann. Full description of a language arts classroom set up for individualizing writing and reading. Includes strategies for organization, use of portfolios, evaluation techniques, and samples of student writing. Although the book shows a middle school classroom, many ideas and attitudes apply to high school reading and writing programs.

ROY, PAULA A., and MOLLY SCHEN. 1987. "Feminist Pedagogy: Transforming the High School Classroom." *Women's Studies Quarterly* 15:3–4 (Fall/Winter). In this very readable article the authors face the following pedagogical questions:

1. How can we make the classroom community a safe place that honors all its voices and silences?

2. How can we fight fragmentation and nurture the wholeness of learning?

3. How can we emphasize process over product while still teaching important skills?

4. How can we honor the private, personal, and subjective as well as the public, impersonal, and objective?

5. How can we redefine the student-teacher relationship in terms of power and authority as we deal with adolescent learners?

SADKER, MYRA, and DAVID SADKER. 1982. *Sex Equity Handbook for Schools.* New York: Longman. Provides concrete suggestions.

THORNE, BARRIE, and NANCY HENLEY, eds. 1975. *Language and Sex: Difference and Dominance.* Rowley, MA: Newbury House. Some of the articles are too esoteric, but several are excellent, though perhaps a little dated. "The Semantic Derogation of Woman" by Muriel R. Schultz shows, among other things, that there are five hundred terms for "prostitute" in English but only sixty-five synonyms for "whoremonger." Also try "Women's Speech: Separate But Unequal?" by Cheris Kramer. All articles thoroughly documented.

VETTERLING-BRAGGIN, MARY, ed. 1981. *Sexist Language: A Modern Philosophical Analysis.* Totowa, NJ: Littlefield, Adams and Company. Twenty-three essays by contemporary philosophers with both pro and con analyses of the feminist claim that much of language is sexist and that it should be replaced by nonsexist language. Recommended for those interested in the philosophical and theoretical aspects of this debate.

THREE

Grades 9 and 10

I was an excellent student until I was ten, and then my mind began to wander.

GRACE PALEY

"Are we going to read all stupid books this year?" Ninth graders are open and spontaneous, and we love them for both qualities. They are willing to try anything, even reading "stupid" books and works by and about women and developing rules or explanations for the use of commas. Curious, they ask out of the blue or in the middle of serious conversation, "Is your sweater new?" or "May I go to the bathroom?" Every fall we have to learn again that if an activity or reading isn't "stupid," it's "boring," and that when questioned about why they think so, they haven't a clue. But ninth graders are ready for anything, open to suggestion, rarely cynical, and, of course, just nervous enough about high school to listen for up to two minutes before their broad and deep interest in their social lives or neighboring classmates draws their attention.

As for tenth graders, we have limited knowledge of them as a classroom group because our English program after the ninth-grade year consists of semester courses where tenth, eleventh, and twelfth graders are together. But we are well aware of their need for encouragement and attention and their desire to gain control over their

English skills. We have found them increasingly interested in thinking clearly about what they read and know although cautious about saying so. We believe most of the works mentioned in this chapter would be appropriate for most ninth or tenth graders.

This chapter will not deal with Young Adult literature, a rich genre for grades 9 and 10. An additional note: we have found it difficult (but not impossible) to find stories about strong, successful young women whose lives turn out to be rewarding, not sad. Sad or not, we need to read about females as well as males. Margaret Carlson, in her article "Teaching Books by and About Women," comments on how most English teachers think that role models in literature "make an important difference to readers' lives . . . that the images of human character revealed in books are an important factor in deciding what to teach. Usually we look for heroism of some degree, journeys of self-discovery, ethical questions . . . and resolutions emerging from personality characteristics" (p. 1). But, she points out, most of the "good books" read in the first years of high school are about boys and men: *Of Mice and Men, A Separate Peace, Julius Caesar*. Where are the role models for young women? Why should they have to settle for the images of women devised by male authors or try to identify with the men in the stories?

Another question needs addressing: Should we do special units of women's literature and so isolate stories about girls, or should we teach these stories right along with the ones about boys? One problem with doing a separate unit on women is that we make them different, odd, or special. And how often do we think of the different as the inferior? We think it's best to mix works by women and men right from the beginning of the year.

In ninth-grade classes, once the students establish some ease with us and some trust among themselves, we begin to discuss gender issues. The next paragraphs describe some activities we use to raise gender concerns. One purpose of this unit is to provide material for students to write an issues paper on, one of several types of papers we expect ninth and tenth graders to be able to write. We are up-front about this paper, telling students that we will be talking, reading, and writing about gender issues for a couple of weeks and that they are responsible for taking notes so they can construct a paper in which they discuss some aspect of this broad topic.

Here's one place to begin this unit: for homework, students write out (list) what they think are some natural differences between men and women and some society-imposed differences. The next day they share these in some way so that every student in the class has a chance to add to the class lists of differences. Discussion may be in small groups with reports to the whole class or we may create lists on the board by going around the room, hearing from everyone in turn. The lists immediately provoke lively agreements and disagreements and observations based on students' personal experiences. We note which differences are more important to boys and which to girls. Having copied the lists, the students write out for homework what, if any, of the items on the list they would change if they could. And the next day we have what always turns out to be one of the most focused and intense classes of the year. For example, one young woman wanted to change the anatomy of women because "it wasn't fair that women had breasts for guys to ogle," nor was it thought fair that girls had to menstruate every month or be the only ones to bear children. Another girl was sick of the double standard for sluts and studs. A young man lamented the macho image he was expected to live up to; he saw himself as sensitive, a rat-race hater who was not looking forward to the "competition out there." Another series of comments turned on how tired the girls were of the expectation to be "little, nice, friendly, clean, and sweet." The bell rang long before an emotional exchange over rape ended: Was it a sexual thing or an issue of power? For once the quiet and disaffected students joined in.

Here are two other ways to begin the unit. Write "Women are made, not born; men are born" on the board and ask students (in a five-minute writing or in small groups followed by whole-class discussion) to what extent they agree with it. Another way to begin would be to have students write a response to the question "How would your life be different if you woke up the opposite sex tomorrow morning?" Again, sharing in small groups first may be the most comfortable way for all students to share their ideas. Putting the changes on the board provokes some analysis of attitudes toward each of the sexes as well as their typical behavior.

Margaret Carlson, of ConVal High School in Peterborough, New Hampshire, has detailed an exercise involving students creating a believable character of the opposite sex (Carlson 1987b). In a paper students describe the appearance and personality of a character of the opposite sex and then write a short scene in which the character *says* and *does* something. In small groups, students analyze how close to reality the descriptions are. Have the boys portrayed the girls accurately? Do boys find the girls' descriptions accurate? In what ways? Not in what ways? Also these small groups come up with lists of the characteristics of the male and female characters. These are reported to the whole class and listed on the board for comments. Can any generalizations be drawn? Further, what activities were the male and female characters engaged in? Any nonstereotypical ones? What do the male and female characters have in common? How do you feel about these characters: Do you like them? admire them? Why or why not?

The next exercise involves some journal writing based on the plot of Phillip Wylie's book *The Disappearance*, describing how, on one day in 1954, all the women in the world disappeared and what happened over the next couple of years. After a few chapters, the book jumps back to that same day, but this time all the men in the world disappear. The women's activities are described before the author brings everyone back. After this brief plot summary, the students pretend that today at 2:00 P.M. all the members of the opposite sex around the world disappear. They write down their first reactions, what they feel, think, do. We go around the room with each student sharing one reaction. After we all settle down again, they write for five minutes about how their lives over the next few days, even a week, would change; again we go around the room, hearing one thing from each student, allowing for some comments and discussion. Depending on the class and the number of comments, this second round-the-room may take a second class period. For homework students write a journal entry from a month later. After some sharing, possibly in small groups, we talk about larger issues and changes in their community, state, nation; in education, government, international affairs, the arts and entertainment, personal relationships, family life. They have to suspend their great interest in reproduction in order to focus on what roles men and women play in the world as they know it. Together we look at the differing assumptions about men and women reflected in these papers. For example, many of the boys see themselves as becoming violent and coarse without women, while some girls see themselves as becoming freer. Why? What self-images are at work here? How are they viewing the opposite sex?

Another activity begins when we read aloud a plot summary and then the last eleven or so pages of Ibsen's *A Doll's House* from the point where Nora and Torvald Helmer get the second letter from Krogstad. The boys are responsible for summarizing Nora's arguments and reasons for leaving, while the girls are responsible for Torvald's point of view, eventually writing these points of view and then explaining where they agree or disagree and what, if anything, has changed since 1880. Small-group and whole-class discussions about the personalities and issues, what's admirable about each character, the roles of men and women, and the assumptions about men and women in that society grow quite lively.

We may read Adrienne Rich's poem "Mother-Right" about another atypical woman running with her son while a man measures his fields. He's content, possessing; she's moving toward "the open" like Nora, her "heart stumbling." What is this "open," this "stumbling"?

A final activity involves reading to the class a story called "X" by Lois Gould. It's about Baby X whose parents, as part of an "Xperiment," refuse to show in any way that the baby is either male or female. Its dress and haircut are neutral; its toys and activities are a mix of typically male and female. Its friends at school, after rejecting it for a few days, join in its activities because they discover it has twice the fun they do. Of course, the other children's parents object (as do many of our students). Giving students some time to write a response before discussion helps to focus their thinking and gives every student something to say. They do get excited about the pros and cons of being or raising a Baby X!

After our Baby X day, the class brainstorms some questions, issues, or topics about gender they would like to address in their papers. These papers allow for very personal comments as well as demand some close reasoning and many helpful specifics from their experience, reading, and imagination to illustrate and support their opinions and conclusions.

The unit we have just described directly addresses gender issues, but less direct ways to create awareness and create gender-balanced classrooms exist. For example, we can weave in the women even when we teach grammar. Every time we use a sentence to illustrate or practice a point of grammar, we need to examine the sentence's content. Is the sentence about people in general? Fine. If it is about just a male or just a female, is it reinforcing stereotypes? If it is, change it or discard it or use an androgynous name. Other possiblities come from classroom structure. First, insist that the boys and girls mix themselves up in the circle: we ask that no more than two boys or two girls sit next to each other. Second, make sure that small groups have at least one male and one female in them. Third, use what we call a "structured discussion" to enable every student in the class to have uninterrupted time to speak. It works this way: before general discussion, go around the circle once (include yourself), having each person address the topic; no one may respond or question until everyone has spoken. (Students need to prepare more than one comment or response so that everyone will have something different to say; we can avoid repeats this way. Students always have the option to pass.) This process works well for almost anything: students may complete a statement (such as "I like poetry because . . ."); they may respond to a question about a reading or topic; they may say what they think the reading is about or explain what word in the piece is the most significant one to them; they may introduce themselves at the beginning of a course; they may read and explain a passage from a reading they found interesting or puzzling. The listeners jot down comments or questions for the ensuing discussion. Fourth, create an inner and an outer circle with the inner group discussing the reading or the topic while the outer group takes notes and writes down questions so they can participate during the last fifteen minutes of class in open discussion. The next day, reverse roles. Fifth, keep track of who's talking: If students are answering questions, alternate, consciously, between boys and girls; if students are talking to each other, remind them to invite the quieter ones in. (In some classes you may have to say that you've heard only one female voice in the last ten minutes, or only one male's.) Sixth, pay attention to responses to student comments; try to react in similar ways to both boys and girls. And finally, try using core groups. In this scheme, a single member of each small group is assigned to a new group, which is to monitor one aspect of the work at hand—for example, a comma rule or a character in a story. These new groups accomplish their particular task; then everyone returns to their original group, where each "teaches" their original group about their particular aspect of the work. This way, every student serves as an expert and contributes to the group's understanding.

We think techniques of this sort are important for ninth and tenth graders as they begin their high school years and grow into their mature selves, exploring their values and identities. Why not set up expectations for balanced consideration of the males and females in the classroom and in the literature? And speaking of literature, let's look at some works by women for young high school students, beginning with short stories. (Also see "Suggested Books for Students" at the end of the chapter.)

More recent anthologies include more women and minority writers. Some are listed at the end of this chapter. But we can't always rely on anthologies; we need to photocopy, share limited copies for in-class reading, make transparencies (some copy machines can do this), or even read stories to our classes in order to bring in the women. Here are some possibilities.

"The Return of Mr. Wills" by Mary Austin, originally published in 1909, concerns a family relocated in the wild west. Upright Mr. Wills, seduced by the legends of lost mines, drifts off for months and finally years in search of sudden wealth. Mrs. Wills, equally respectable, sinks but then rises with newfound independence and spirit, only to lose it when Mr. Wills returns and settles, like a blight, upon his family. Questions of responsibility, character change, motivation, and values all arise. This marriage and its members' roles connect at many points with current marriages and issues. Although the vocabulary challenges the students, the one-liners and humor hold their interest. Asking students to write about a single sentence they find significant for the character of either Mr. or Mrs. Wills gives them another way to focus and develop a paper.

Two stories involving older people by women are Mary Wilkins Freeman's "A Mistaken Charity" (written in 1887) and Anne Tyler's "With All Flags Flying." The former describes the meager lives of two old women, Harriet and Charlotte Shadduck, who live in a "mouldering" old shack penetrated by both wind and water. Neighbors look after them in quiet ways—leaving them a batch of doughnuts, a sack of potatoes, a bit of pork, some firewood—until one of the pair decides they would be more comfortable in an old folks' home. Once there, these feisty old women, though one is quite deaf and the other blind, escape from the fancy food, lace caps, and hovering attentions of the home, which put them "slantendicular" to heaven. On the other hand, Mr. Carpenter, the main character in the Tyler story, wants to go to an old folks' home. Why? Because he's gotten weak. He leaves his tiny house and his independence to walk to his daughter's house so she can make the arrangements. Picked up by a hippie, he thoroughly enjoys his ride on a motorcycle. He enters the home ramrod straight, only relaxing when the family leaves. What does he gain? What does he lose? Incidentally, Tyler's original title was "You Choose What You Lose." These three characters compare and contrast nicely and raise questions about the elderly, students' grandparents, and great-grandparents.

Two other stories about grandparents connect even more with students' lives because grandchildren tell the tales. In Paule Marshall's "To Da-duh, in Memoriam" a fierce young girl visits her grandmother in Barbados; it is their first and only meeting. The two walk daily in the fruit groves, each proclaiming the beauty and power of their world, the grandmother incredulous and finally defeated by the visions of New York City conjured up by her granddaughter, the granddaughter both triumphant and sad at her apparent victory. The other story, "Blues Ain't No Mockin Bird" by Toni Cade Bambara, is funny, and the grandparents triumph over the invading white county government officals who have come to take pictures of their property in conjunction with an article about food stamps. Granny hums low or high, depending upon her estimate of the status of things. She "talks with her eyebrows," and when they address her as "aunty," her response, spoken "real low through her teeth," is a simple, "Your mama and I are not related." Granddaddy Cain, "tall and silent and like a king" with a hand big enough to carry a baby to its mother as if on a tray, asks for the camera with his extended hand, gets it, and pulls the top off the camera in one easy motion, exposing the film. When he points out to the men that they are "standin in the misses' flower bed," Granny starts humming high, watching them retreat facing Mr. Cain. Students enjoy comparing and contrasting their grandparents with one or more of the older people in these four stories.

Another pair of stories to compare and contrast is "Bad Characters" by Jean Stafford and "The Animals' Fair" by James Gould Cozzens, both about young people getting into mischief. In the Stafford story, Emily Vanderpool admits that she had a bad character before she met Lottie Jump, a master thief. Both girls show wit, outspokenness, and a lively spirit, which teenagers find amusing. The unusual friendship between these girls comes to a screeching halt when Lottie is caught shoplifting: she uses Emily as a distraction for the clerk while she reaches up as if to scratch her head under a magnificent felt hat used to store the stolen goods. The hat, dull-colored and brimless but with some flowers sewn on the front, "rose staight up to a very considerable height, like a monument. . . . It looked, in a way, like part of her." It was; but when Lottie tried to stuff one last item, a string of pearls a little too long to go up under it easily, just as Emily's courage to continue the game dissolves, the clerk detects the theft and hollers for the floorwalker who lifts the hat "to reveal to the overjoyed audience that incredible array of merchandise." Within days, Emily, only an accomplice, decides to make many friends to avoid the temptation of disdainful solitude that had led to her fascination with Lottie in the first place. The Cozzens story entertains students with tales of Hicksey, another "bad character." Hicksey, small, freckle-faced, and impudent, routinely appears in and then disappears from private schools. He, like Lottie, draws an innocent into "crime." Both stories offer humorous situations and unusual but fascinating main characters.

Another unusual female main character is Annie John in Jamaica Kincaid's novel *Annie John*. Chapter 5 could be used as a short story in itself. We get to know this spunky, rebellious character at school, with a brief look at her relationship with her mother who, at the end of the chapter, smiles, showing off "big, shiny, sharp white teeth . . . as if [she] had suddenly turned into a crocodile." Annie's depictions of her teacher, Miss Edwards, and her unmodel student behavior delight and provoke students into thinking about their education, their parents, and what makes some people rebellious.

A great favorite with young high school students is "The Scarlet Ibis" by James Hurst. Equally fine, and also about siblings, one of whom is handicapped, is Toni Cade Bambara's "Raymond's Run." Both stories are in many anthologies and collections. In the Bambara story, Raymond's sister, Squeaky, is a runner. She lives for running and doesn't mind people's knowing it. Cocky and independent, she looks after Raymond who mimics her even to the point of running a race alongside her but on the other side of a fence. He keeps up; she realizes the one thing he can do is run; she decides she'll coach him. In the meantime, she comments on people in general, especially on girls who need to learn to smile because "we don't practice real smiling everyday, you know, cause maybe we too busy being flowers or fairies or strawberries instead of something honest and worthy of respect . . . you know . . . like being people." At first some students don't like Squeaky (or Hazel Elizabeth Deborah Parker, as she tells Mr. Pearson when he calls her Squeaky but she can't call him Beanstalk) with her blustery, candid, pugnacious attitude, but most of them change their minds. At any rate, she's unforgettable and she has a strong self-image.

Another girl with self-esteem is Sylvia in Sarah Orne Jewett's "The White Heron." Like Freeman's "A Mistaken Charity," this story at first turns some students away with its late 1800s vocabulary and strong New England dialect, but the humor of Sylvia's cow Mistress Moolly and a closer look at Sylvia's personality, age, and remarkable decision to be silent in the face of great pressure to reveal the where-abouts of the heron's nest elicit at least interest, if not respect, from most of the students in the end. In discussing and ranking the courage of several young people from short stories, students usually put Sylvia in the top two. Sylvia comes from a large, poor, city family that has given her up to the grandmother in an effort to make ends meet. Afraid of the neighborhood bullies, shy in the confusion and noise of her family, Sylvia welcomes the solitude of her grandmother's isolated farm, a place she never wishes to leave. A young taxidermist interrupts their peacefulness when he comes upon them and discovers Sylvia can locate the elusive white heron he wants to add to his collection so everyone can see all the birds of the area in a museum. When she climbs a giant pine at dawn, the heron, "like a single floating feather," comes to rest briefly on a limb just a few feet from her, then flies off "like an arrow" to its home in the marshes. In spite of her grand-mother's rebukes and the kind young man's pleading eyes, Sylvia does not speak a word. What Sylvia gains and loses interests students.

Two other stories of gains and losses are Eugenia W. Collier's "Marigolds" and Kay Boyle's "Winter Night." The first involves poverty and a teenage girl's response to her awareness of bleak condi-tions for her neighborhood and family. For many reasons she strikes out by uprooting an old woman's carefully tended marigolds, "a bril-liant splash of sunny yellow against the dust." By this destructive act, Lizabeth loses her innocence but gains compassion; according to Collier, we cannot have both innocence and compassion. One loss in "Winter Night" is the father to World War II and the consequent loss of the mother to work and a new social life. Felicia fascinates a new babysitter, a woman who knew but lost a young girl in a Nazi concen-tration camp. As the woman's story of that little girl comes out in response to Felicia's questions, the two grow closer and closer, and after midnight Felicia's mother returns to find them asleep on the sofa, her daughter entwined in the woman's arms. The sight is "as startling as a slap across her delicately tinted face." What happens thereafter? Students wonder.

A story to compare with "Winter Night" is Cynthia Ozick's "The Shawl." The shawl wraps around Magda, a little girl, dying in a concentration camp. In just a few pages Ozick captures the agony and brutality of these camps with unforgettable vividness. The story may be too strong for some young teenagers.

We'll mention just one more story. This last story has the advantage of having been adapted to film, a thirty-minute video. "Boys and Girls" by Alice Munro exposes the crushing expectations for boys and girls as we read about a brother and sister on a fox farm in Canada in the 1940s. The daughter loves to feed the foxes and generally do all the kinds of work the father does. Her little brother has less interest and stomach for it all. The women of the household do their best to bring cooking and lace into the affections of the daughter, but with little success. Neither the boy nor the girl grows comfortably in the traditional roles designed for them. When a horse goes to be slaughtered for fox food, all the tensions break loose.

Before going on to some novels, poems, and plays by and about women, let's review some open-ended pedagogical strategies that make it easier for the less talkative students to participate. They also encourage a wide range of perspectives. To begin discussion of a reading, ask students about the way or ways the work connected with their experience, or have two to five minutes of free writing on the work. In either case, go around the class, giving every student the chance to speak. At the end of class, especially on difficult works, have a two- or five-minute writing on what they learned and what they would like to discuss the next day; then collect the papers and decide on topics with which to begin the next day's class. If students come to class with three or five written questions or topics about the reading, in a very few minutes you can find two or three, put them on the board, and have students write for five minutes or so on one of their choice before beginning the talking in small groups or as a whole class. Or students can select one of their ideas to pass to a neighbor, who then writes a response. The originator of the topic may write a response to the response; then move to the whole class to share ideas. If students write a reaction to a work, they can meet in small groups, share all their papers, discuss the material in them, and then summarize the interesting, important, or puzzling points for the whole class. Or small groups might try writing an extension of the story. After reading their piece to the class, they can give their rationale and compare and contrast it with the other groups', all of this leading to a variety of interpretations. Or read a story to a class and have students formulate questions or topics they're interested in, including such questions as "I think she/he should have. . . . What do you think?" Collect all the papers, type a list of them (as many as the number of students in the class), and assign one to each student the next day to write an answer to. Then, go around the class discussing each item, beginning with the written comments of each student. After reading a poem, ask students to write what they pictured when they read the poem, what issue(s) the poem raised, and what single word best describes what they felt when they read the poem. By the time every student has responded, the size and shape of the poem will have expanded wonderfully.

Two other activities are a little more elaborate. One is to have students write about the following four areas in response to a reading: what they liked, what they didn't like, what puzzled them, and what patterns they found. These four topics are broad enough for prose or poetry, for short or long works. The patterns can range from elements of style to behavior of characters. With such written responses in hand, most students feel relatively confident in speaking up. The next activity worked well when a ninth-grade class was reading Buchi Emecheta's novel *The Bride Price*. The students had read the first six chapters, and although they had been forewarned that the book would be a challenge and hard to get into, clearly they were restless. The names were odd, the culture (Nigeria) connected little to their experiences, the plot line disappeared for them into long and (you guessed it) "stupid" descriptions of Aku-naa's family life in Lagos, her father's funeral, and the family's return to their traditional, remote village where Aku, a young teen, did not fit in at all. Students at that point were asked to write for fifteen minutes, free writing. They knew a classmate would read what they wrote, though it would be anonymous. At the end of fifteen minutes, they passed the papers around until they had no idea whose paper they had. After reading their classmate's paper, they selected and underlined a passage in it to share with the class. Then we spent the rest of the period and all of the next reading these selected passages and discussing them. By the time we finished, the students' frustrations with the book were out and we had touched upon key episodes, looked at important passages, dealt with questions, made comparisons with our lives, and talked about the difficulties of reading about very different cultures. The comments were often emotional, but we all had found a way to deal with the slow beginning of the book. The remaining five chapters moved rapidly and interested the students. (Aku crosses her uncle, now her stepfather, by falling in love with Chike, the son of a former slave. She is kidnapped into a forced marriage by a rival to Chike, but Aku cleverly avoids consummating it and escapes with Chike's help. They marry and live happily until all comes crashing down on them, a sad ending students don't like much, even though they remember Aku and Chike well.)

I Heard the Owl Call My Name by Margaret Craven and *The Planet of Junior Brown* by Virginia Hamilton tell the stories of nontraditional men. In *Owl* a young priest with an incurable disease takes a parish in remote Indian country along the coast of Alaska where the waves of contemporary civilization invade traditional lives and beliefs. Mark, the priest, is an exception. In *Junior Brown* Buddy, a familyless, street-smart mathematics whiz, provides a home (a planet) for other homeless boys. Only in junior high school, he is a caregiver who takes on Junior Brown, a lonely musical prodigy and artist whose mother strips his piano of its strings. Both boys find support from Mr. Pool, a former progressive teacher demoted to janitor at their school.

Now to look at some poets.

Many female poets, especially twentieth-century ones, appeal to young high schoolers. Again, the secret is just to count the number of male and female poets to insure an equal number of each. Here are some names: Maya Angelou, Elizabeth Bishop, Gwendolyn Brooks, Lucille Clifton, Emily Dickinson, Carolyn Forché, Nikki Giovanni, Susan Griffin, Louise Glück, Nigase Kiyoko, Denise Levertov, Mekeel McBride, Thylias Moss, Mary Oliver, Marge Piercy, Sylvia Plath, Adrienne Rich, Muriel Rukeyser, Kay Smith, Mary Tall Mountain, Alice Walker. Of course, dozens more would be just as exciting. At any rate, these authors are published, and many of their poems are anthologized. *Reading Poetry,* edited by Robert DiYanni and published by Random House, is a balanced collection of male and female poets from several centuries and ethnic groups with poems by most of the above-named poets.

To begin a unit on poetry, students select a favorite poem from a group of poems and talk to the class about why they picked it. Classmates add their ideas until responses and comments dwindle. Some analysis and some study of poetic techniques happens along the way. Each year we become more convinced that trying their hand at composing poems expands students' responses to and appreciation for others' poems. Students alternate writing their own poems with formally studying specific aspects of poetry, such as lining and use of sounds.

At the end of work on poems, in lieu of taking a test, students spend a week or so designing and putting together a poetry anthology of ten to twelve poems. Sometimes they must choose poems in certain categories, such as regional poets or English poets; sometimes students simply pick whatever poems they want. The anthologies must have the following: a title and subtitle; a sturdy cover; a table of contents; a preface or running commentary, explaining why they chose each poem, why they put each poem in the place they did, and what sort of response they had to each poem; and the source of each poem. They might also include some biographical information about the poets, create a special design for their anthology, or illustrate their collection. Students are encouraged to use friends' poems and their own poems. Usually students discover some common thread in their collection. When they have these projects to do in the warm days of June, students relax, share their finds with each other, and enjoy showing their anthologies to the class, reading a favorite poem or two and explaining the title and organization during the last day or two of school.

As for novels by women, we couldn't name all the novels by women available these days; many are in permabound or other hardcover. A colleague found a few novels to use in a multicultural unit where small groups of students worked on different novels, then found ways to involve their classmates with their books. They used visuals, games, panels, and reports. Four books by women that work for this type of activity are the above-mentioned *The Bride Price* by Emecheta, *The Good Earth* by Pearl S. Buck, *Nectar in a Sieve* by Kamala Markandaya, and *Shabanu* by Suzanne Fisher Staples. All four reveal the rebellion of women against well-established conventions in Nigeria, China, India, and Afghanistan respectively. *The Good Earth* and *Nectar in a Sieve* each follow a woman from her teenage years through marriage and into late middle age during the early twentieth century; the two others describe the lives of teenage girls. Poverty and riches, small triumphs and tragedies, history and family life, grief and joy and pain all work their way into these tales. *Earth* is the longest, *Shabanu* the shortest and by far the easiest to read. *Shabanu* especially appeals to young men, who are drawn to the story, which involves camels, the desert, villains, a wonderful and complex father, an eccentric aunt, and the spirited, clever Shabanu, who loves the camels. Some students think *Nectar* is an Indian version of *The Grapes of Wrath.* The stories are similar: a chronicle of the plight and near devastation of a farming family with a strong mother, caught in the vast political, religious, and economic network of the country. In all four books the roles of women and the relationships between the men and the women illuminate not only these four cultures but our own by the obvious contrasts and the more subtle similarities. (Other novels that tell lively stories and offer atypical men or women are listed at the end of the chapter.)

When Carol Gilligan described the different voices of men and women in *In a Different Voice,* did she have the play *Antigone* in mind? We find it exemplifies the conflicting voices of duty and the law, of caring and rights, of mercy and justice. In fact, having students discuss definitions of these in small groups before delving into the play provides a point of entry into Antigone's and Creon's dilemmas. We use Jean Anouilh's adaptation of Sophocles' play: its contemporary vocabulary and brisk pace clarify the conflicts and draw the students in quickly. Since we also study *Lord of the Flies* and *Julius Caesar,* the political threads from these two works find themselves tied up in *Antigone,* but with the happy addition of a strong female character. Once students have understood the family history of Oedipus, Antigone's and Creon's motives make more sense; and students seem to enjoy these legends or mythlike stories. The more feminist-minded students quickly see Antigone as one of them, angry at being "only a girl," who can be herself at last but only when she is handcuffed and doomed to die. She tells Creon that he cannot make her do what she doesn't want to. In reflecting on what her happiness would be like if she goes along with Creon's plan to save her, she says softly: "What base things will she [Antigone] have to do, day after day, in order to snatch her own little scrap of happiness? Tell me—who will she have to lie to? smile at? sell herself to? Who will she have to avert her eyes from, and leave to die?" Later she adds, "I don't want to be sensible, and satisfied with a scrap—if I behave myself!" She fights and dies, speaking "in a different voice."

Two other plays show different and strong women: *The Miracle Worker* by William Gibson and *The Effects of Gamma Rays on Man-in-the-Moon Marigolds* by Paul Zindel. *The Miracle Worker* shows up in anthologies, and *Marigolds* is available in paperback, a short work and inexpensive. Although these are written by men, the female characters invite us to look at women as having some control, power if you will, not because of their gender but because of their personalities and minds. Annie Sullivan's and Kate's (Helen's mother) control is clearly positive. All of the characters in *Worker* change as Annie works her miracle with Helen; one student reasoned that she works miracles with all the others as well. On the other hand, the control may be negative, as it is with Beatrice (nicknamed Betty the Loon by her high school classmates), the alcoholic mother of Tillie and Ruth. The effect of Beatrice on her daughters is less subtle. Tillie, the younger child, loves science and wins a prize at the school science fair for her experiment, exposing marigolds to varying amounts of gamma rays. As her mother and sister laugh, shout, and berate her, she drifts along with her experiment, just out of their reach. Too many rays stunt the plants, too few create mutations, such as double blossoms. Students wonder about the parallels between these plants and the three characters: Who's stunted? Who's a mutant? Who's more or less okay? The mother can't keep a job, care for the aged woman boarding at their house (a source of income), or tolerate Tillie's pet rabbit (she kills it). The play ends enigmatically, with Tillie reciting lines from her speech at the science fair about the future, leaving room for students to puzzle out what might happen to these people.

Another genre often used with ninth and tenth graders is autobiography/biography. We suggest finding a way to make sure an equal number of males and females are read about. Some years we just divide the class in half alphabetically, by seating arrangement, or by counting off by two's. Some years the boys read about a woman and the girls read about a man. Other times they find a person whose last name begins with the same letter theirs does. Anything we do to show that we take women's lives just as seriously as men's will support a gender-balanced classroom and curriculum and help empower the women in the class.

But what can we do differently when we study works by and about men? How can we re-vision these works, look at them from male *and* female perspectives? The following are some suggestions.

Ask students what the images of women are in the work. What roles are they playing? Describe their personalities, the kinds of things they say and do, their relationships to other people in the work or how they are defined by the male characters. Ask how accurate the portraits of the men and the women are, based on their experiences. In conjunction with these questions, we can ask, "Whose story is *not* told? What would this person's story be like?" Along the same lines, we can ask what we think the women in the story are thinking, doing, and feeling while the rest of the story is going on.

Curley's wife in John Steinbeck's *Of Mice and Men* is a perfect example of a woman seen only in relation to a man. She doesn't even have a name! She is known only as Curley's wife. Once students look more closely at her situation—her isolation, her vitality and curiosity restricted to things in the house, a jealous and cocky husband, her loneliness so acute as to drive her to Lennie for some social life—their scorn turns to acceptance, if not sympathy. All of the questions posed in the above paragraph can be asked of Curley's wife. Re-visioning her story highlights dramatically the necessity and rewards of establishing some new ways to think about the stories we read. After all, everyone's story ought to have a fair hearing.

Another fruitful question is "Where are *you* in the story?" Sometimes students admit they are not in the story; sometimes a male student will indentify with a female character or a female student with a male character. As students describe the ways they relate to these characters and why they do or don't, they come to see the story very differently. Students might look at the events from a female character's point of view rather than the author's (or whatever point of view the author has selected). Ask students to change a male main character to a female and discuss what would change, what wouldn't, and why. For example, in working with *Lord of the Flies*, students may speculate about events had the group been all girls. How would they have dealt with their fear? How would they have organized themselves? Does Golding think the savage rests securely in the hearts of females as well as males? (After all, he wrote only about males.)

Once we started looking for works to balance our curriculum and for learning activities to spread class participation around more evenly, our teaching was more fun, and the unexpected comment pleased and stimulated us all. We found that more ideas were put on the table. It may well be that for some students almost all the books, stories, poems, and plays will still be "stupid," but it is also likely that fewer minds will be bored and have to "wander" the way Grace Paley's did.

Works Cited

ANOUILH, JEAN. 1958. *Antigone*. In *Five Plays*, Vol. I. Trans. Lewis Galantiere. New York: Hill and Wang.

AUSTIN, MARY. 1987. "The Return of Mr. Wills." In Marjorie Pryse, ed., *Stories from the Country of Lost Borders*. American Women Writers series. New Brunswick, NJ: Rutgers University Press.

BAMBARA, TONI CADE. 1972. "Blues Ain't No Mockin Bird." In *Gorilla, My Love*. New York: Random House.

———. 1972. "Raymond's Run." In *Gorilla, My Love*. New York: Random House.

BOYLE, KAY. 1975. "Winter Night." In Susan Cahill, ed., *Women and Fiction: Short Stories by and About Women.* New York: Mentor.

BUCK, PEARL S. 1931. *The Good Earth.* New York: Pocket Books.

CARLSON, MARGARET. 1987a. "Teaching Books by and About Women." *Slate* (May). Urbana, IL: National Council of Teachers of English.

———. 1987b. "Unit on Gender Concerns in Literature: Pairing Stories for Gender Balance in High School English Classes." Unpublished paper.

COLLIER, EUGENIA W. 1992. "Marigolds." In *African American Literature: Voices in a Tradition.* Austin, TX: Holt, Rinehart and Winston. (First published in *Negro Digest,* November 1969.)

COZZENS, JAMES GOULD. 1937. "The Animals' Fair." In *Children and Others.* New York: Harcourt Brace Jovanovich.

CRAVEN, MARGARET. 1973. *I Heard the Owl Call My Name.* New York: Dell.

DIYANNI, ROBERT. 1989. *Reading Poetry: An Anthology of Poems.* New York: Random House.

EMECHETA, BUCHI. 1976. *The Bride Price.* New York: George Braziller.

FREEMAN, MARY WILKINS. 1979. "A Mistaken Charity." In Barbara H. Solomon, ed., *Short Fiction of Sarah Orne Jewett and Mary Wilkins Freeman, Including the Country of the Pointed Firs.* New York: Signet.

GIBSON, WILLIAM. 1962. *The Miracle Worker.* New York: Bantam.

GOULD, LOIS. 1980. "X." Ms. (May):61–64.

HAMILTON, VIRGINIA. 1971. *The Planet of Junior Brown.* New York: Collier Books.

HURST, JAMES. 1960. "The Scarlet Ibis." *The Atlantic Monthly* (July).

IBSEN, HENRIK. 1950. *A Doll's House.* Trans. Eva Le Gallienne. New York: Modern Library.

JEWETT, SARAH ORNE. 1988. "The White Heron." In Charles G. Waugh, Martin H. Greenberg, and Josephine Donovan, eds., *Best Stories of Sarah Orne Jewett.* Augusta, ME: Lance Tapley.

KINCAID, JAMAICA. 1983. *Annie John.* New York: Plume.

MARKANDAYA, KAMALA. 1954. *Nectar in a Sieve.* New York: Signet.

MARSHALL, PAULE. 1983. "To Da-duh, in Memoriam." In *Reena and Other Stories.* New York: Feminist Press.

MUNRO, ALICE. 1968. "Boys and Girls." In *Dance of the Happy Shades.* New York: Penguin.

OZICK, CYNTHIA. 1986. "The Shawl." In Susan Cahill, ed., *New Women and New Fiction: Short Stories Since the Sixties.* New York: Mentor.

PALEY, GRACE. 1974. "Art Is on the Side of the Underdog." Interview. Ed. Harriet Shapiro. *Ms.* (May):43-45.

RICH, ADRIENNE. 1978. "Mother-Right." In *The Dream of a Common Language.* New York: Norton. (Also in *The Fact of a Doorframe: Poems Selected and New, 1950-1984.* New York: Norton.)

STAFFORD, JEAN. 1954. "Bad Characters." In *Bad Characters.* New York: Farrar, Straus & Giroux.

STAPLES, SUZANNE FISHER. 1991. *Shabanu: Daughter of the Wind.* New York: Borzoi Sprinter.

STEINBECK, JOHN. 1972. *Of Mice and Men.* New York: Bantam Pathfinder.

TYLER, ANNE. 1982. "With All Flags Flying." In Edmund J. Farrell, et al., eds., *Arrangement in Literature.* Glenview, IL: Scott, Foresman.

WYLIE, PHILLIP. 1952. *The Disappearance.* New York: Pocket Books.

ZINDEL, PAUL. 1971. *The Effects of Gamma Rays on Man-in-the-Moon Marigolds.* New York: Bantam.

Suggested Books for Students

ANONYMOUS. 1971. *Go Ask Alice.* New York: Avon. Fictional account in diary form of Alice, explaining how and why she experimented with drugs and how she tried to stop.

AUEL, JEAN. 1980. *The Clan of the Cave Bear.*

———. 1983. *The Valley of Horses.*

———. 1985. *The Mammoth Hunters.*

————. 1990. *The Plains of Passage.* (All) New York: Bantam. Stories of conflicts between different prehistoric peoples with one girl as the central character.

CARTER, FORREST. 1976. *The Education of Little Tree.* Albuquerque: University of New Mexico Press. Set in the 1930s, the book relates in a humorous and moving way the growing up of Little Tree under the hands of his Cherokee grandparents.

CATHER, WILLA. 1974. *Obscure Destinies: Three Stories of the West.* New York: Vintage. (Written around 1930.) We recommend "Neighbor Rosicky" and "Old Mrs. Harris." Anton Rosicky, a Bohemian farmer, exemplifies a sensitive person who values relationships with both men and women. The longer "Old Mrs. Harris" raises questions about the roles of women as Mrs. Harris serves her daughter and grandchildren, reducing her independence, while her daughter struggles with her five children and her desire for a university education.

————. 1988. *O Pioneers!* Boston: Houghton Mifflin. The pioneer is Alexandra Bergson, better able than her brothers to run the family farm. Along with the hardships, the novel includes romantic love, murder, and refusals to marry. Vivid images, easy to read, and available in video form.

CHILDRESS, ALICE. 1973. *A Hero Ain't Nothin' But a Sandwich.* New York: Avon.

EMECHETA, BUCHI. 1974. *Second Class Citizen.* New York: George Braziller. Nigerian woman joins her husband in England, rebels against the strict tribal rules for women her husband tries to force her to obey, and wins for herself and her five children some education and financial independence. Clear statement of what it means to be a second class citizen. References to marital sex may be unsuitable.

FRANK, ANNE. 1952. *Anne Frank: The Diary of a Young Girl.* New York: Pocket Books.

FREEDMAN, BENEDICT, and NANCY FREEDMAN. 1947. *Mrs. Mike.* New York: Berkley. A woman finds personal courage in fighting for a new life in the wilds of Alaska.

GAINES, ERNEST J. 1971. *The Autobiography of Miss Jane Pittman.* New York: Bantam. The book covers approximately one hundred years, from the

Civil War to the Civil Rights Movement of the 1960s, depicting the violence done to recently freed slaves, the prison of sharecropping, and the loves and bonds holding the hopes and courage of Miss Pittman as she walks and works her way to freedom. Short chapters. The movie supports the text well.

GEORGE, JEAN C. 1972. *Julie of the Wolves.* New York: Harper & Row.

GREEN, HANNAH (Joanne Greenberg). 1964. *I Never Promised You a Rose Garden.* New York: Signet. Bright teenaged girl saved from insanity by sensitive woman psychiatrist.

GREENBERG, JOANNE. 1970. *In This Sign.* New York: Avon. Novel about hearing daughter of deaf parents.

GREENE, BETTE. 1973. *Summer of My German Soldier.* New York: Dial. Patty, a lonely Jewish girl, protects an escaped German soldier, creating problems for her family. *Morning Is a Long Time Coming* is a sequel.

GUEST, JUDITH. 1976. *Ordinary People.* New York: Ballantine. When one son dies accidentally while sailing, the other son, Conrad, feels responsible. His mother, in her grief, turns cold while Conrad and his father get counseling. In the end Conrad acknowledges his innocence and his rage, squaring himself with his father and himself in spite of his mother's as yet unresolved feelings.

GUY, ROSA. 1973. *The Friends.* New York: Bantam. The ups and downs of a friendship between two black girls, growing up in an urban setting.

HANSBERRY, LORRAINE. 1959. *A Raisin in the Sun.* Many editions and commonly anthologized.

HARRIS, MARILYN. 1973. *Hatter Fox.* New York: Bantam. About a young Native American's rage against American society.

HOFFMAN, ALICE. 1989. *At Risk.* New York: Berkley. Effects on a family when a young girl contracts AIDS from a transfusion.

KELLER, HELEN. 1954. *The Story of My Life.* New York: Dell.

LEE, HARPER. 1960. *To Kill a Mockingbird.* New York: Popular Library.

LEFFLAND, ELLA. 1979. *Rumors of Peace.* New York: Harper & Row. Suse Hansen, ten years old in 1941, grows to hate all things German and Japanese as she experiences World War II. Her fear leads to racism for her Japanese-American neighbors before she works through her prejudice.

LE GUIN, URSULA K. 1968. *A Wizard of Earthsea.* New York: Bantam. The first in a four-part series about the world of Earthsea and Ged (or Sparrowhawk), its chief wizard. This book details Ged's growing up and training as a wizard.

————. 1971. *The Tombs of Atuan.* New York: Bantam. Tenar is taken to the tombs to become a priestess in this underground land. Ged arrives, searching for the missing half of an amulet. With both their lives at stake, they join forces.

————. 1973. *The Farthest Shore.* New York: Bantam. The equilibrium of Earthsea grows unbalanced as some force drains off the power of the wizards. Sparrowhawk and Arren, Prince of Enlad, roam the distant islands to find the source of the evil. They do, and Sparrowhawk uses up his powers to repair the damage.

————. 1990. *Tehanu: The Last Book of Earthsea.* New York: Bantam. Tenar, a grown woman now, returns to aid an abused child and a dying wizard.

L'ENGLE, MADELEINE. 1980. *A Ring of Endless Light.* New York: Dell. Deals with the values of friendship as a young girl copes with the death of her grandfather and the attention of three boys.

MCCAFFERY, ANN. 1971. *Dragonsinger.*

————. 1976. *Dragonsong.*

————. 1979. *Dragondrums.* (All) New York: Bantam. Interesting, strong female characters in science fiction adventures with themes of good versus evil.

MCCULLERS, CARSON. 1940. *The Heart Is a Lonely Hunter.* New York: Bantam. When Mick learns that the possibilities in life are not unlimited, she changes: something, a music in her head, dies.

————. 1963. *The Member of the Wedding.* New York: New Directions. Frankie discovers she's not as important as she thought. She struggles with her identity as her brother's wedding day approaches.

O'BRIEN, ROBERT C. 1975. *Z for Zachariah.* New York: Collier. At the end of World War III, Ann lives alone in a valley until a stranger arrives, at first giving her hope but later fear as she sees that all she's worked for might be destroyed.

PATERSON, KATHERINE. 1980. *Jacob Have I Loved.* New York: Avon. Louise Bradshaw's coming of age is complicated by her seemingly perfect twin sister, Caroline. Set in the 1930s and 1940s.

PORTIS, CHARLES. 1968. *True Grit.* New York: Signet. Teenager defies tough lawman in accompanying him in pursuit of her father's murderer, and she earns his respect and affection.

SIEGAL, ARANKA. 1981. *Upon the Head of a Goat: A Childhood in Hungary, 1939–1944.* New York: Farrar, Straus & Giroux. A young Jewish girl narrates the daily lives of her family and friends, the women left behind. Their strength is emphasized over the horrors of Auschwitz. Autobiographical.

SMITH, BETTY. 1943. *A Tree Grows in Brooklyn.* New York: Perennial. An Irish girl grows up in Brooklyn at the turn of the century.

SPEARE, ELIZABETH G. 1986. *The Witch of Blackbird Pond.* New York: Dell.

TAYLOR, MILDRED. 1976. *Roll of Thunder, Hear My Cry.* New York: Puffin. The first of two novels about the members of the Logan family, whose land is an island in plantation country peopled with sharecroppers. Cassie, the narrator, learns about racism and the courage, pride, and strength it takes to resist the night riders, white girls who would degrade her, and the imprisoning of T.J., a family friend. Unsentimental.

———. 1981. *Let the Circle Be Unbroken.* New York: Bantam. Set in 1935, one year after *Thunder,* Cassie's family works through the depression and the blatant attempts to drive them off their land. T.J. is found guilty by an all-white jury and Stacey, Cassie's brother, goes off to work on a sugar plantation to earn money to pay the taxes on their land only to find himself cheated and imprisoned for robbery before his family finds him.

VOIGT, CYNTHIA. 1982. *Dicey's Song.* New York: Atheneum. Sequel to *Homecoming.* Two strong personalities in Dicey and her grandmother who, independent, learn about reaching out to others and accepting their affection in return.

WHITE, ANTONIA. 1933. *Frost in May.* New York: Dial Press. Nanda Grey's coming of age takes place in a Catholic boarding school outside of London, but her rebellions against the rules and her oppressive father lead to a diminished sense of self-worth.

Useful Books for Teachers

DiYANNI, ROBERT, ed. 1988. *Reading Fiction: An Anthology of Short Stories.* New York: Random House. Well-balanced collection of stories by male and female, white and nonwhite, American and non-American authors. Stories are of various reading levels, from Margaret Atwood's "Giving Birth" to Ursula Le Guin's "The Wife's Story." Of the forty-five stories, eighteen are by women and nineteen are by non-American writers.

ROSENBLATT, LOUISE. 1970. *Literature as Exploration.* New York: Noble and Noble.

SAFIER, FANNIE, ed. 1986. *Impact: Fifty Short Short Stories.* Orlando: Harcourt Brace Jovanovich. Stories divided into sections with such focuses as plot, tone, theme, and total effect.

WARRINER, JOHN E., ed. 1981. *Short Stories: Characters in Conflict.* Orlando: Harcourt Brace Jovanovich. Twenty-three stories, only four by women, but including "Raymond's Run," "Bad Characters," "The Animals' Fair," "The Scarlet Ibis," Munro's "Red Dress," and Doris Lessing's "A Sunrise on the Veld."

FOUR

American Literature
Seventeenth and Eighteenth Centuries

I am obnoxious to each carping tongue
Who says my hand a needle better fits;
A poet's pen all scorn I should thus wrong,
For such despite they cast on female wits.
If what I do prove well, it won't advance;
They'll say it's stol'n, or else it was by chance.

ANNE BRADSTREET
"The Prologue"

The next four chapters cover two semester courses we teach, American Literature I and American Literature II. This chapter concerns the first quarter of American Literature I. The anthology we use is Ginn's *American Literature* (1984), chosen for its multicultural, gender-balanced selections. Unfortunately, it is short on historical and biographical information, and it is likely to have only one or two poems by any given poet. However, since our course is extensive rather than intensive, we welcome its range of authors. In this and the next three chapters on American literature, the text we refer to will be this anthology.

How does one approach the balancing of men and women writers in early American literature? Must we defer to the traditionalists and say, "What established male writers can we afford to drop in order to bring in worthy women writers?" We think not. The questions have

69

to be revised, the norms re-established, the standards for "literature" recast. We must not ask who the good women writers were in Colonial America; instead we begin with "What were early American women writing about?" Since we have rediscovered Anne Bradstreet and unearthed Mary Rowlandson, no doubt we would find that many other women were busy writing; they just weren't published.

One who was published is Anne Bradstreet. Her poem "The Author to Her Book" offers hearty food for thorough chewing by nascent scholars. We often point out to students that a recurring and widespread theme of poets is the art of writing poetry. In this early Bradstreet poem, she explains this theme with wit, charm, expert technique, and irony. The central metaphor, the "ill-formed off-spring," is developed so that we see the author's lack of confidence in her poem/child and at the same time her pride in her own creation:

> I cast thee by as one unfit for light,
> Thy visage was so irksome in my sight;
> Yet being mine own, at length affection would
> Thy blemishes amend, if so I could:
> I washed thy face, but more defects I saw,
> And rubbing off a spot still made a flaw.
> I stretched thy joints to make thee even feet,
> Yet still thou run'st more hobbling than is meet.

What, then, is a woman poet to do? We see in the above excerpt the dilemma raised in the epigraph for this chapter, only from a different angle.

One problem we've run into with "The Author to Her Book" is that some students misread the poem and think the speaker is some sort of child abuser, forgetting that the poem is an extended metaphor. So sometimes we teach this more deductively than inductively and encourage students to be prepared for this metaphor—to note how well it is sustained, to find all the places where it is used. Ultimately students can see why the metaphor is one that a woman would choose much more readily than a man.

Bradstreet wrote a series called "Meditations Divine and Moral" for her son Simon. He had asked for something from her he could read after she died, and these meditations, along with a dedicatory letter dated 20 March 1664, were her response. They consist of aphorisms on such topics as personal improvement, the need for balance, and spiritual equanimity. They can be usefully compared with the maxims from *Poor Richard's Almanac* and contrasted with the deadly witticisms from Ambrose Bierce's *The Devil's Dictionary*. Here is a taste:

#4

A ship that bears much sail and little or no ballast is easily overset, and that man whose head hath great abilities and his heart little or no grace is in danger of foundering.

#9

Sweet words are like honey: a little may refresh, but too much gluts the stomach.

#10

Diverse children have their different natures: some are like flesh which nothing but salt will keep from putrefaction, some again like tender fruits that are being preserved with sugar. Those parents are wise that can fit their nurture according to their nature.

#12

Authority without wisdom is like a heavy axe without an edge: fitter to bruise than polish.

Bradstreet's father, Thomas Dudley, had managed the estates of the earl of Lincoln before emigrating to America, where he became an early governor of Massachusetts. At age sixteen, Anne married Simon Bradstreet, a literate and thinking person nine years older than she, who had worked as the earl's steward. (He, too, became a governor of Massachusetts.) When Anne was eighteen, she and Simon journeyed to America with her parents. Since she had been educated by private tutors and had free access to the earl's library, it would have been entirely natural for her to write, to jot things down, to keep a journal, to record her moral meditations, to craft poems, to express her feelings. At the same time, of course, she would have been full of ambivalence and guilt: a Puritan woman writing poems! Bad enough for a Puritan man to do so. Bradstreet wrestled with the problem of her desire to write poetry and her knowledge that literature and art were forbidden; after all, work and leisure were supposed to be devoted to prayer and worship of God. Still, she persisted; and when her brother-in-law took her volume of poems to England and had them published there in 1650, she complained but at the same time went on writing, revised some of the poems, and looked forward to a second edition, which appeared after her death in 1678.

Information in the above paragraph is important for today's teenagers, especially young women. If a teacher spends some time with Anne Bradstreet, a grounding in one of the fundamental inequities in American literature can be made clear: female literary genius was not at all encouraged; male talent often was. Students will see a link between the situations of Bradstreet, Emily Dickinson, Amy Lowell, and more modern writers such as Sylvia Plath and Adrienne Rich: the silencing of the woman poet. Anthologies now regularly include a poem or two of Bradstreet's, often "To My Dear and Loving Husband" and "The Author to Her Book." Both, in Ginn, are accessible to high school students, as are "The Prologue" and "Upon the Burning of Our House July 10, 1666." Students need to know how someone like Bradstreet struggled with her Puritan beliefs and her wanting to be a dutiful wife and mother. They need to see this part of early times as surely as they need to see William Bradford's journal of early Indian encounters at Plymouth or Jonathan Edwards's hellfire and damnation approach to Christianity.

Speaking of Jonathan Edwards, we could well use a journal entry from his daughter Esther, ". . . The Awful Sweetness of Walking with God." Esther's letter is wonderfully refreshing after Jonathan's gloominess. At nine or ten she comments on her mother's seeming "very old" at thirty-three, and she wonders if she will live that long. In another entry on what a "singing family the Edwards family is," she says, "Our home is more like an aviary than the dwelling of a Colonial parson," after cataloguing the various voices of the household members and pointing out that her father's low spirits can be revived by her mother's voice, which is to him "like medicine, as David's harp was to King Saul." At the end of the final entry in this excerpt, Esther's probing mind comes through clearly; she has written about their abundant flower and vegetable garden, which her "honored father, of course, has not time to give attention to." She notes that the husband of Rose, the colored cook, tends the garden: "We hire her services from one of the prominent people in Father's parish, who owns both her and her husband. That word 'owns' sounds strange about people."

Students find Esther Edwards fascinating: "How could she think like that at such a young age?" "I admire her for being aware of the racism in her culture from her remark at the end of the excerpt."

Students can compare and contrast Bradstreet with Mary White Rowlandson. She wrote an account of her capture by Wampanoags in 1675. The full title of the book, published in 1682 after her death, is *The Sovereignty and Goodness of God, Together with the Faithfulness of His Promises Displayed: Being a Narrative of the Captivity and Restoration of Mrs. Mary Rowlandson*. The following passage, more graphic than Ginn's selection, suggests very well both the vivid power of her description and her reliance on God for survival:

O the doleful Sight that now was to behold at this House! *Come, behold the works of the Lord, what desolation he has made in the earth.* Of thirty-seven Persons who were in this one House, none escaped either present Death or a bitter Captivity save only one, who might say as he, *Job i. 15, And I only am escaped alone to tell the news.* There were twelve killed, some shot, some stabb'd with their Spears, some knock'd down with their Hatchets. . . . There was one who was chopped into the Head with a Hatchet, and stripp'd naked, and yet was crawling up and down. It was a solemn Sight to see so many Christians lying in their Blood, some here and some there, like a company of Sheep torn by Wolves; all of them stript naked by a company of hell-hounds, roaring, singing, ranting, and insulting, as if they would have torn our very hearts out; yet the Lord, by his Almighty power, preserved a number of us from death, for there were twenty-four of us taken alive; and carried Captive.

Even though Bradstreet and Rowlandson wrote in different genres, they each report on their own experiences. They both praise God, but in separate ways: Rowlandson credits her survival to God; Bradstreet struggles to maintain faith in a God who would be so harsh and punitive to the Massachusetts settlers. Rowlandson, lacking Bradstreet's humor, is ready to believe that God had her captured to test her faith. Bradstreet shows in her poems her conflict over caring too much about temporal things like houses, property, children. If this life is just a preparation for eternity, then how is one justified in placing so much value on temporal belongings?

Students, always quick to read everything from their enlightened late-twentieth-century perspective, often criticize Mary Rowlandson's eagerness to attribute her survival entirely to God. Today's young women want to see these early women giving themselves and their own strength and courage more credit. Bradstreet seems a little more human to them because she wrestled with her competing values: Puritanism and love of family or Puritanism and a desire to write poems.

Sarah Kemble Knight, writing somewhat later, traveled from Boston to New York in 1704 and recorded her experiences in "The Journal of Madam Knight," which was eventually published in 1865. Knight, a woman of robust physical strength and assertiveness, writes a journal which mentions God but does not give him the frequent thanks he gets in Rowlandson's narrative. Knight can easily be compared and contrasted with Rowlandson. These two women have different values and traveled a different road; yet both, in their separate ways, wrote graphically and revealed much about women's thoughts and behavior at the time. For example, Madam Knight reports that when she and her guide arrived in Billings, a colonial village south of Boston where they were to spend the night, she was disgusted with the questions of the eldest daughter of her hostess because the woman seemed totally thunderstruck that a woman should be traveling through the countryside: "I told her she treated me very rudely, and I did not think it my duty to answer her unmannerly Questions." The daughter, apparently in the midst of questioning Madam Knight, goes upstairs and puts on some jewelry in an effort to impress Mrs. Knight, who comments, "But her Granam's new-rung sow [a sow with a ring through its snout], had it appeared, would [have] affected me as much."

Two more additions for this unit of early American writers are Phillis Wheatley and Abigail Adams. Much of Wheatley has been printed in the past ten years, so she is now quite often available in anthologies, including the Ginn. In a course that tries to be multicultural as well as gender-balanced, Wheatley, an African American, is essential. Depending on how much time you have, you can include her more formal poem, "To the Right Honorable William, Earl of Dartmouth" (in Ginn) and the more simple "On Being Brought from Africa to America." Other Wheatley titles that are accessible to high school students are "To S.M., a Young African Painter, on Seeing His Works" and "To Maecenas." In the former, Wheatley praises the skill of the painter:

> To show the lab'ring bosom's deep intent,
> And thought in living characters to paint.
> When first thy pencil did those beauties give,
> And breathing figures learnt from thee to live,
> How did those prospects give my soul delight,
> A new creation rushing on my sight?

In the latter poem, Wheatley as the speaker wishes she had the talent of a Virgil or a Maecenas: "Then should my song in bolder notes arise, / And all my numbers pleasingly surprise."

For a contemporary perspective, we may teach Margaret Walker's "Ballad for Phillis Wheatley," which focuses on her childhood, or Robert Hayden's "A Letter from Phillis Wheatley (London, 1773)," showing the tokenism of the English who entertained her at dinner:

> At supper—I dined apart
> like captive Royalty—
> the Countess and her Guests promised
> signatures affirming me
> True Poetess, albeit once a slave.

75

It's important in dealing with Wheatley to help students avoid a revisionist reading of this brilliant prodigy who profited from the education the Wheatleys gave her, but who did not write poetry decrying the treatment of slaves or calling for abolition. Her genius, her poverty, the tragedy of her short life are all compelling. We are grateful to the Wheatleys, whose name she took; without them she probably would not be known to us today. She is the precursor to later American black female poets, such as Frances Watkins Harper, Gwendolyn Bennett, Helene Johnson, Margaret Walker, Gwendolyn Brooks, and Alice Walker. (More about these later.)

Abigail Adams also makes it into some anthologies. She can be used to link Jefferson's "Declaration of Independence" and Elizabeth Cady Stanton's "Declaration of Sentiments" from the Women's Rights Convention at Seneca Falls in 1848. Adams is an early feminist, and we need to spend time on her letters—not just the famous one of 31 March 1776 to John about remembering the ladies. Seventy-five years before Stanton makes much of the fact that women were left out of the "Declaration of Independence," Adams reminded her husband and others not to forget the women. Her letter of 7 May 1776 is eloquent on attitudes toward women; she reminds John that "whilst you are proclaiming peace and good will to men, emancipating all nations, you insist upon retaining an absolute power over wives." She goes on to warn him that arbitrary power exercised by husbands "is like most other things which are very hard, very liable to be broken." Other letters suitable for high school students include hers of 20 April 1771 in which she laments the fact that women have been unable to travel much in other countries, something she would have liked. She writes knowingly of the tendency of power to corrupt in her letter of 27 November 1775: "I am more and more convinced that man is a dangerous creature, and that power, whether vested in many or a few, is ever grasping and like the grave cries give, give. The great fish swallow up the small, and he who is most strenuous for the rights of the people, when vested with power, is as eager after the prerogatives of government."

Adams is an appropriate person to use to talk further about letters as a literary genre. Letters were very important in an age without radio, telephone, telegraph, TV, and transatlantic cable. Journals, diaries, and letters are very much a part of early American literature; diary entries for less well known women can be found in such books as *A Day at a Time: The Diary Literature of American Women from 1764 to the Present,* edited by Margo Culley. Two excerpts bear special interest for high school students: those of Elizabeth Sandwith Drinker and Nancy Shippen Livingston. Drinker provides an eyewitness's view from her family's house overlooking the Delaware River as the British and the colonists vied for control there in 1777. The Livingston diary records the predicament of one of Philadelphia's leading debutantes at the time of the Revolution. She falls in love with a Frenchman who supports the colonists. Her family rushes her into marriage with one of her suitors, from a wealthy New York family. He turns out to be a tyrant with several mistresses and some illegitimate children. In her entry for 15 May 1783, Livingston writes a series of statements about what a woman should not expect or hope for. Of husbands she writes: "They are naturally tyrannical; they will have pleasures & liberty, yet insist that Women renounce both: do not examine whether their rights are well founded; let it suffice to you that they are established."

In addition to adding these women to the curriculum, it's important to develop new pedagogical strategies for teaching them. One we use in doing Bradstreet is to assign small groups on various topics, such as historical and biographical background, individual poems, and meditations. They do group presentations with each member contributing in some way. A roundtable discussion with Bradstreet, Rowlandson, Wheatley, and Abigail Adams is worth trying, too. Once a student wrote a play in which Sarah Kemble Knight stumbled into Jonathan Edwards's church; she took him to task for his sternness, his cruelty, his overdoing of the themes of hellfire and damnation and images of snake pits and spiders in his metaphors of God's wrath.

Another interesting possibility would be to imagine a meeting between Benjamin Banneker and Phillis Wheatley. Banneker was the brilliant black man who confronted Jefferson about his paradoxical situation: a framer of the "Declaration of Independence," which demanded the colonists' freedom from the British, yet a man who owned slaves himself. Banneker's letter to Jefferson, quoted in our text, is remarkable for its eloquence and logical reasoning. After pointing out that if God created all beings, then blacks are equal to whites, and reminding him of his commitment to the idea of freedom and the "free possession of those blessings to which you were entitled by nature," Banneker says:

> But, sir, how pitiable is it to reflect that although you were so fully convinced of the benevolence of the Father of mankind and of his equal and impartial distribution of those rights and privileges which he had conferred upon them, that you should at the same time counteract his mercies in detaining by fraud and violence so numerous a part of my brethren under groaning captivity and cruel oppression, that you should at the same time be found guilty of that most criminal act which you professedly detested in others with respect to yourselves.

Wheatley and Banneker were contemporaries, but they were from different parts of the country, he from Baltimore and she from Boston. Students could imagine what their conversation might have consisted of; they would have to base their writing on their knowledge of the two persons. Would Banneker have tried to raise Wheatley's consciousness? What might he have felt about the intellectual capabilities of a black woman in the mid-1700s? Would he have been sexist?

Having raised the question of sexism on the part of a man like Benjamin Banneker, we need to look at Nathaniel Hawthorne—at not only his sexism but also his achievement in the creation of Hester Prynne. We use *The Scarlet Letter* early in the course because the setting is Puritan New England, even though chronologically Hawthorne belongs in the second quarter as a nineteenth-century writer. We go through this novel quite slowly and deliberately; after that, we won't ever be so painstaking, but students will have learned how to do a close reading of a challenging novel.

We begin with a minilecture on Hawthorne with a bit about his life and something on his literary techniques, such as use of dark and light, reflection, and purposeful ambiguity. Sometimes we tell students about one of Hawthorne's ancestors, a judge who burned women at the stake for supposed witchcraft. We model discussion and analysis using the first three chapters (we skip "The Custom House" but summarize it). After outlining the plot of these three chapters, we look closely at each. We may read the first one, "The Prison Door," together out loud; it's very short, and we can easily show students the importance of each word, helping to disabuse them of thinking Hawthorne is too long-winded, uses too many difficult vocabulary words, and spends too much time on description. We ask many questions, about his use of color, for instance. Will this concentration on black, gray, and red prevail throughout the novel? Should we watch for it? What about the wild rosebush near the threshold of the prison close to the ugly weeds? Is it important? Why the reference to Anne Hutchinson? We don't have definitive answers to these questions, but we encourage students to keep the questions in mind as they read. We define the more difficult words, sometimes putting definitions on the board.

We look at the people assembled in Chapter 2, "The Market Place." How is Hester treated by the women? We ask students to describe Dimmesdale. Then we ask them to examine the difficult passage with Hester ruminating about her past in England. What is her connection with the "misshapen scholar"? Why does she go to Amsterdam with him? We clarify the difficult places in Chapter 3, "The Recognition," that can be misread and we ask students to explicate them. If they can't, we do so, and then ask what these passages tell us about plot, about character. We review any literary techniques we've found so far.

At this point students, having been assigned to teach the remaining chapters either alone or with one other person, take over the teaching. We remind them that nothing in this book can be skipped with impunity, warning them, "If you miss one sentence in a paragraph, you are lost." (Sometimes they find this out the hard way.) We look closely at Hester: Is she an early feminist heroine? What about the intriguing Chapter 13, "Another View of Hester"? What is Hawthorne saying here? Sometimes we acquaint students with Hawthorne's famous attack on the "scribbling women" writers of his time.

How does this jibe with his view of Hester? The enigmatic Pearl is a provocative character for teenagers of today. And they are quite thorough in their investigation of just how realistic a little girl in Puritan New England she is. Is she an imp or a devil or a messenger from Satan? Or is she just a precocious child suffering from isolation and Puritan censure?

An additional pedagogical strategy, and one of our most important assignments in American and English literature courses, is the extended essay or position paper. Students read a book or play from or about the period we're studying. We give them a list of possible works to read. We vary among our staff as to what to call this paper. Some of us prefer "extended essay" because, as we tell our students, it is just another, but longer, analytical essay. We want them to extend their thinking so they can write a paper of from 1,500 to 2,000 words *at their level of authority*. We have conferences about possible topics for this paper, and we schedule progress reports for the two or three weeks before it is due. Students need to learn how to organize material for a longer paper, how to deepen their thinking about a topic, and how to weave in the quotes. They have to discover what process works for them: composing several drafts, writing in longhand, or composing on the computer. They must do their own thinking, their own puzzling. They explain an idea fully; they do analysis that they've practiced in shorter papers but in more detail and at greater depth. And they are on their own—no reading of secondary sources, no class notes to bolster their ideas. They need to learn the process so they don't come in the day the paper is due to say they haven't been able to write 1,500 words. Different students have different needs and diverse methods in tackling this assignment. That's fine. Students have to find a focus and make a point—we don't want a book review or a biographical sketch of the author.

In conclusion, using well-written works by unknown women writers adds to the tapestry of the curriculum and makes it more truly inclusive, more fully American. Whenever we find them, we would be wise to consider the letters, journals, and diaries of ordinary women. Look what happened with Laurel Ulrich and Martha Ballard's diary: she won the Pulitzer Prize in history for *A Midwife's Tale*:

The Life of Martha Ballard, Based on Her Diary, 1785–1812! Ulrich selected entries from each month over the twenty-seven-year period the diary covers, from the time Martha Ballard is fifty years old until shortly before her death. The entries themselves are laconic, factual, and terse, but Ulrich, through her meticulous research, cross-referencing, and extraordinary thinking, has expanded on these entries not only to give us a portrait of the remarkable midwife but also to paint an indelible picture of the complex community of Hallowell, Maine, in the late eighteenth century. Students can learn the importance of searching out the histories of their own ancestors. Maybe they'll find diaries going back, if not to the seventeenth and eighteenth centuries, perhaps to the nineteenth. (A male student recently reported on a diary from his great-great-great-grandfather's Civil War experiences.) Such study makes letters, diaries, and journals legitimate literature and establishes the presence of women right from the beginning. Pairing writings of women with those of men will show differences and similarities—the same subjects presented from different points of view; the same abilities, but with different focus. Students will feel validated, encouraged to write their own diaries; through these writings they can make more connections between life and literature. We can see how the dailiness of life accumulates to become the stuff of literature. We can all be Madam Knights as well as Henry Thoreaus. Only *we* can record our experiences. As they look back at the array of women they've studied during the first quarter of the American Literature course, girls can say: "Aha! We have a literary history, too!"

Works Cited

ADAMS, ABIGAIL. 1988. Letters. In Alice S. Rossi, ed., *The Feminist Papers: From Adams to De Beauvoir*. Boston: Northeastern University Press.

BANNEKER, BENJAMIN. 1984. Letter to Thomas Jefferson. In Porter, Terrie, and Bennett.

BIERCE, AMBROSE. 1979. *The Devil's Dictionary*. New York: Crowell.

BRADSTREET, ANNE. 1984. "The Author to Her Book" and "To My Dear and Loving Husband." In Porter, Terrie, and Bennett.

———. 1990. "Meditations Divine and Moral," "The Prologue" from *The Tenth Muse,* and "Upon the Burning of Our House July 10, 1666." In Paul Lauter et al., eds., *The Heath Anthology of American Literature,* v. 1. Lexington, MA: D. C. Heath.

CULLEY, MARGO. 1985. *A Day at a Time: The Diary Literature of American Women From 1764 to the Present.* New York: Feminist Press.

EDWARDS, ESTHER. 1982. ". . . The Awful Sweetness of Walking With God." In Edmund J. Farrell et al., eds., *Arrangement in Literature.* Glenview, IL: Scott, Foresman.

HAWTHORNE, NATHANIEL. 1985. *The Scarlet Letter.* New York: Bantam.

HAYDEN, ROBERT. 1985. "A Letter for Phillis Wheatley (London, 1773)." In Frederick Glaysher, ed., *Collected Poems.* New York: Liveright.

KNIGHT, SARAH KEMBLE. 1990. "The Journal of Madam Knight." In William L. Andrews, ed., *Journeys in New Worlds: Early American Women's Narratives.* Madison: University of Wisconsin Press.

PORTER, ANDREW J., JR., HENRY TERRIE, JR., and ROBERT A. BENNETT. 1984. *American Literature.* Lexington, MA: Ginn and Company.

ROWLANDSON, MARY. 1990. "A True History of the Captivity and Restoration of Mrs. Mary Rowlandson." In William L. Andrews, ed., *Journeys in New Worlds: Early American Women's Narratives.* Madison: University of Wisconsin Press.

ULRICH, LAUREL THATCHER. 1990. *A Midwife's Tale: The Life of Martha Ballard, Based on Her Diary, 1785-1812.* New York: Knopf.

WALKER, MARGARET. 1989. "Ballad for Phillis Wheatley." In *This Is My Century: New and Collected Poems.* Athens: University of Georgia Press.

WHEATLEY, PHILLIS. 1916. "On Being Brought from Africa to America," "To Maecenas," and "To S.M., a Young African Painter, on Seeing His Works." In G. Herbert Renfro, ed., *Life and Works of Phillis Wheatley, Containing Her Complete Poetical Works, Numerous Letters, and a Complete Biography of This Famous Poet of a Century and a Half Ago.* Washington, DC: Robert L. Pendleton.

———. 1984. "To the Right Honorable William, Earl of Dartmouth." In Porter, Terrie, and Bennett.

Suggested Books for Students

FARNHAM, ELIZA W. 1988. *Life in Prairie Land.* Urbana: University of Illinois Press. A New Yorker who became a feminist, Farnham spent five years in the prairie land of Illinois and gives us a complex picture of the midwestern wilderness during the 1830s. Table of contents gives detailed summaries of actual chapters.

KARLSEN, CAROL F., and LAURIE CRUMPACKER, eds. 1984. *The Journal of Esther Edwards Burr, 1754–1757.* New Haven: Yale University Press. A comprehensive look at three years in the life of the adult Esther whom we saw briefly in ". . . The Awful Sweetness of Walking With God" in her youth. Offers a rare perspective on an ordinary woman's life in the eighteenth century in America; shows the importance of religion, intellectual thought, and personal relationships.

SEAVER, JAMES E., ed. 1990. *A Narrative of the Life of Mrs. Mary Jemison.* Syracuse, NY: Syracuse University Press. A captivity narrative to compare and contrast with that of Mary Rowlandson. Jemison was taken by Indians at the age of twelve, in 1755. The narrative contains an account of the murder of Jemison's father and his family, her sufferings, her marriage to two Indians, and her troubles with her children.

WILSON, HARRIET. 1983. *Our Nig: Sketches from the Life of a Free Black.* New York: Random House. As a servant to a northern white family, "Nig" is treated as badly as a slave.

WITHEY, LYNNE. 1981. *Dearest Friend: A Life of Abigail Adams.* New York: Free Press.

Useful Works for Teachers

FETTERLEY, JUDITH. 1978. *The Resisting Reader: A Feminist Approach to American Fiction.* Bloomington: Indiana University Press. Teachers can dip into this for instruction in a feminist reading of several classic American texts; includes sections on "Rip Van Winkle," Hawthorne's "The Birthmark," Hemingway's *A Farewell to Arms,* among others.

MILLER, JAMES E., JR., et al., eds. 1979. *United States in Literature.* Glenview, IL: Scott, Foresman. A complement to the Ginn anthology; strong multicultural emphasis.

SHOCKLEY, ANN ALLEN. 1988. *Afro-American Women Writers, 1746–1933: An Anthology and Critical Guide.* New York: Meridian.

FIVE

American Literature
Nineteenth Century

*Women have been called queens for a long time, but the
kingdom given them isn't worth ruling.*

LOUISA MAY ALCOTT
An Old-Fashioned Girl

Nineteenth-century American literature is covered in the second
quarter of our American Literature I course. Two excellent sources of
nineteenth-century material are *Hidden Hands: An Anthology of
American Women Writers, 1790–1870*, edited by Lucy M. Freibert and
Barbara A. White, and *Provisions: A Reader from 19th-Century American Women*, edited by Judith Fetterley. The writers in these collections, who were very popular in their day, include women who
describe women's lives as they were as well as women who offered
criticism, sometimes scathing satire. Alcott isn't the only one who
didn't think much of the kingdom.

One of the most successful ways to illustrate gender inequities in
the literature itself is to teach a pair of early-nineteenth-century
works: "Rip Van Winkle" by Washington Irving and "Hilda Silfverling" by Lydia Maria Child. Everyone knows the former; the latter is
a longer story set in Sweden and Norway, a fantasy in which Hilda,
after being unjustly convicted of infanticide, instead of being exe-
cuted, is frozen for a hundred years as a scientific experiment. When
she is awakened, she is still sixteen, but the world is a century older.

She feels alienated, but a kind man arranges for her to go to Norway to a friendly family, the Hansens, for a fresh start. Hilda's story is very complicated: she falls in love with someone who turns out to be her own great-grandson; her daughter hadn't died or been killed but had been taken to Norway by the woman to whom the young, unwed Hilda had entrusted her. The story contains some satire, a look at whether or not the world has improved for women in the one hundred years Hilda has slept. Alerik, her new lover, combines in an interesting way a practical jokester and Loki, the mythic trickster of Nordic folklore. After reading "Hilda Silfverling," students are asked to come in with three written questions that they want discussed. The teacher tries to stay completely out of the discussion as students question each other about the story. They compare and contrast the sleeps Rip and Hilda experience. They look at the two characters and come to see that Rip was essentially lazy and irresponsible as a family person. Much can be gleaned, too, about the unfair treatment by Irving of Dame Van Winkle. She is repeatedly termed a "shrew" and a "termagant," but the irony is that Irving gives her no words of her own; she never speaks in the story. Students see that the world Hilda awakens to remains an unfriendly place for women.

A colleague pairs "The Revolt of 'Mother'" by Mary Wilkins Freeman with "Rip." In it, Father builds a barn for his new cows and horse, but Mother, promised a new house forty years ago when first married, questions how necessary it is and reiterates her need for a bigger house. When Father goes off to Vermont for a few days to purchase a new horse, Mother, with unexpected boldness, seizes this opportunity to move her entire household into the barn. When Father returns, he's dumbfounded, but agrees, after a hearty meal, to build the partitions to complete the conversion of the barn to a house, saying to Mother that he "hadn't no idee you was so set on't as all this comes to." Just looking at the ways husbands and wives communicate will fill a class period, and as an added bonus, good humor lives in both stories.

Another book, by Lydia Maria Child, is *Hobomok*, in which a young white American sees her fiancé, Charles, leave for England after her father has forbidden her to marry him because he's not a

Puritan. In her loss and grief, she is befriended by a decent and kind Indian named Hobomok. Eventually she marries him, has his child, and is banished from the Puritan circle. However, when Charles returns from England, Hobomok decides to leave, knowing that Mary has always loved Charles, and that clears the path for Charles to be reunited with his beloved Mary. Presumably he adopts the half-Indian child who is socialized as a white person and given a Puritan New England name: Charles Hobomok Conant. He eventually graduates from Cambridge. (Excerpts from this book appear in *Hidden Hands* along with a helpful introduction.) The treatment of the Indian is too sanitized; he seems too much a white man in Indian clothes. Still, when we compare and contrast excerpts from *Hobomok* with an excerpt from James Fenimore Cooper's *The Deerslayer,* we can easily see that in the latter the Indians are idealized even more. The poems and speeches the students read by real Native Americans contrast nicely with the Child and Cooper selections.

When we move further into the second quarter of American Literature, we tackle the transcendentalists, Emerson and Thoreau, but we don't get involved with Margaret Fuller. She doesn't appeal to our high school students. Though her ideas are feminist, her writing is dull and labored. We tell students about her, however, and some of them enjoy reading a biography of her, for her life was colorful. We talk about Emerson's writing "Self-Reliance" in his room while downstairs women are fixing lunch for him. (We're indebted to Peggy McIntosh for this anecdote.) In studying the two great male anti-transcendentalists or dissidents, Melville and Hawthorne, the only way to bring in the women, since Melville didn't include them, is to look at the women in Hawthorne's short stories. We read "The Minister's Black Veil," "Dr. Heidegger's Experiment," and "Rappaccini's Daughter." Usually the women are emblems of faith (Elizabeth in "Black Veil") and innocence (Beatrice in "Daughter"). But in "Heidegger," Hawthorne's woman, Dame Wycherly, is old and foolish and wishes to be young again.

The next group of writers and thinkers and speakers we call Reformers. They include blacks writing about slavery, women speaking up for women's rights, and a more amorphous group, some of whom are social reformers, consisting of Louisa May Alcott, Harriet Robinson, and Elizabeth Peabody. Altogether they provide a rich blend of fiction, slave narrative, poetry, journals, and speeches. If we had to pick the most popular work from this group, it would be Sojourner Truth's "Ain't I a Woman?" It doesn't always sink in with students that Truth (born Isabella Baumfree) was illiterate, but that luckily a woman at the Women's Rights Convention in Akron, Ohio, in 1851 wrote her speech down. Students are impressed with the tightness of Truth's logic, her choice of examples, and her amazing ability to turn the arguments of the men in the audience upside down with irrefutable comebacks:

> Then that little man in black there, he says women can't have as much rights as men, 'cause Christ wasn't a woman. Where did your Christ come from? From God and a woman! Man had nothing to do with Him.

The feistiness and clarity of Sojourner Truth look forward to her descendants (more literary perhaps, but with her courage and presence) Toni Morrison, Alice Walker, Toni Cade Bambara. Truth, Harriet Jacobs, and Frances Harper are a powerful triumvirate of black women writers of this time period. Often a student will choose Harper's novel *Iola Leroy* for an outside extended essay. In class we read two powerful poems of hers. In "Bury Me in a Free Land," the speaker decries the slaves' lot, asking only for a humble burial in a land without slaves. These stanzas make clear the female slaves' dehumanization:

> I could not rest if I heard the tread
> Of a coffle gang to the shambles led,
> And the mother's shriek of wild despair
> Rise like a curse on the trembling air.

> I could not sleep if I saw the lash
> Drinking her blood at each fearful gash,
> And I saw her babes torn from her breast,
> Like trembling doves torn from their parent nest.

In her poem "A Double Standard" a white man and a black woman have an affair, but only she has to suffer the consequences:

> Crime has no sex and yet today
>   I wear the brand of shame;
> Whilst he amid the gay and proud
>   Still bears an honored name.

Students are quick to point out that the double standard is alive and well today.

For a full-length book we read *Incidents in the Life of a Slave Girl* by Harriet Jacobs, written under her pseudonym, Linda Brent. Jacobs records the particular horrors that black female slaves experienced at the hands of the white plantation owners. They received no mercy from their white mistresses, who had little power and could not vent their wrath against their unfaithful husbands. Several editions of *Incidents* are available now; Jane Yellin's provides the real names of the people in the narrative: the notorious Dr. Flint, from whom Jacobs escaped by living for seven years in a crawl space in her grandmother's attic; and the senator by whom she chose to have children in order to escape rape at the hands of Flint, both men upstanding white citizens of their time.

Reading Jacobs and Harper creates a context for fully appreciating something like the contemporary novel *Beloved* by Toni Morrison. *Beloved* looks back to the time of slavery and includes the devastating tale of a mother, Sethe, who does the unthinkable to avoid the unlivable life, and thereby hangs her tragic tale. (We won't divulge the plot!) Morrison makes us understand Sethe's pain and agony; Jacobs and Harper prepare us in less anguished ways for that unthinkable horror. We must own this particular horror, just as we must own the horrors described in the slave narratives of Frederick Douglass and James Pennington, if we are ever to come to terms with our country's history of racism. Some students choose to read Harriet Beecher Stowe's *Uncle Tom's Cabin,* another useful book, for extended essays.

Louisa May Alcott, another reformer, is a must for nineteenth-century American literature. Some students may choose to read *Little*

Women for their extended essay; some years we have taught it to the whole class. Students can be introduced to the thrillers that Alcott wrote anonymously, collected and published recently under the title *Behind a Mask.* In these stories Alcott takes pleasure in getting back at the patriarchy that forced her to write the Pollyannish *Little* books to provide for her mother and sisters when her father wasn't up to anything as mundane as making a living and supporting his family. Alcott's *Early Diary at Fruitlands* is wonderfully revealing of the young girl's genius between the ages of ten and thirteen, and it can be compared and contrasted with that earlier journal of Esther Edwards. Alcott's diary reveals her character, her efforts to be good and please her mother:

> As I went to bed the moon came up very brightly and looked at me. I felt sad because I have been cross today, and did not mind Mother. I cried, and then I felt better, and said that piece from Mrs. Sigourney, "I must not tease my mother." I get to sleep saying poetry,—I know a great deal.

The reference to Lydia Howard Sigourney, a popular writer to whom women looked for the latest in etiquette and proper behavior, provides a chance to consider the writers, magazines, and other media that dictate correct behavior, clothes, and cosmetics for today's teenage girls.

Through Alcott's writings, we begin to appreciate the depth of her struggle. She was a brilliant woman in a century when brilliance in women was not accceptable, so she had to be subversive. We've also used excerpts from her satiric look at the whole Fruitlands experience, her comment on the limitations of the rural communal Utopia with its terrifically apt title, *Transcendental Wild Oats.*

Harriet Robinson's *Loom and Spindle* shows a spirited young woman's refusal to be badgered and beaten down. She leads the strike at the Lowell, Massachusetts, cotton mills in 1836: the girls in upper rooms started first and when it got to Robinson's floor, people were indecisive:

And not one of them having the courage to lead off, I, who began to think they would not go out, after all their talk, became impatient, and started on ahead, saying, with childish bravado, "I don't care what you do, I am going to turn out, whether any one else does or not"; and I marched out, and was followed by the others.

The Lowell Offering, a magazine published at the time and in some ways seen as propaganda for the mill owners, contains, nevertheless, much honest and revealing writing from the girls who worked in the mills. A collection of these writings, edited by Benita Eisler, is available. Occasionally a student likes Lucy Larcom's *A New England Girlhood,* useful in showing the experience of living in the mills. If you live close enough, try a trip to the Lowell mills, where the times and conditions have been well re-created.

Some years we have used an excerpt from Elizabeth Peabody's "Plan of the West Roxbury Community," a report on what later came to be known as Brook Farm. Intellectual and manual skills were to be valued equally; Brook Farm never succeeded, but Peabody's report of it is interesting for what it reveals about her idealism. Of special interest to students is what she says about education. After pointing out that instruction in agriculture will be of paramount importance, she also mentions natural sciences and mathematics.

> But to classical learning justice is also to be done. Boys may be fitted for our colleges there, and even be carried through the college course. The particular studies of the individual pupils, whether old or young, male or female, are to be strictly regulated, according to their inward needs.

A noble experiment in equality, the reality could not live up to the ideal. Hawthorne's *The Blithedale Romance* points out some of the problems. For one, farm work was too strenuous and tedious for some of the resident intellectuals (like Hawthorne himself). They also didn't take manual labor seriously enough—they more valued lofty intellectual pursuits.

All of the foregoing writers are excellent preparation for the next reformer, Elizabeth Cady Stanton and her "Declaration of Sentiments," which appears in the Ginn anthology we use. Since this anthology also has the "Declaration of Independence," we compare and contrast the two. Students are always impressed with Stanton's cleverness in basing her declaration on the earlier, famous one. Stark, clear, revealing, the repetition of "he" in listing the rights women don't have is compelling:

> The history of mankind is a history of repeated injuries and usurpations on the part of man toward woman, having in direct object the establishment of an absolute tyranny over her. To prove this, let facts be submitted to a candid world.
>
> He has never permitted her to exercise her inalienable right to the elective franchise.
>
> He has compelled her to submit to laws, in the formation of which she had no voice.
>
> He has withheld from her the rights which are given to the most ignorant and degraded men—both natives and foreigners.

And so on, with the same irrefutable logic shown by Sojourner Truth. Here, the eloquence includes literary skill as well as oratorical acumen. Stanton provides many opportunities for the teacher to connect past and present as students, sometimes in small groups, look at what has happened to and for women in the years since 1848. Many students haven't as yet had U.S. history, where they learn, usually from a paragraph in an outdated history text, that women were "given" the vote in 1920. The reality was a long, hard fight culminating in women finally winning the franchise in 1920.

The last, long unit of our American Literature I course includes writers from the last half of the nineteenth century. The women writers we select speak honestly about their lives, and, thanks to Rutgers University Press's American Women Writers series, many of the works excerpted in *Hidden Hands* are now available in their entirety. One writer whom students can enjoy is Sara Willis Parton, writing under the pseudonym Fanny Fern. Her autobiographical novel *Ruth Hall* is one students can read independently; the Rutgers edition includes a generous selection from Fanny Fern's newspaper columns.

The following three passages illustrate her wit and may whet your appetite for more. In one column, "Awe-ful Thoughts," Fanny writes about "that awe, which is the most delicious feeling a wife can have toward her husband."

> *AWE!*—awe of a man whose whiskers you have trimmed, whose hair you have cut, whose cravats you have tied, whose shirts you have "put into the wash," whose boots and shoes you have kicked into the closet, whose dressing-gown you have worn while combing your hair; who has been down cellar with you at eleven o'clock at night to hunt for a chicken-bone; who has hooked your dresses, unlaced your boots, fastened your bracelets, and tied on your bonnet; who has stood before your looking glass, with thumb and finger on his proboscis, scraping his chin; whom you have buttered, and sugared, and toasted, and tea-ed; whom you have seen asleep with his mouth wide open! Ri—diculous!

In another column, "Male Criticism on Ladies Books," Fern quotes from the *New York Times*, which says that courtship, marriage, servants, and children provide the substance of novels by women and "we have no right to expect anything else." Fern goes on to say (after pointing out that the great male writers like Thackeray and Dickens have included those topics in their novels):

> Would a novel be a novel if it did not treat of courtship and marriage? And if it could be recognized, would it find readers? When I see such a narrow, snarling criticism as the above, I always say to myself, the writer is some unhappy man, who has come up without the refining influence of mother, or sister, or reputable female friends; who has divided his migratory life between boarding-houses, restaurants, and the outskirts of editorial sanctums; and who knows as much about reviewing a woman's book, as I do about navigating a ship, or engineering an omnibus from the South Ferry, through Broadway, to Union Park. I think I see him writing that

paragraph in a fit of spleen . . . in his small . . . upper chamber. . . . Perhaps, in addition, his boots hurt, his cravat-bow persists in slipping under his ear for want of a pin, and a wife to pin it (poor wretch!).

Fern also writes about "The Modern Old Maid," contrasting her with the stereotype:

The modern "old maid" is round and jolly, and has her full complement of hair and teeth, and two dimples in her cheek, and has a laugh as musical as a bobolink's song. She wears pretty, nicely fitting dresses too, and cunning little ornaments around her plump throat, and becoming bits of color in her hair, and at her breast, in the shape of little knots and bows; . . . and she goes to concerts and parties and suppers and lectures and matinees, and she don't go alone either; and she lives in a nice house, earned by herself, and gives jolly little teas in it. She don't care whether she is married or not, nor need she. She can afford to wait, as men often do, till they have "seen life," and when their bones are full of aches, and their blood tamed down to water, and they have done going out, and want somebody to swear at and to nurse them—then marry!

Another writer of the period is Rose Terry Cooke, whose *How Celia Changed Her Mind and Selected Stories* has also been published by Rutgers. The title story and her "Dely's Cow" are both highly suitable for secondary students. "Dely's Cow" tells of a young woman married to a decent man who goes off to fight in the Civil War. She suffers from loneliness and isolation with only her baby and Biddy, the cow, for company. She and the cow brave the long winters; a firm bond between the two females forms. In the other story, Cooke makes clear one of her recurring themes: women themselves have to change their attitude toward men before real equality can occur because women seem to think that being attached to a man—any man—is preferable to being a spinster. For instance, when the parson's wife tells Celia that many of her best friends were maiden ladies, Celia retorts that old maids are "cumberers of the ground" and includes herself among them. Convinced of the blessings of marriage, she goes to bat for her young friend Rose and Rose's beloved Amos Barker:

> Miss Celia was ready to do anything for Amos Barker, and she considered it little less than a mortal sin to stand in the way of any marriage that was really desired by two parties. That Amos was poor did not daunt her at all; she had the curious faith that possesses some women, that any man can be prosperous if he has the will so to be; and she had a high opinion of this youth, based on his civility to her. It may be said of men, as of elephants, that it is lucky they do not know their own power; for how many more women would become their worshipers and slaves than are so to-day if they knew the abject gratitude the average woman feels for the least attention, the smallest kindness, the faintest expression of affection or good will. We are all, like the Syrophenician woman, glad and ready to eat of the crumbs which fall from the children's table, so great is our faith—in men.

Celia later marries Deacon Everts and, soon disenchanted, changes her mind about marriage:

> As her husband's mean, querulous, loveless character unveiled itself in the terrible intimacy of constant and inevitable companionship, she began to look woefully back to the freedom and peace of her maiden days. She learned that a husband is by no means his wife's defender always, not even against reviling tongues. It did not suit Deacon Everts to quarrel with any one, whatever they said to him, or of him and his; he "didn't want no enemies," and Celia bitterly felt that she must fight her own battles. . . . She became not only defiant, but also depressed; the consciousness of a vital and life-long mistake is not productive of cheer or content; and now admitted into the freemasonry of married women, she discovered how few among them were more than household drudges, the servants of their families, worked to the verge of exhaustion, and neither thanked nor rewarded for their pains.

We recommend these late-nineteenth-century women writers for use in a variety of courses and with all high school age groups. Here are three others.

Kate Chopin has been resurrected in the last twenty-five years; her novel *The Awakening* is now readily available. Some of her stories are anthologized; "The Story of an Hour" is in *By Women* and "The Storm" is in Ginn's *American Literature*. "Désirée's Baby" appears in *Story*, a short story collection published by D.C. Heath. Chopin focuses on women's lives, women's feelings, women's thoughts *not* filtered through males' authority. She dared to write about what women actually felt and thought when they chose divorce or chose to see their husbands as something less than the perfect entity for the center of their lives. She was frowned upon, and her writing was ultimately banned.

Elinore Pruitt Stewart, a strong, independent woman, moved to Burnt Fork, Wyoming, in 1909 to take up ranching. *Letters of a Woman Homesteader* captures her life in this new country. It has been made into a film called *Heartland*, always a big hit with high school students. Here are some samples to give you the flavor of Stewart's writing.

She writes to a former employer in Denver:

> Well, I have filed on my land and am now a bloated landowner. I waited a long time to even *see* land in the reserve, and the snow is yet too deep, so I thought that as they have but three months of summer and spring together and as I wanted the land for a ranch anyway, perhaps I had better stay in the valley. So I have filed adjoining Mr. Stewart and I am well pleased. . . . I thought it would be very romantic to live on the peaks amid the whispering pines, but I reckon it would be powerfully uncomfortable also.

Later she describes naming the newborn calves with Mr. Stewart:

> As fast as a calf was vaccinated it was run out of the chute and he or I called a name for it and it was booked that way. The first two

he named were the "Duke of Monmouth" and the "Duke of Montrose." I called my first "Oliver Cromwell" and "John Fox." The poor "mon" had to have revenge, so the next ugly, scrawny little beast he called the "Poop of Roome." This morning I had the startling news that the "Poop" had eaten too much alfalfa and was all "swellit oop," and, moreover, he had "stealit it." I don't know which is the more astonishing, that the Pope has stolen alfalfa, or that he has eaten it.

A fascinating comparison might be made between *Letters of a Woman Homesteader* and the very contemporary nonfiction book by Gretel Ehrlich about her own experiences in Wyoming, *The Solace of Open Spaces.* She writes:

Space has a spiritual equivalent and can heal what is divided and burdensome in us. My grandchildren will probably use space shuttles for a honeymoon trip or to recover from heart attacks, but closer to home we might also learn how to carry space inside ourselves in the effortless way we carry our skins. Space represents sanity, not a life purified, dull, or "spaced out" but one that might accommodate intelligently any idea or situation.

We Americans are great on fillers, as if what we have, what we are, is not enough. We have a cultural tendency toward denial, but, being affluent, we strangle ourselves with what we can buy. We have only to look at the houses we build to see how we build *against* space, the way we drink against pain and loneliness. We fill up space as if it were a pie shell.

Things happen suddenly in Wyoming, the change of seasons and weather; for people, the violent swings in and out of isolation. But good-naturedness is concomitant with severity. Friendliness is a tradition. Strangers passing on the road wave hello. A common sight is two pickups stopped side by side far out on a range, on a dirt track winding through the sage. The drivers will share a cigarette, uncap their thermos bottles, and pass a battered cup, steaming with coffee, between windows.

Among accessible novels for independent study is *The Story of Avis* by Elizabeth Stuart Phelps. In it a talented artist gives up her art to marry the love of her life. As the marriage progresses, Avis questions her decision. Before her marriage she had been determined *not* to marry and give up her art. But Philip insisted he needed her and assured her that she could still paint and be married. Avis can be compared to Sybylla in Miles Franklin's *My Brilliant Career*, an Australian novel. In it, the heroine refuses to marry the man in love with her because she can't become a part of someone else's life without finding out about herself first. Also try Mollie Dorsey Sanford's journal, *Mollie: The Journey of Mollie Dorsey Sanford in Nebraska and Colorado Territories*.

The course ends with four major writers, two humorists and two poets. Emily Dickinson is paired with the other nineteenth-century great, Walt Whitman. It's useful to refer to Adrienne Rich's provocative article from her *On Lies, Secrets, and Silence*, "Vesuvius at Home: The Power of Emily Dickinson." Dickinson was a poet ahead of her time, using not strictly traditional verse forms; in fact, T. W. Higginson, the editor of *The Atlantic Monthly*, didn't like her approximate rhymes, didn't quite approve of them. Luckily, Dickinson knew she was a poet and kept on writing, putting those packets in her drawer; and her sister, Lavinia, finding them after Emily's death, did not destroy them. If Dickinson had read Anne Bradstreet, she would have empathized, we feel sure.

Finally, we come to Marietta Holley, a wonderful counterpart to Mark Twain at the end of the century: a true humorist who created the character of Samantha to write scathingly yet gently of women's rights in surefire dialect. Samantha is the wife of Josiah Allen, and Josiah is clearly no intellectual match for his wife. The contemporary feminist scholar Jane Curry has collected some of Holley's work in *Samantha Rastles the Woman Question*, a compendium of the over fourteen novels Holley published between 1887 and 1914. (An audiotape is also available.) From this collection we used "The Woman Question," "On the Tuckerin' Nature of Pedestals," "On Looking to Nature for Woman's 'Spear'," and "On Soothin', Clingin', and Cooin'." The latter includes another recurring character, one Betsy

Bobbet, who plays Phyllis Schlafly to Samantha's Gloria Steinem. Bobbet, content with the way things are, has no interest in fighting for women's rights. Many students love these Holley pieces, and boys especially often appreciate the humorous way she makes her point. The females usually delight in both approaches to the problem of women's inequality.

In concluding this chapter, we can't resist quoting from Holley's "On the Tuckerin' Nature of Pedestals." Samantha is speaking.

> How under the sun can I or any other woman be up on a pedestal and do our own housework, cookin', washin' dishes, sweepin', moppin', cleanin' lamps, blackin' stoves, washin', ironin', makin' beds, quiltin' bed quilts, gittin' three meals a day, day after day, biled dinners and bag puddin's and mince pies and things, to say nothin' of custard and pumpkin pies that will slop over on the level, do the best you can; how could you keep 'em inside the crust histin' yourself up and down?

By now students have encountered a variety of women who have redefined the "kingdom" mentioned by Alcott in the epigraph. Our tapestry is enhanced with vivid colors and innovative designs as we weave in the diverse strands from Lydia Maria Child to Marietta Holley. By the end of the nineteenth century, women were no longer to be confined to the domestic kingdom while men prevailed in the public domain. Women had made their way into the political and public arenas; there would be regression from time to time, but there would be no going back.

Works Cited

ALCOTT, LOUISA MAY. 1979. *Early Diary at Fruitlands.* Excerpted in James E. Miller, Jr., et al., eds., *United States in Literature.* Glenview, IL: Scott Foresman.

————. 1984. *Behind a Mask: The Unknown Thrillers of Louisa May Alcott.* Ed. Madeleine Stern. New York: Quill.

————. 1988. *Transcendental Wild Oats.* In Elaine Showalter, ed., *Alternative Alcott.* American Women Writers series. New Brunswick, NJ: Rutgers University Press.

CHILD, LYDIA MARIA. 1846. "Hilda Silfverling." In *Fact and Fiction: A Collection of Stories.* New York: C. S. Francis.

————. 1986. *Hobomok and Other Writings on Indians.* Ed. Carolyn L. Karcher. American Women Writers series. New Brunswick, NJ: Rutgers University Press.

CHOPIN, KATE. 1972. *The Awakening.* New York: Avon.

————. 1976. "The Story of an Hour." In Marcia McClintock Folsom and Linda Heinlein Kirschner, eds., *By Women: An Anthology of Literature.* Boston: Houghton Mifflin.

————. 1984. "The Storm." In Porter, Terrie, and Bennett.

————. 1985. "Désirée's Baby." In Boyd Litzinger and Joyce Carol Oates, eds., *Story: Fiction Past and Present.* Lexington, MA: D. C. Heath.

COOKE, ROSE TERRY. 1986. *How Celia Changed Her Mind and Selected Stories.* Ed. Elizabeth Ammons. American Women Writers series. New Brunswick, NJ: Rutgers University Press. Contains eleven stories, published together for the first time, that reflect the whole range of Cooke's career from the 1850s to the 1890s. We recommend writing to Rutgers for their catalogue of their American Women Writers series.

EHRLICH, GRETEL. 1986. *The Solace of Open Spaces.* New York: Viking.

EISLER, BENITA, ed. 1977. *The Lowell Offering: Writings by New England Mill Women, 1840–1845.* New York: Lippincott. This magazine was published from 1840 to 1845, written and edited by women factory workers. Included editorials, columns, fiction, and pictures. Available at the Lowell Mills museum in Lowell, MA.

FETTERLEY, JUDITH, ed. 1985. *Provisions: A Reader from 19th-Century American Women.* Bloomington: Indiana University Press. Selections from sixteen writers, many of whom were involved in movements for social change. Editor provides literary and historical context. Section on each writer includes critical analysis plus selected bibliography.

FRANKLIN, MILES. 1984. *My Brilliant Career.* New York: Washington Square.

FREEMAN, MARY WILKINS. 1983. "The Revolt of 'Mother'." In Marjorie Pryse, ed., *Selected Stories of Mary Wilkins Freeman*. New York: Norton.

FREIBERT, LUCY M., and BARBARA A. WHITE, eds. 1980. *Hidden Hands: An Anthology of American Women Writers, 1790–1870*. New Brunswick, NJ: Rutgers University Press. Excerpts of popular women writers of the time made available in concise form; biographical sketches, annotation, introductory material, and excerpts from critical articles provided to place works in historical context.

HARPER, FRANCES WATKINS. 1981. "A Double Standard." In Erlene Stetson, ed., *Black Sister: Poetry by Black American Women, 1746–1980*. Bloomington: Indiana University Press.

———. 1984. "Bury Me in a Free Land." In Porter, Terrie, and Bennett.

———. 1987. *Iola Leroy*. Boston: Beacon. Written during the black women's renaissance of the 1890s, this novel traces Iola's search for community and her commitment to bettering the conditions of blacks' lives. New introduction by Hazel Carby. Good for students' outside reading for extended essay.

HAWTHORNE, NATHANIEL. 1973. "Dr. Heidegger's Experiment" and "The Minister's Black Veil." In James Early, ed., *Adventures in American Literature*. New York: Harcourt Brace Jovanovich.

———. 1974. "Rappaccini's Daughter." In *Mosses from an Old Manse*. Columbus: Ohio State University Press.

———. 1983. *The Blithedale Romance*. New York: Penguin.

HOLLEY, MARIETTA. 1983. *Samantha Rastles the Woman Question*. Ed. Jane Curry. Urbana: University of Illinois Press.

IRVING, WASHINGTON. 1984. "Rip Van Winkle." In Porter, Terrie, and Bennett.

JACOBS, HARRIET (Linda Brent). 1973. *Incidents in the Life of a Slave Girl*. Ed. Walter Teller. New York: Harcourt Brace Jovanovich. Other editions now available.

LARCOM, LUCY. 1986. *A New England Girlhood*. Boston: Northeastern University Press. Excerpts include description of Lucy's mother's boarding house, Lucy's own entry into the mills, and her first efforts at publishing her own writing.

MORRISON, TONI. 1987. *Beloved.* New York: New American Library.

PARTON, SARA WILLIS (Fanny Fern). 1986. *Ruth Hall.* American Women Writers series. New Brunswick, NJ: Rutgers University Press. A novel believed to be quite autobiographical; this edition includes a good sampling of Fanny Fern's columns.

PEABODY, ELIZABETH. 1980. "Plan of the West Roxbury Community." (*The Dial*, January 1842.) In Elaine and William Hedges, eds., *Land and the Imagination.* Rochelle Park, NJ: Hayden.

PHELPS, ELIZABETH STUART. 1985. *The Story of Avis.* New Brunswick, NJ: Rutgers University Press.

RICH, ADRIENNE. 1979. "Vesuvius at Home: The Power of Emily Dickinson." In *On Lies, Secrets, and Silence: Selected Prose, 1966–1978.* New York: Norton.

ROBINSON, HARRIET H. 1976. *Loom and Spindle, or Life Among the Early Mill Girls.* Rev. ed. Kailua, HI: Press Pacifica.

SANFORD, MOLLIE DORSEY. 1976. *Mollie: The Journal of Mollie Dorsey Sanford in Nebraska and Colorado Territories, 1857–1866.* Ed. Donald F. Danaker. Lincoln, NE: Bison. Accessible for students; very personal and vivid. Mollie endured many adventures with rattlesnakes, blizzards, mining camps, and "Pike's Peak Fever." We see her courage, humor, and common sense.

STANTON, ELIZABETH CADY. 1984. "Declaration of Sentiments." In Porter, Terrie, and Bennett.

STEWART, ELINORE PRUITT. 1982. *Letters of a Woman Homesteader.* Boston: Houghton Mifflin.

TRUTH, SOJOURNER. 1984. "Ain't I a Woman?" In Porter, Terrie, and Bennett.

Suggested Books for Students

ALCOTT, LOUISA MAY. 1977. *Work.* New York: Schocken. Autobiographical novel dealing with problems of the American working girl in the mid-nineteenth century. The protagonist assumes a number of different jobs, including maidservant, governess, seamstress, and actress. She eventually finds her true calling as a women's rights advocate.

CHOPIN, KATE. 1986. *At Fault*. Cambridge, MA: Green Street Press. Chopin's first novel and the first one published in the United States that treats divorce in a disinterested, nonjudgmental way. Strong-willed heroine, Therese, tries to impose order on her life; has to reexamine her assumptions about life and love.

CUMMINS, MARIA SUSANNA. 1988. *The Lamplighter*. American Woman Writers series. New Brunswick, NJ: Rutgers University Press. A mid-nineteenth-century novel of female development in which a woman who begins as an abandoned child learns to meet life with courage and honesty.

DAVIS, REBECCA HARDING. 1985. *Life in the Iron Mills and Other Stories*. New York: Feminist Press. Very short—about sixty-five pages—with a long discussion by Tillie Olsen afterwards. Hard, stinging account of brutal lives of people in a nineteenth-century steel town like the one in Virginia, where the author grew up.

PHELPS, ELIZABETH STUART. 1983. *The Silent Partner*. New York: Feminist Press. Focuses on problems of women in the machine age. Raises such questions as how those who are denied access to speech might express themselves and how those who have access to speech use it.

———. 1987. *Doctor Zay*. New York: Feminist Press. Explores the struggle experienced by a woman trying to choose between a career in medicine and marriage.

STERLING, DOROTHY, ed. 1984. *We Are Your Sisters: Black Women in the Nineteenth Century*. New York: Norton. Divided into five parts plus an epilogue, the book includes a rich array of primary source material; examples of section titles are "Slavery Time" up through "The Postwar North." Students may read selections centered on a theme. Also a valuable reference tool for teachers.

STOWE, HARRIET BEECHER. 1988. *Pink and White Tyranny*. New York: Plume. Ahead of its time in 1871, the novel comments on the limited position of women, socially and economically. Stowe criticizes a society that demands of its women only that they have charm and beauty.

Useful Works for Teachers

DUBLIN, THOMAS, ed. 1981. *Farm to Factory: Women's Letters, 1830–1860.* New York: Columbia University Press. A selection of the letters of six of the thousands of single women who left rural New England to work in the factory towns of the region and later returned home, moved west, or settled in urban centers. The letters give different perspectives on early industrial capitalism and its effect on women.

HOFFMAN, NANCY, ed. 1981. *Woman's "True" Profession: Voices from the History of Teaching.* New York: Feminist Press. An excellent collection of primary source material about teaching. In the 1840s, 1850s, and 1860s, theorists believed women were better fitted to be teachers than men because teaching "unlocked" their instincts for motherhood and prepared them for that later undertaking.

KESSLER, CAROL FARLEY, ed. 1984. *Daring to Dream: Utopian Stories by United States Women, 1836–1919.* Boston: Pandora. Extraordinary collection of stories showing women's yearnings for a future that has yet to be realized even today. Collection includes great variety, from women running businesses in sober suits while the men do housework to blueprints for a nonsexist society; in one story, men get up in the night to comfort crying children.

KOLODNY, ANNETTE. 1975. *The Lay of the Land: Metaphor as Experience and History in American Life and Letters.* Chapel Hill: University of North Carolina Press. Explores frontier metaphors from Cooper's *The Deer-slayer* to Bellow's *Henderson the Rain King.* Provocative reading for teachers interested in a new way of looking at western literature.

———. 1984. *The Land Before Her: Fantasy and Experience of the American Frontiers, 1630–1860.* Chapel Hill: University of North Carolina Press. Examination of three centuries of women's writing about the frontier. Whereas the American frontiersman saw the land before him as a wilderness to be conquered, the woman saw it as a garden to be cultivated.

KOPPELMAN, SUSAN, ed. 1984. *Old Maids: Short Stories by Nineteenth Century U.S. Women Writers.* Boston: Pandora. Often written by unmarried women, these stories reveal attitudes about spinsterhood, seen by some as negative and by others as a chance for welcomed independence.

MᴄSʜᴇʀʀʏ, Fʀᴀɴᴋ Jʀ., Cʜᴀʀʟᴇs G. Wᴀᴜɢʜ, and Mᴀʀᴛɪɴ Gʀᴇᴇɴʙᴇʀɢ, eds. 1988. *Civil War Women: The Civil War Seen Through Women's Eyes in Stories by Louisa May Alcott, Kate Chopin, Eudora Welty, and Other Great Women Writers.* New York: Simon & Schuster. Also includes stories by Rose Terry Cooke, Constance Fenimore Woolson, and Elizabeth Stuart Phelps Ward.

Mʏᴇʀsᴏɴ, Jᴏᴇʟ, and Dᴀɴɪᴇʟ Sʜᴇᴀʟʏ, eds. 1987. *The Selected Letters of Louisa May Alcott.* Boston: Little, Brown.

———. 1989. *The Journals of Louisa May Alcott.* Boston: Little, Brown.

Rᴏɢᴇʀs, Kᴀᴛʜᴀʀɪɴᴇ M., ed. 1991. *The Meridan Anthology of Early American Women Writers from Anne Bradstreet to Louisa May Alcott, 1650–1865.* New York: Penguin. Includes writings by Sarah Kemble Knight, Mary Rowlandson, Abigail Adams, Phillis Wheatley, "Fanny Fern," and many others. Also includes the short story "The Angel Over the Right Shoulder" by Elizabeth Stuart Phelps, which is very accessible to students. In it, a well-meaning husband tries to let his wife have a couple of hours a day to herself for writing or studying, but this fails as gradually everyone in the house comes to interrupt her with their needs.

Rᴏss, Nᴀɴᴄʏ Wɪʟsᴏɴ. 1944. *Westward the Women.* San Francisco: North Point Press. A vivid, surprising, and intriguing account of the diverse accomplishments of women from all levels of society in the westward settlement. This book proves Spengler's maxim "Women are history." Ross did extensive research in primary sources.

Sᴄʜʟɪssᴇʟ, Lɪʟʟɪᴀɴ. 1982. *Women's Diaries of the Westward Journey.* New York: Schocken. Pioneering was in fact a family matter, and the westering experiences of American women must be read about in order to get a clear picture of the frontier. Schlissel provides analysis, pictures, tables, commentary and, in the latter part of the book, whole diaries or sections of diaries women wrote on their westward journeys.

Sʜᴏᴡᴀʟᴛᴇʀ, Eʟᴀɪɴᴇ, ed. 1988. *Alternative Alcott.* American Woman Writers series. New Brunswick, NJ: Rutgers University Press. Contains *Transcendental Wild Oats*, *Work*, and *Behind a Mask*.

Sᴛᴀɴᴛᴏɴ, Eʟɪᴢᴀʙᴇᴛʜ Cᴀᴅʏ. 1974. *The Woman's Bible.* Seattle, WA: Seattle Coaliton on Women and Religion. Stanton and others' effort to reveal the sexism of the Bible. Fourteen printings of this book through March 1989 attest to its popularity.

STRATTON, JOANNA L. 1981. *Pioneer Women: Women from the Kansas Frontier*. New York: Simon & Schuster. A tribute to women's strength, independence, and wisdom during the nineteenth century in Kansas. Created from a rediscovered collection of autobiographical accounts written by hundreds of pioneer women.

WOOLSON, CONSTANCE FENIMORE. 1988. *Women Artists, Women Exiles: "Miss Grief" and Other Stories*. American Woman Writers series. New Brunswick, NJ: Rutgers University Press. The author was the great-niece of James Fenimore Cooper and a good friend of Henry James. She was very conscious of the situation of women writers at this time, and her stories probe the marginality of women writers who saw themselves as artists.

SIX

American Literature
Early Twentieth Century

*I found that I had no need of either class or race
prejudice, those scourges of humanity. The solace of easy
generalization was taken from me, but I received the
richer gift of individualism. When I have been made to
suffer or when I have been made happy by others, I have
known that individuals were responsible for that, and not
races. All clumps of people turn out to be individuals on
close inspection.*

ZORA NEALE HURSTON
Dust Tracks on a Road

As the twentieth century in America advances, its literature reflects
the increasing variety of people, people loving freedom, discovering
their heritage, and trying to create a world complex enough to integrate and accommodate them all without prejudice. Langston
Hughes, echoing the spirit of Zora Neale Hurston, talks in "Daybreak
in Alabama" of composing a world where everybody touches everybody "with kind fingers" naturally, whether these hands are black or
brown or white or yellow. Anyone teaching a twentieth-century
American literature course opens that world, and the richness of the
literature makes choosing which people to include a pleasure. This
chapter will suggest a number of women authors writing during the
first half of the century (enough to make a course in themselves)

whose writing can be mixed into the tasty stew of twentieth-century American literature.

The women's stories written at the turn of the century during the so-called Age of Realism strike as forcefully as the men's in the opinion of students who remember them well over the semester. These stories act in some ways as touchstones for later literature. One of them, the first story we present in the course, is "The Hiltons' Holiday" by Sarah Orne Jewett. She once called it her favorite. The entire plot consists of John Hilton's taking his two daughters, Susan Ellen and Katy, ages eleven and nine, to Topham Corners some seventeen miles away, where they meet both a judge and an old friend, see the local academy, and get their picture taken. The day, "famous" and "great" to them, came about because the father (a nontraditional man, typical of the men in Jewett's stories) wanted his daughters to "know the world, an' not stay right here on the farm like a couple o' bushes." When his wife says they are contented enough, John responds: "Contented ain't all in this world; hopper-toads may have that quality an' spend all their time a-blinkin'. . . . Ambition's somethin' to me." Indeed, the journey changes the course of Katy's life: she, the "shy-feelin' and wishful" one who "lives right with herself," loves roving around outside, and may well be one not to get married, comes to see that she can attend the academy and become a teacher like her grandmother Hilton. When she sees the academy, and the judge, a classmate of her grandmother, remarks on Katy's resemblance to her grandmother, Katy experiences an epiphany. We warn students that at first glance nothing much appears to happen in the story, but a second reading will show that something does. Students talk about similar discoveries they have made about who they are, might be, or where they've come from.

To encourage close reading and class participation, we divide the class into four groups, assigning each group someone or something to think about and the task of finding supporting passages for that person or thing in the story for homework. This way every student gets to talk and is encouraged to take notes and read the story at least twice, activities we expect all the time in this course. The assignments include characterizing the mother, the father, or Susan Ellen; comparing and contrasting the two sisters; and discussing the changes in Katy. Students do not meet in groups; rather, when they come to class, each member of each group says one thing, using the text for evidence, until all the members of the group have said all they have prepared. They may disagree; if so, they talk to each other. Then their classmates join in with additions, questions, more evidence, and general reactions to the story as a whole before we move on to the next group. We as teachers stay out of it except to ask a student to hold a comment until later where it may be more helpful. You may be wondering why we're going into this detail about the way we conduct the class; it's because we want to show how we build up to having student groups conduct the class entirely on their own at the end of the semester.

The second story we read is "A Church Mouse" by Mary Wilkins Freeman, found in the Ginn anthology. Since both Jewett and Freeman have been categorized as local colorists, we explain the term *local colorist* and ask students to decide for themselves if this and the Jewett story fit the definition. As with the Jewett story, we assign students to think about topics ranging from characterizing Hetty, the protagonist, to finding issues raised by her story; all students come to class prepared to compare and contrast these two writers.

In "A Church Mouse" a feisty, belligerent, stubborn, prickly, outspoken, homeless old woman demands that the town do something about her. "Always taking her own way, and never heeding the voice of authority," Hetty "was held in the light of a long thorned brier among the beanpoles, or a fierce little animal with claws and teeth bared." She outfoxes the head selectman and church deacon, Caleb Gale, into setting herself up as the live-in church sexton. When the men try to force her out (the smells of her cabbage and turnip outweigh in their minds her masterful cleaning of the church), Mrs. Gale and the women find the solution: let Hetty use the little room off to the side where the preacher stows his hat; let the minister find another place for his headgear. All of the students enjoy the humor and liveliness of this story.

The next works also involve rural, local scenes: autobiographical essays by W. E. B. DuBois and Zitkala-Ša, a native American.

DuBois's piece "Of the Meaning of Progress" can be compared with a selection from Ida B. Wells's autobiography, *Crusade for Justice*. Students are as grieved by the death of Josie in DuBois's essay as they are angered by Zitkala-Ša's description of the herding of the Indian children in the white missionary school and the insult thrown at Wells for refusing to sit in the unoffical black section of the train. Zitkala-Ša is forced to wear what she considers immodest dresses and hard, noisy shoes, and must have her hair shingled, the sign of a coward in her culture. She first hid, then fought, before she was tied to a chair while the shears gnawed off her thick braids. Both DuBois and Zitkala-Ša ask if white people's civilization brings with it "real life or long-lasting death" (Zitkala-Ša). Progress for the blacks in a distant hill of Tennessee shines in a new school; but when DuBois returns to see it and his former students, although he finds a few families with more acres of land, he finds many of his students dead or running from the law. "How many heartfuls of sorrow shall balance a bushel of wheat?" he asks, here "where the dark-faced Josie lies."

In preparing these two or three readings, students write a paper based on a quote. We call this our "generic writing assignment" because it can be used with stories, essays, novels, plays, or poems. It has four parts. First, students choose a passage that made a deep impression on them, and they write it down. Second, they explain the context, where it appears in the whole piece. (Some students give us a page and column number rather than the surrounding events!) Third, they explain their reaction to the passage: how they identified with it, how it made them feel, what it made them think about. Students are warned to explain themselves thoroughly, because no one else will have their reaction. The point is for them to just write honestly about their response. And fourth, they relate their passage to the rest of the work. They're asked to explain how this passage helps them understand the whole piece. Then they're asked to find some connection between the selected passage and the work as a whole. What are the implications of the passage? How does it illuminate a purpose and meaning of the whole?

We usually just divide the class to insure an equal number of students on each reading, but everyone reads all the selections. In class, the discussion circles around the papers as each student in turn reads or summarizes her or his paper. Each work gets one day of discussion. We, the teachers, have little to do except enjoy what the students have to say. Sometimes we join in with one of our favorite passages, as the ground rules include jumping in if you have the same or a related passage.

Another story about an outsider concerns the loneliness of the immigrant caught between two worlds, a member of neither. "Children of Loneliness" by Anzia Yezierska vividly describes the disgust Rachel, a recent college graduate, has for the slovenly, dirty ways of her immigrant parents. She decries the heaped dirty dishes, the noisy crunching of bones as her father devours his dinner, the greasy food, and the cramped quarters. "They're ugly and gross and stupid" to Rachel. Students hate her yelling at her parents as she refuses to be a pillow for their old age. "My life is my own; I'll live as I please," she cries as she slams the door, leaving home for good. But Rachel's heart is torn: she looks in the window at them, seeing their despair at losing her and wanting desperately to move back home. But she can't. She doesn't want to abandon them, she just wants to get to a place where she belongs: "I only want to get to the mountain-tops and view the world from the heights, and then I'll give them everything I've achieved." When Rachel discovers that her college friend Frank has romanticized the squalid reality of her parents' ghetto, she finds herself misunderstood by the Americans as well as by her parents. The story ends with her sitting in her spotlessly clean, white-walled room wondering how she will live as an American but wanting to do so, even if she must be utterly alone like so many other immigrant children, wandering between two worlds, one too old and the other too new to live comfortably in. Yezierska's sharp, distinctive vocabulary draws sharp responses from the students. For example, Rachel thinks as she flees from her parents: "Vampires, bloodsuckers fastened on my flesh! Black shadow blighting every ray of light that ever came my way! . . . They put dead stones in front of every chance I made for myself."

Since this story has three sections, it is easy to make three groups of students responsible for coming to class with questions/topics pertinent to their section and helping their classmates discuss what they found important. Such a student-led discussion runs more smoothly if the students meet briefly in their groups to organize their questions; the advantage of not organizing first lies in having each student offer a question—there's no hiding behind the well-prepared classmate.

Three other women who wrote during this period are Willa Cather, Edith Wharton, and Kate Chopin. All wrote intriguing short stories about a woman's identity. Cather's "A Wagner Matinée" is about Aunt Georgiana, who returns to Boston on business and attends a matinee with her nephew after living thirty years on a bleak Nebraska farm. Before eloping and disappearing into the prairie, she had been a pianist and music teacher. Living in a "tall, naked house . . . , black and grim as a wooden fortress" in this flat world of hard labor, her hands "had been stretched and twisted into mere tentacles to hold and lift and knead with." Her passion for music had withered, but as the concert swelled, so did her passion until at the end she cries, "I don't want to go!" Not home to that farm with its "crook-backed ash seedlings" and "the gaunt, moulting turkeys picking up refuse about the kitchen door."

Students do some writing before we begin talking about this story: they may respond to their favorite single sentence or address a question, such as whether this concert had been a positive or a negative experience for Georgiana, or whether the harsh life on the plains had strengthened or weakened her. Other questions raised in discussion include: What do you think will happen to her if she goes home to her children and animals and husband? Will she go back? What about a person's central passion, for music in this story—can it be killed without killing the person? How whole can the person be without expressing it? In addition to raising these and other questions about the frontier versus civilization or rural versus urban environments, the story offers strong images, packed in one right after another.

Edith Wharton's "The Other Two" takes us to New York and the aristocracy of the times. Alice Waythorn, complying with the expectations of society in order to raise her social class, has moved into her third marriage, having adopted the acceptable mannerisms and remolded herself to fit each husband. Mr. Waythorn, at first loving her for her elasticity, her calmness, her absolutely right demeanor, grows restless with her too-easy transformations. One afternoon her other two husbands (one the father of her child and the other working through a business deal with Waythorn) appear at the house at the same time her husband comes home, all just in time for tea. Alice Waythorn, easily up to the occasion, offers tea all around, even remembering who takes milk, lemon, or sugar. Her husband chuckles, finally, his perturbations over; after all, he has molded one third of her. But who *is* Alice? This story, humorous as it may be, underscores the tenuousness of women's identity in a society of limited options for them.

A third woman's identity story, and one about racism, is Kate Chopin's "Désirée's Baby." In it, an arrogant man marries Désirée, though her family background is somewhat mysterious. When their son is born, his dark skin summons latent racial hatred in the husband, who assumes Désirée is black and casts her out. Later her husband discovers that his family is the one carrying the detested genes.

Henry James's story "Four Meetings" offers a look at Carolyn Spencer, "a charming little figure" of innocence and New England conscience. She saves and saves for a trip to her beloved Europe to see the art and buildings and drink of the atmosphere of quaint and beautiful streets. But, alas, as the male narrator tells us, her nephew, an artist, dupes her with a tale of woe and borrows all her money, sending her home within twenty-four hours of her arrival. A few years later, this nephew's wife, a self-styled countess, appears in Grimwinter, claiming Miss Spencer's hospitality. This fake countess, demanding her coffee with cognac every morning, is all Miss Spencer gets to see of her dear old Europe. (This character connects nicely with Aunt Georgiana.)

For this period, there are too many stories to teach. (At least we have many works by women to choose from!) Some years students choose one to read independently; or we have them read one for a unit test, asking them to apply their analytical skills and make connections to the stories they've studied; or we suggest they might try a collection of short stories by one of the authors for their extended essay.

Our next unit is the Harlem Renaissance. Zora Neale Hurston delights students with her straightforward, independent commentaries excerpted from *Dust Tracks on a Road.* Who can resist someone who sees "no curse in being black, nor no extra flavor by being white" or that "all clumps of people turn out to be individuals on close inspection." Hurston continues: "Negroes are just like anybody else. Some soar. Some plod ahead. Some just make a mess and step back in it—like the rest of America and the world." Besides her imagery, her prose is a relief from all the poetry in the unit. Many students read this autobiography or her novel *Their Eyes Were Watching God* (see Chapter 10) for their extended essays.

After graduating from Barnard College, Hurston pursued her interest in folklore, traveling extensively in the South to gather tales later collected in *Mules and Men.* These stories could be used in a unit or course on myths, legends, or folktales for any grade level. Her language is that of the storytellers she interviewed, filled with the "varmints" and "ker ploogums" of the local dialects. And no wasted words.

Two of the Harlem Renaissance poets we teach are women: Gwendolyn Bennett and Helene Johnson. We found them and many other black women poets in *Black Sister* edited by Erlene Stetson and in *Shadowed Dreams* edited by Maureen Honey. The following poems speak for themselves. By Bennett:

Song[1]

I am weaving a song of waters,
Shaken from firm, brown limbs,
Or heads thrown back in irreverent mirth.
My song has the lush sweetness
Of moist, dark lips
Where hymns keep company
With old forgotten banjo songs.
Abandon tells you
That I sing the heart of a race
While sadness whispers
That I am the cry of a soul. . . .

---

[1]Published in *Opportunity* 4 (October 1926). Appeared in *The New Negro* edited by Alain Locke (New York: Albert and Charles Boni, 1925).

A-shoutin' in de ole camp-meetin' place,
A-strummin' o' de ole banjo.
Singin' in de moonlight,'
Sobbin' in de dark.
Singin', sobbin', strummin' slow . . .
Singin' slow; sobbin' low.
Strummin', strummin', strummin' slow. . . .

Words are bright bugles
That make the shining for my song,
And mothers hold brown babes
To dark, warm breasts
To make my singing sad.

A dancing girl with swaying hips
Sets mad the queen in a harlot's eye.
   Praying slave
   Jazz band after
   Breaking heart
   To the time of laughter. . . .
Clinking chains and minstrelsy
Are welded fast with melody.
   A praying slave
   With a jazz band after . . .
   Singin' slow, sobbin' low.
   Sun-baked lips will kiss the earth.
   Throats of bronze will burst with mirth.
   Sing a little faster,
   Sing a little faster!
   Sing!

Also by Bennett:

To Usward[2]

Let us be still
As ginger jars are still

---

[2]Published in *Opportunity* 2 (May 1924) and *The Crisis* 28 (May 1924)

Upon a Chinese shelf,
And let us be contained
By entities of Self . . .

Not still with lethargy and sloth,
But quiet with the pushing of our growth;
Not self-contained with smug identity,
But conscious of the strength in entity.

If any have a song to sing that's different from the rest,
Oh, let him sing before the Urgency of Youth's behest!

And some of us have songs to sing
Of jungle heat and fires;
And some of us are solemn grown
With pitiful desires;
And there are those who feel the pull
Of seas beneath the skies;
And some there be who want to croon
Of Negro lullabies.
We claim no part with racial dearth,
We want to sing the songs of birth!

And so we stand like ginger jars,
Like ginger jars bound round
With dust and age;
Like jars of ginger we are sealed
By nature's heritage.
But let us break the seal of years
With pungent thrusts of song,
For there is joy in long dried tears,
For whetted passions of a throng!

Another poem by Bennett students have responded readily to is
"Hatred," about hating with the sharpness of steel darts and "swift
arrows" and the coolness of hands playing a game until "you . . .
understand / my hatred." Another is "Heritage" with its five clear
images of Africa, composing the soul of her "sad people . . . hidden by
a minstrel-smile."

The following two poems are by Helene Johnson.

Bottled[3]

Upstairs on the third floor
Of the 135th Street library
In Harlem, I saw a little
Bottle of sand, brown sand
Just like the kids make pies
Out of down at the beach.
But the label said: "This
Sand was taken from the Sahara desert."
Imagine that! The Sahara desert!
Some bozo's been all the way to Africa to get some sand.

And yesterday on Seventh Avenue
I saw a darky dressed fit to kill
In yellow gloves and swallow tail coat
And swirling a cane. And everyone
Was laughing at him. Me too,
At first, till I saw his face
When he stopped to hear a
Organ grinder grind out some jazz.
Boy! You should a seen that darky's face!
It just shone. Gee, he was happy!
And he began to dance. No
Charleston or Black Bottom for him.
No sir. He danced just as dignified
And slow. No, not slow either.
Dignified and *proud*! You couldn't
Call it slow, not with all the
Cuttin' up he did. You would a died to see him.

The crowd kept yellin' but he didn't hear,
Just kept on dancin' and twirlin' that cane
And yellin' out loud every once in a while.
I know the crowd thought he was coo-coo.

---

[3]From *Caroling Dusk* edited by Countee Cullen (New York: Harper and Brothers, 1927).

117

But say, I was where I could see his face,
And somehow, I could see him dancin' in a jungle,
A real honest-to-cripe-jungle, and he wouldn't have on them
Trick clothes—those yaller shoes and yaller gloves
And swallow tail coat. He wouldn't have on nothing.
And he wouldn't be carrying no cane.
He'd be carrying a spear with a sharp fine point
Like the bayonets we had "over there."
And the end of it would be dipped in some kind of
Hoo-doo poison. And he'd be dancin' black and naked
   and gleaming.
And he'd have rings in his ears and on his nose
And bracelets and necklaces of elephants' teeth.
Gee, I bet he'd be beautiful then all right.
No one could laugh at him then, I bet.
Say! that man that took that sand from the Sahara desert
And put it in a little bottle on a shelf in the library,
That's what they done to this shine, ain't it? Bottled him.
Trick shoes, trick coat, trick cane, trick everything—
   all glass—
But inside—
Gee, that poor shine!

Magalu[4]

Summer comes.
The ziczac[5] hovers
'Round the greedy-mouthed crocodile.
A vulture beats away a foolish jackal.
The flamingo is a dash of pink
Against dark green mangroves,
Her slender legs rivalling her slim neck.
The laughing lake gurgles delicious music in its throat
And lulls to sleep the lazy lizard,
A nebulous being on a sun-scorched rock.

---

[4]From *Caroling Dusk* edited by Countee Cullen (New York: Harper and Brothers, 1927).

[5]An Egyptian species of plover who warns the crocodile of approaching danger by its cry.

In such a place,
In this pulsing, riotous gasp of color,
I met Magalu, dark as a tree at night,
Eager-lipped, listening to a man with a white collar
And a small black book with a cross on it.
Oh, Magalu, come! Take my hand and I will read you poetry,
Chromatic words,
Seraphic symphonies,
Fill up your throat with laughter and your heart with song.
Do not let him lure you from your laughing waters,
Lulling lakes, lissome winds.
Would you sell the colors of your sunset and the fragrance
Of your flowers, and the passionate wonder of your forest
For a creed that will not let you dance?

Students also enjoy Johnson's short poem "The Road." After describing the "little road, brown as my race is brown," the speaker insists that "they must not bruise you down." Rather, the road is exhorted to "rise" with its "cry" spilling over. Johnson's "Trees at Night" summons up beautiful images with its vocabulary: lacy, slumbrous, quivering, tremulous, stencilled, spluttered, pinnacles, webs. The man in her "Sonnet to a Negro in Harlem" is splendid, his "head thrown back in rich, barbaric song" as he refuses to whine for wages even though the scorn of the white folks "will efface each footprint that [he makes]."

During this unit, pairs of students teach poems after we have modeled some ways to draw out responses and analysis from students, such as asking for students' favorite images or for what connections they found between sounds and tone or imagery.

Since there are so many contemporary authors to study as well, we bring them in whenever we can. When we come to the end of the Harlem Renaissance, for example, we add Maya Angelou and Alice Walker as links to the 1980s and 1990s. Paul Laurence Dunbar's caged bird image from his poem "Sympathy" ties into a selection from Angelou's autobiography *I Know Why the Caged Bird Sings*. We add her poems "Still I Rise" and "Phenomenal Woman." The sassy and challenging tone of her autobiography and "Still I Rise" contrasts with the pain and grief of Dunbar. In spite of what others (no doubt whites) may say or do, like dust and the sun and the moon and tides, she'll rise; like a black ocean "leaping and wide" she'll raise her full heritage onto the shore. Alice Walker's long, tough-voiced poem "Each One, Pull One" speaks for all the disenfranchised and insists that each of them must pull their kinsfolk out of the obscurity powerful folk have buried them in. We also look at her "On Stripping Bark From Myself." The bark she strips off, the identity imposed on her by her family and lover, exposes her own "standing self" ready to fight any and all who might kill her.

In lieu of a test, students design a project to show what they have learned and what they feel about the Harlem Renaissance authors and works, including works not studied in class they may find. Projects have included response journals, tapes of poems set to original music or read against familiar music, collages, drawings and paintings, mobiles, a bowl made in pottery class and decorated with images from poems and filled with fruit, and poetry anthologies (some with elaborate designs and illustrations). All of these projects are accompanied by rationales, explaining what and why, the order, the purpose, the connections to the works. One young man enchanted us all for twenty minutes as he talked quietly about a rich, complex collage based on the "Bottled" motif; another enticed his musical friends to join him in playing his original score while he sang "Bottled." A young woman packed a cutout of Africa with tiny, brilliantly colored pictures of the people, animals, birds, and flora mentioned in works and imagined in her head; another sewed a small quilt incorporating the colors and images of "Magalu." While sharing these projects, one class got to discussing the advantages of projects, the idea that they were creating their own images in response to the images and passions of these works; they amazed themselves. These projects are the highlight of the course for most of us.

Having singled out the black writers from the 1920s through the 1950s, we go back, picking up other writers, prose first, then poetry.

During the first quarter of American Literature II, students read two or three short novels, such as *The Old Man and the Sea, The Great Gatsby,* or *A Lost Lady.* Willa Cather's *A Lost Lady* challenges students to examine how reliable Niel Herbert is as a narrator, as he tells

Marian Forrester's story. She is lost to him, but must she be to us? Her husbands treasured her; can we? Along with showing students the West in the days after the railroads were built and the frontier was crossed, when the moneygrubbers and shysters like Ivy Peters had arrived, the book poses Marian's dilemma: what to do with one's vitality, once nourished by wealth, respect, and social excitement, when one lives stranded in a fading small town. When the banks fail and Captain Forrester, Marian's husband, suffers a stroke and finally dies, Marian takes a downward turn. She becomes, for Niel, one of the "lilies that fester." His heroine falls from her pedestal. But he was the one who put her there; he was the one who lost her. Others see her as strong, a survivor; she may drink too much and even take up with Ivy Peters, but she does what she has to to work her way out of Sweet Water, back to the life she needs. She marries a rich man in Buenos Aires, and even Niel is relieved to know she is well taken care of. This second husband surprises us when he sends money for the perpetual care of Captain Forrester's grave in Marian's memory after Marian dies. Students come to class prepared with comments and questions and interesting passages to talk over with each other, and they write short papers on the novels on topics of their own choosing.

Even if students have read it before, they enjoy Shirley Jackson's "The Lottery." Its proclamations against following unexamined tradition speak to their own energy for change. Eudora Welty, Katherine Anne Porter, and Ann Petry all wrote many stories that appeal to teenagers. Sometimes we pair Welty's "A Visit of Charity" with Porter's "The Jilting of Granny Weatherall" for a look at older people, the subtle uses of religious images, and expert characterization. In Welty's story, a campfire girl, Marion, visits an old folks' home to earn points. Not knowing what to expect, she grows increasingly disoriented by the impersonal nurse, the uneven linoleum floor, the cramped room, and the old women's arguing. A bedridden woman invites her to come over close; Marion peers at her, seeing every detail, including her tears. Shocked, she flees the building, grabbing her red apple from its hiding place under a bush outside the door and hailing a bus. In Porter's story, Granny Weatherall's deathbed monologue, reflecting on her life and the condition of her soul, gradually reveals her character and values. In the end, having been jilted a second time, she blows out the light of her life, asserting her independence and control. Petry's "Like a Winding Sheet" shocks students, and its violence, first society's to the husband and then his to his wife, reminds students of current domestic violence even though the motivation may differ. Stories by these people balance those by Faulkner, Hemingway, Steinbeck, Fitzgerald, and Wright. Every student writes one short paper on some topic or question on one of the stories. The students who write the papers begin the discussion.

Among the female poets of this time period, the students particularly enjoy Amy Lowell, the imagist. Lowell's "Patterns," a strong antiwar poem, exemplifies many of her hallmarks: bright images, sharp and painful experiences, contrasting worlds of the ideal and harsh reality, and mixed or irregular meters and rhymes. Having described the irritations of the patterns in her life (a stiff brocade gown, proper behavior, and formal gardens), the young woman reveals the death of her fiancé in battle. The poem ends with the question "What are patterns for?" Other antiwar poems of Lowell's include "Misericordia" and "The Fort." We also study "Taxi," with the speaker asking why she should leave when it causes her so much pain, and "Fugitive" with its "brittle pleasures" that will not last. In "Music" a neighbor's flute's notes "flutter and tap about the room" of a listener who imagines the player is a young man dressed in a blue coat with silver buttons. In fact, he is bald and eats onions with his bread. Students work in groups, one group for each of these poems. They study their poem and prepare a way to present it to the class. They also find ways to connect their poem to one or more of the other groups' poems.

Edna St. Vincent Millay also wrote many poems high school students relate to, for example, "Spring." In it she asks April why it returns, for though spring may be beautiful, she knows that "not only underground" are maggots eating the brains of men. In fact, the speaker in the poem finds April quite an idiot. Millay, like Housman, writes a poem "To a Poet that Died Young"; she also wrote of love: "Never May the Fruit Be Plucked." And she writes an angry poem when she discovers the world is preparing to go to war again, "Apostrophe to Man." She's disgusted with the human race's energy to place "death on the market," to "expunge" itself and "die out." All of these poems are spirited.

Other poets to read include Elizabeth Bishop, with her detailed descriptions of gas stations and fish with implied commentaries about the world and the way people think and work in it. Or try a pair of poets: Sara Teasdale and Elinor Wylie. Teasdale may be better known for her war poems, but she also addresses the benefits of standing strong for oneself, even if that means being alone. In her "Advice to a Girl" she comments that a thing or person that can be possessed may not be worth possessing. In "The Solitary" she says that because her heart's "grown rich" she doesn't have the same need to "share" herself with others: she is as "self-complete as a flower or a stone." "On a March Day" pinpoints the sharpness of March weather in New England and then adds that she loved all aspects of her life, the pleasant and hurtful, and now sees no reason to fear her final entombment in the earth. "The Answer" sounds a similar note. These work well with the better-known "There Will Come Soft Rains." Wylie has similar themes of contentment in the face of death (in "Prophecy") and independence (in "Let No Charitable Hope"). In the latter she is fearless, amused by life even though "being human, born alone" and "being woman, hard beset" she has had to squeeze "from a stone" what meager "nourishment" she gets. In "Unfinished Portrait" she refuses to limit or freeze her loved one by painting a portrait; rather, she prefers an uncaptured lover, free.

Two others to weave in are Gwendolyn Brooks and Margaret Walker. In "truth," Brooks says that truth has a hard time penetrating the snug "thick shelter" of what we're used to. "Life for my child is simple, and is good" is about her son, who "never has . . . been afraid to reach" for things. Brooks has many accessible poems. A sonnet we like is "Fight First. Then Fiddle" in which she advises people to clear a situation of animosity before playing their violins, for violins need civilized space—space without malice, murder, or hate—to sound with grace.

Margaret Walker's poems reflect on her childhood and her people. In "Childhood" her description of the mining town and surrounding shacks seems straightforward enough until the last lines push us back into the poem as we realize that hate still governs and only the bitterness in the land itself has been washed away. Similarly, the excitement of going home in "October Journey" dims the closer she gets to her unchanged land, where the stagnant water is "full of slimy things." On the other hand, she admires her grandmothers in "Lineage." In "Iowa Farmer" the speaker implies the stark contrast of her life with that of the farmer. And finally, in "For My People" (which can be compared in interesting ways with Sandburg's "The People Will Live On") Walker piles up images of her people in their vitality and confusion and victimization and laughter and dying "of consumption and anemia and lynching." The sweep of the first nine stanzas ends in the pulsing rhythms of the last stanza about people who are hopeful and loving but who have to fight for freedom. In this last stanza, "my people" has become "a people" who she hopes will rise and take control.

These women writers of the first fifty years of our century are an energizing group. They have many of the qualities of Margaret Walker's new generation, who she says will build a new world for all the people.

Works Cited

ANGELOU, MAYA. 1969. *I Know Why the Caged Bird Sings*. New York: Bantam.

———. 1981. "Phenomenal Woman" and "Still I Rise." In *Poems*. New York: Bantam.

BENNETT, GWENDOLYN. 1981. "Hatred," "Heritage," "Song," and "To Usward." In Stetson.

BISHOP, ELIZABETH. 1955. *The Complete Poems*. New York: Farrar, Straus & Giroux.

BROOKS, GWENDOLYN. 1963. "Fight First. Then Fiddle." *Selected Poems*. New York: Harper & Row.

———. 1984. "truth" and "Life for my child is simple, and is good." In Porter, Terrrie, and Bennett.

CATHER, WILLA. 1972. *A Lost Lady.* New York: Vintage.

———. 1984. "A Wagner Matinée." In Porter, Terrie, and Bennett.

CHOPIN, KATE. 1985. "Désirée's Baby." In Boyd Litzinger and Joyce Carol Oates, eds., *Story: Fiction Past and Present.* Lexington, MA: D. C. Heath.

DUBOIS, W. E. B. 1984. "Of the Meaning of Progress." In Porter, Terrie, and Bennett.

DUNBAR, PAUL LAURENCE. 1984. "Sympathy." In Porter, Terrie, and Bennett.

EARLY, JAMES, ed. 1973. *Adventures in American Literature.* New York: Harcourt Brace Jovanovich.

FREEMAN, MARY WILKINS. 1984. "A Church Mouse." In Porter, Terrie, and Bennett.

HONEY, MAUREEN, ed. 1989. *Shadowed Dreams: Women's Poetry of the Harlem Renaissance.* New Brunswick, NJ: Rutgers University Press.

HUGHES, LANGSTON. 1959. "Daybreak in Alabama." In *Selected Poems of Langston Hughes.* New York: Vintage.

HURSTON, ZORA NEALE. 1935. *Mules and Men.* New York: Perennial.

———. 1978. *Their Eyes Were Watching God.* Urbana: University of Illinois Press.

———. 1984. *Dust Tracks on a Road.* Ed. Robert Hemenway. Urbana: University of Illinois Press.

JACKSON, SHIRLEY. 1973. "The Lottery." In Early.

JAMES, HENRY. 1984. "Four Meetings." In Porter, Terrie, and Bennett.

JEWETT, SARAH ORNE. 1980. "The Hiltons' Holiday." In Cynthia Griffin Wolff, ed., *Classic American Women Writers.* New York: Perennial.

JOHNSON, HELENE. 1981. "Bottled," "Magalu," "The Road," and "Trees at Night." In Stetson.

———. 1989. "Sonnet To a Negro in Harlem." In Honey.

LOWELL, AMY. 1955. "Fugitive," "Misericordia," "Music," "Patterns," "Taxi," and "The Fort." In *The Complete Poetical Works of Amy Lowell.* Boston: Houghton Mifflin. ("Patterns" also in Porter, Terrie, and Bennett)

MILLAY, EDNA ST. VINCENT. 1975. "Apostrophe to Man," "Never May the Fruit Be Plucked," "Spring," and "To a Poet that Died Young." In *Collected Poems*. New York: Harper & Row.

PETRY, ANN. 1989. "Like a Winding Sheet." In *Miss Muriel and Other Stories*. Boston: Beacon.

PORTER, ANDREW J., JR., HENRY L. TERRIE, JR., and ROBERT A. BENNETT, eds. 1984. *American Literature*. Lexington, MA: Ginn and Company.

PORTER, KATHERINE ANNE. 1984. "The Jilting of Granny Weatherall." In Porter, Terrie, and Bennett.

SANDBURG, CARL. 1984. "The People Will Live On." In Porter, Terrie, and Bennett.

STETSON, ERLENE, ed. 1981. *Black Sister: Poetry by Black American Women, 1746–1980*. Bloomington: Indiana University Press.

TEASDALE, SARA. 1937. "Advice to a Girl," "On a March Day," "The Answer," "The Solitary," and "There Will Come Soft Rains." In *The Collected Poems of Sara Teasdale*. New York: Macmillan.

WALKER, ALICE. 1984. "On Stripping Bark from Myself." In *Good Night, Willie Lee, I'll See You in the Morning*. San Diego: Harvest/Harcourt Brace Jovanovich. All of her previously published poems through *Horses Make a Landscape Look Better* plus some unpublished and new poems are now available in *Her Blue Body Everything We Know: Earthling Poems 1965-90*. San Diego: Harcourt Brace Jovanovich.

———. 1986. "Each One, Pull One." In *Horses Make a Landscape Look More Beautiful*. San Diego: Harvest/Harcourt Brace Jovanovich.

WALKER, MARGRET. 1989. "Childhood," "For My People," "Iowa Farmer," "Lineage," and "October Journey." In *This Is My Century: New and Collected Poems*. Athens: University of Georgia Press.

WELLS, IDA B. 1992. Excerpt from *Crusade for Justice*. In *African American Literature: Voices in a Tradition*. Austin, TX: Holt, Rinehart and Winston.

WELTY, EUDORA. 1980. "A Visit of Charity." In *The Collected Stories of Eudora Welty*. New York: Harcourt Brace Jovanovich; also in Early.

WHARTON, EDITH. 1975. "The Other Two." In Susan Cahill, ed., *Women and Fiction*. New York: Mentor.

WYLIE, ELINOR. 1930. "Let No Charitable Hope," "Prophecy," and "Unfinished Portrait." In *Collected Poems*. New York: Knopf.

YEZIERSKA, ANZIA. 1981. "Children of Loneliness." In Nancy Hoffman, ed., *Woman's "True" Profession: Voices from the History of Teaching*. New York: Feminist Press.

ZITKALA-ŠA. 1985. "The School Days of an Indian Girl." In *American Indian Stories*. Lincoln: University of Nebraska Press.

Suggested Books for Students

AUSTIN, MARY. 1987. *Western Trails: A Collection of Stories*. Ed. Melody Graulich. Reno: University of Nevada Press. Helpful, well-written introductory essay. Includes six unpublished stories and others.

BROOKS, GWENDOLYN. 1953. *Maud Martha*. New York: Harper & Row. Narrated by teenaged girl growing up in Chicago.

CATHER, WILLA. 1971a. *Death Comes for the Archbishop*. New York: Vintage. Cather's personal favorite. Two French priests bring Catholicism to New Mexico.

———. 1971b. *The Troll Garden*. New York: Plume. A collection of Cather's early short stories, highlighting the conflicts between sensitive, artistic people and the barren prairie or the mechanistic urban environment.

———. 1973. *The Professor's House*. New York: Vintage. The professor builds a new house and a new life, learning from his children and students.

———. 1975. *Youth and the Bright Medusa*. New York: Vintage. Short stories with many female protagonists whose careers suffer even though they have talent and ambition.

———. 1988. *O Pioneers!* Boston: Houghton Mifflin. (See Chapter 3 for annotation.)

CHILDRESS, ALICE. 1979. *A Short Walk*. New York: Bard. Story of a woman's life, her "short walk" from birth to death, and Black America's road from 1900 to 1950. Includes minstrel shows, the Bible Belt, vaudeville, and poker games.

ELLIS, ANNE. 1990. *The Life of an Ordinary Woman*. Boston: Houghton Mifflin. Daily life of intelligent, articulate woman who lived in the mining camps of Colorado and ran for public office. Reveals Ellis's wit, courage, and humanity.

FIELDS, MAMIE GARVIN, with KAREN FIELDS. 1988. *Lemon Swamp and Other Places*. New York: Free Press. A look at the South from a black woman who taught in a one-room schoolhouse and worked in a Boston sweat shop. Shows what it was like to be an educated black woman in the early twentieth century.

HULL, GLORIA T., ed. 1984. *Give Us Each Day: The Diary of Alice Dunbar-Nelson*. New York: Norton. The widow of Paul Laurence Dunbar, Alice had her own career as poet, journalist, lecturer, and activist for civil rights.

JEWETT, SARAH ORNE. 1986. *The Country Doctor*. New York: Meridian. A young woman fights tradition to fulfill her ambitions to be a doctor. Jewett's quiet style will not appeal to all students, but some will enjoy this novel, her many short stories, and her novel *The Country of the Pointed Firs* (available in several editions), set in a Maine coastal village (little plot but large cast of characters).

LARSEN, NELLA. 1987. *Quicksand* and *Passing*. American Women Writers series. New Brunswick, NJ: Rutgers University Press. Two short novels students enjoy. In *Quicksand* Helga Crane struggles to find her identity in both the white and black worlds, in Denmark and Harlem, only to find herself locked into a miserable marriage. *Passing* documents the life of Clare, a very light black, trying to pass as white, yet loyal to and loving her black heritage. Her life ends when her white husband discovers her black background.

LESUEUR, MERIDEL. 1982. *Ripening: Selected Work, 1927–1980*. Ed. Elaine Hedges. New York: Feminist Press. Compilation of work by articulate working-class woman; includes photographs.

O'CONNOR, FLANNERY. 1971. *The Complete Stories*. New York: Farrar, Straus & Giroux.

PAGE, MYRA. 1986. *Daughter of the Hills: A Woman's Part in the Coal Miners' Struggle*. New York: Feminist Press. Straightforward account.

PETRY, ANN. 1985. *The Street.* Boston: Beacon. Novel set in 1940s Harlem. Lutie tries to fend off the curses of her street in Harlem, but the street finally takes away her son and her soul. Gripping. Clear prose. For mature students. (See Chapter 10 for more discussion.)

PORTER, KATHERINE ANNE. 1958. *The Collected Stories.* New York: Harvest/Harcourt Brace Jovanovich. Students who enjoyed "Rope" and "The Jilting of Granny Weatherall" will find others in this collection to enjoy.

SCHLISSEL, LILLIAN, BYRD GIBBENS, and ELIZABETH HAMPSTEN. 1989. *Far from Home: Families of the Westward Journey.* New York: Schocken. Using diaries and letters, the authors pieced together the stories of three families who traveled West in the period from the mid-nineteenth to the early twentieth century.

SOLOMON, BARBARA H., ed. 1979. *Short Fiction of Sarah Orne Jewett and Mary Wilkins Freeman, Including "The Country of the Pointed Firs."* New York: Signet. Nine Jewett stories, four related to the *Pointed Firs*; and fourteen Freeman stories, including "A Mistaken Charity," "The Revolt of 'Mother'," and "Old Woman Magoun."

WALKER, MARGARET. 1966. *Jubilee.* New York: Bantam. Novel based on true story of Walker's great-grandmother. Contrasts with *Gone with the Wind.* A little too long, but first half is excellent.

WELTY, EUDORA. 1980. *The Collected Stories of Eudora Welty.* New York: Harcourt Brace Jovanovich.

———. 1984. *One Writer's Beginnings.* Cambridge, MA: Harvard University Press. Welty describes learning to write as a three-part process: "Listening," "Learning to See," and "Finding a Voice."

WHARTON, EDITH. 1980. *Summer.* New York: Harper & Row. An amazingly modern novel, dealing with female sexuality in a way that honors the complexity of the issue. More accessible for high school students than *The Age of Innocence* or *The House of Mirth.*

———. 1987. *Roman Fever and Other Stories.* New York: Collier. Eight of Wharton's longer stories.

———. 1990. *The Muse's Tragedy and Other Stories.* New York: Signet. Includes twenty stories, list of Wharton's works in chronological order, and selected bibliography.

YEZIERSKA, ANZIA. 1991. *How I Found America: Collected Short Stories of Anzia Yezierska.* Ed. Vivian Gornick. New York: Persea.

Useful Works for Teachers

CULLEN, COUNTEE. 1993. *Caroling Dusk: An Anthology of Verse by Black Poets of the Twenties.* New York: Carol Publishing Group. First published in 1927, this collection of Harlem Renaissance poets includes a number of women poets.

HULL, GLORIA T. 1987. *Color, Sex, and Poetry: Three Women Writers of the Harlem Renaissance.* Bloomington: Indiana University Press. A biographical/critical study of Alice Dunbar-Nelson, Angelina Weld Grimké, and Georgia Douglas Johnson. Hull had access to unpublished letters, diaries, and manuscripts.

MORRISON, TONI. 1992. *Jazz.* New York: Knopf. Her latest novel, set in Harlem in the twenties.

O'CONNOR, FLANNERY. 1979. *The Habit of Being: Letters.* Ed. Sally Fitzgerald. New York: Farrar, Straus & Giroux. Letters are warm, witty, funny, wise, and often intellectually challenging. Worth dipping into here and there; for long stretches of reading, too.

WELTY, EUDORA. 1979. *The Eye of the Story: Selected Essays and Reviews.* New York: Vintage. Divided into sections: "On Writers," "On Writing," "Reviews," and "Personal and Occasional Pieces." Good essays on Cather and Porter. Especially interesting is "Is Phoenix Jackson's Grandson Really Dead?" in which she answers the question most frequently asked her about her short story "A Worn Path."

SEVEN

Contemporary American Literature

> So all that is in her [Emily] will not bloom—but in how many does it? There is still enough left to live by. Only help her to know—help make it so there is cause for her to know—that she is more than this dress on the ironing-board, helpless before the iron.
>
> TILLIE OLSEN
> "I Stand Here Ironing"

Just as groups of contrasting notes create harmonies, literary works of authors from diverse cultural groups create the vibrant patterns of contemporary American literature. Themes and counterthemes, melodies and pulsing rhythms, chords and discords weave together, and students respond freely. These are some of the images, some of the voices, of the world they are maturing in. Students easily hear the voices similar to their own, those agreeing with them, but they need help to hear the voices truly unlike their own, to be curious about and even relish the voices contradicting theirs or offering experiences they can never have. We purposely select as diverse a group of works as we can, and if they require us to reason carefully, expand our sympathies and sensibilities, and extend our notions about how language can work, then they are helpful, valuable, and good.

The last quarter of American Literature II begins with an investigation of Amy Tan's *The Joy Luck Club*, a novel tracing four Chinese families from pre-1949 China through late-twentieth-century America. Their Chinese heritage twines around and through the grandmothers, mothers, and American-born daughters, liberating and binding, strengthening and chafing all at once. We learn about the importance of Chinese names and the year one is born in, the invisible winds giving cleverness and victory strong enough to confound a chess opponent, a mother (and third concubine) who commits suicide to guarantee a respectable life for her daughter, a mother who sees things before they happen, a mother who temporarily abandons her twin baby daughters only to have them saved unbeknownst to her, and daughters finding power and strength when they open themselves to the power and strength in the heritage of their mothers. These are stories about identity: losing it and turning piece by piece into a ghost, or hiding it, or the difficulty of showing one's Chinese face in America. The book is also funny. For example, Waverly Jong, on the outs with her mother, talks with her friend Marlene.

> "You know, I really don't understand you," said Marlene. . . . "You can tell the IRS to piss up a rope, but you can't stand up to your own mother."
>
> "I always intend to and then she says these little sneaky things, smoke bombs and little barbs, and . . ."
>
> "Why don't you tell her to stop torturing you," said Marlene. "Tell her to stop ruining your life. Tell her to shut up."
>
> "That's hilarious," I said with a half-laugh. "You want me to tell my mother to shut up?"
>
> "Sure, why not?"
>
> "Well, I don't know if it's explicitly stated in the law, but you can't *ever* tell a Chinese mother to shut up. You could be charged as an accessory to your own murder."

The book is also wise: "Your tears do not wash away your sorrows. They feed someone else's joy. And that is why you must learn to swallow your own tears." Or: "Unlike my mother, I did not believe I could be anything I wanted to be. I could only be me." Students who love this book often read Tan's second novel, *The Kitchen God's Wife*, for fun or for an extended essay.

Since the structure of *The Joy Luck Club* confuses students (each of the four chapters in each of the four sections deals with one of the four families), students divide into four groups, one for each family. Students read the entire book family by family, reading about their family twice. These groups meet for a class period to plan how they will involve their classmates in looking more closely at their particular family. Each group has one class period for its activities, which range from minitalks to small-group work. After two or three class periods, patterns emerge: students apply the section titles and the short introductory stories for each section to their family's story. In addition, similarities in the stories shine clearly, proving Tan's own theory that when you want to know the truth about a thing, listen to one hundred stories about it.

After Tan, but before getting into some short stories and poems, we read some nonfiction pieces. Some years we have time to read as many as five, two or three by women along with two by men, James Baldwin and N. Scott Momaday. "Rachel," by Dorothy West, describes her mother, Rachel, and the "thinness in the air" when she dies, leaving her children confused over their feelings of relief and loss. Rachel was a dominating, compelling mother, easing the loneliness and tempering the fear of her children but meddling, too, in their "intimate affairs." Margaret Mead, in "On Being a Granddaughter," reveals the influence of her grandmother, who taught Mead at home until high school. Grandmother "thought that memorizing mere facts was not very important and that drill was stultifying." Instead she set Mead to analyzing plants and going on treasure hunts in the woods to find plants matching descriptions. In addition, her grandmother told wonderful stories and made Mead comfortable being a woman with brains, a career, and a family.

A third essay is called "Seeing," an excerpt from Annie Dillard's *Pilgrim at Tinker's Creek*. "What you see is what you get" is only one comment on several kinds of seeing Dillard describes. She points out the difference between seeing what you expect to see and seeing what's actually there. After discussing some experiences of newly sighted people, she concludes with two kinds of seeing, "walking with and without a camera." Sometimes she pries and probes; other times she lets go and becomes "an unscrupulous observer." Her essay is a fine companion piece to Momaday's "A Vision Beyond Time and Place," which is also about seeing, seeing both forward and backward in time, seeing both to the horizon and into oneself. James Baldwin's essay on the responsibilities of the artist and Martin Luther King, Jr.'s "I Have a Dream" speech add further kinds of seeing. All of these essays set up a foundation, or backdrop, for the stories and poems to come.

With so many contemporary stories to choose from, we made the decision to use pretty much what our Ginn anthology offers, adding only Alice Walker's "Everyday Use." We chose a total of six stories, two by Latinos, two by white Americans, and two by African Americans; of these six, three are by women, and these are the ones we will discuss.

Walker's "Everyday Use" introduces a mother, the narrator, and her two daughters, Maggie and Dee. A question of heritage—what it includes, what it means, and what's important about it—dominates the story of the day Dee brings her boyfriend and camera home to the plain wooden, dirt-yarded cabin to see and cart off her heritage. But Dee, now called Wangero and draped in a sun-bright dress to celebrate her African heritage, may not have more than the butter churn top and dasher, carved by Uncle Buddy and Aunt Dee's first husband, to decorate her city apartment. Mama, "a large, big-boned woman with rough, man-working hands" strong enough to kill a bull calf with one blow of a sledge hammer, and Maggie, like "a lame animal," shuffling, slow, and awed by Dee all of her life, keep the family's quilts for everyday use. When Dee drives off, hiding behind her oversized sunglasses and muttering that they just don't understand their heritage, Mama and Maggie sit and smile "just enjoying" with a "dip of snuff" until bedtime. Contrasts in values, family relationships, and three incisively drawn characters constitute interesting tangents to the heritage theme.

Another story about mothers and daughters involves Emily, "a child of anxious, not proud love," a child "of depression, of war, of fear." Tillie Olsen tells the story "I Stand Here Ironing" as an internal monologue. The mother, only nineteen when Emily was born, receives a note from the school guidance counselor suggesting that

Emily needs help and requesting a meeting. As the mother reviews Emily's life, she realizes she cannot "total it all." Emily, a lively, sensitive child, stiffens under the early care she gets from grandparents, a neighbor, and a convalescent home when poverty drives her mother, at first deserted by her husband and later remarried with four more children, to these choices. But Emily, though not glib or pretty like her sister, finds her voice as a stand-up comic, winning a talent show and giving performances here and there to wildly applauding audiences. At nineteen she is lovely, moody, and cynical about how long the world will survive given the atom bomb—indeed, she is a child of her time, born in the depression years and growing up during World War II. Will Emily survive? Is this the mother's or the daughter's story? Was the mother a good mother? Who is "helpless before the iron"? Students inevitably disagree on answers to these questions.

The third story is actually an excerpt from Toni Morrison's *The Bluest Eye*. For many students this excerpt about Maureen Peal with her "summery" complexion, long brown braids, and rich-people clothes exposes them for the first time to status based on color within the African American community. Maureen enchants everyone. Even the rowdies teasing Pecola, the very dark main character, stop more because Maureen comes over than because Pecola's friend Frieda crowns one of them with her books. Suddenly, Maureen befriends Pecola and offers to buy her some ice cream, but when she asks if Frieda and her sister Claudia (as poor as Pecola) will buy some for themselves, they say "no," and their hatred for Maureen rises up again.

Discussions of all six of the contemporary stories engage the students more than earlier ones. We teachers sit outside the circle just watching and enjoying. The high level and the independence of their discussion demonstrates the success of our student-centered pedagogy. The unit goes this way: We divide the class into groups, assigning one to each story. These groups meet for one class period to discuss their story, assign their members each a different topic to write a short paper on, and plan activities for the period the class will deal with their story. The papers are due the day they're in charge of class, so they will have reviewed the story very carefully. Without the teacher available for help, students plan all sorts of questions, small-group work, and homework assignments. They do not ask for written work because they don't want to grade it. Sometimes we've had to step in and say we didn't hear enough voices, or we ask a question to think about, but as a rule, the students cover the stories wonderfully well and with an openness only possible when the teacher isn't sitting there to respond, redirect comments, ask follow-up questions, and encourage. Some students also learn that teaching isn't all that easy. At the very beginning of the unit, on the assignment sheet, the test is written out: "Find a way to connect any three of the stories and write an essay explaining the connection using details from the texts to support your thinking." Students connect by contrast and similarity; they connect values, characteristics, and themes (such as imprisoned or free people); they apply quotes from one story to two others; they are clever, sometimes wise, and usually insightful.

This quarter's extended essay has to be on a contemporary book. (Some of the favorites by women are listed at the end of the chapter.) While they are busy with this paper, we end the course with contemporary poets. In teaching this unit, we ask students to keep a response log, writing about any two of the poems assigned each day. Each student also signs up for a poet—two, if we have only one or two poems by two poets assigned for one day. They are to write a more in-depth response to this poet and include some analysis. Some students ferret out poems other than those studied in class to write about. In class, students volunteer to share their responses; we talk about only the poems the students choose. We assign anywhere from three to seven poems by a poet, knowing we won't discuss them all but hoping to expose students to a wide variety. We also read around twenty poets. The idea is to just enjoy the poems, to see where they take us, and to encourage students to connect these poems with works read earlier in the course as a way to review for the final exam. We jump in with our comments too, but not as experts, just as other readers. Besides, the seniors leave class approximately one week before the underclasspeople, so the whole unit turns into a relaxing but stimulating what-do-you-make-of-it conversation.

What women poets do students like?

Denise Levertov's political outspokenness and striking images impress students. Born and educated at home in England, she served as a nurse in a London hospital during World War II. She has lived in America since 1948. In "Fragrance of Life, Odor of Death," about the Vietnam War, she surprises us with not smelling death in the Mekong Delta, but in America, where no bodies have been shredded, no "earth-guts" exposed, and she finds the "faint seepage" everywhere. Just the word "seepage" provokes reactions. Her poem "May Our Right Hands Lose Their Cunning" denounces the smart bombs that can slip right into kitchens, "bite . . . into perfect bodies," chew them into bloody bits. She wants us to keep a part of us "blunt, soft, slow," so we won't be so smart in that way. "Thinking About El Salvador" describes how she is made silent every time someone's head is chopped off. Picture rotting heads floating down a river in El Salvador, then sinking, mute. Her images cry out as much when she writes in "Urgent Whisper" of the earth itself shuddering as if she is terrified by the pollution and exploitation inflicted upon her. Levertov asks, "Isn't the earth our mother?" And here we have terrorized her. In "From the Image-Flow—South Africa 1986," Levertov likens Africa itself to a "gigantic slave-ship." Two other poems to try are "Scornful Reprieve" and "Movement."

Every year we decide on different Adrienne Rich poems. We'll mention only a few here. Her poems find their way into almost every class that deals with poetry. "Aunt Jennifer's Tigers" is used in classes for ninth and tenth graders. In it her wedding ring "sits heavily" on Aunt Jennifer's finger, but her embroidered tigers prance, "proud and unafraid." In American Literature II the first Rich poem we read is "A Woman Mourned by Daughters." At first it puzzles many students, for they aren't sure just how the daughters feel about their mother as they groan beneath her weight. Although dead, her "solid assertions" dare them to do any little thing "save exactly" the way she would have wanted. In "Song" Rich sings of breaking through traditions and expectations and finding herself alone but not lonely. Having left a dull life behind or being the first one awake in the house at dawn, she could well be lonely, but she's not because, like a wooden boat held "ice-fast on the shore," she knows her potential, the latent passion; she's not asleep, not inanimate, not like everyone else or like what everyone else expects her to be. This poem picks up the challenge of "Prospective Immigrants Please Note." The question here is whether or not to go through the door to a new kind of life; it's risky but empowering, but even if you do not, you may still "live worthily." "The Lioness" reiterates one of Rich's central themes: women especially get into trouble when they stray outside the set boundaries, boundaries set by society and men, and even by themselves when they accept "bars" and limits. The lioness paces back and forth to the edges of her cage, but her eyes reflect the rivers and spaces of her own country. In a 1988 poem, "Divisions of Labor," Rich looks around the world at the plight of women who sit "in the back rows of politics" still laboring without electricity or endlessly fixing tiny wires into silicon chips. She feels the scorching on the finger and thumb of the poor woman snuffing out candles, and she praises these women "whose labor remakes the world" day after day after day.

A third white female poet is Sylvia Plath, whose technical virtuosity and control focus the rage underneath. In this course we look at "Kindness," "Cut," and "Daddy." "Kindness" crystallizes Plath's conflict between her equally compelling drives to be mother and poet. Students pick up her sarcastic tone easily enough, but the images confuse them somewhat. Usually one or two students see that the unstoppable "blood jet" of poetry overwhelms Dame Kindness's "little poultice" of a sugary cup of tea but cannot drown out the cries of her children. "Cut" is a sort of fascinating, even funny, exercise on all the things a severely cut thumb with its flap of skin reminds her of: a hat, a scalped pilgrim, a babushka, a homunculus; the blood is like "a million . . . redcoats" running and like pulp. Even the setup of the poem—long with short lines and the quick, hard *t*'s and *k*'s—fits the images of this wounded thumb. "Daddy" is an impressive poem no matter what we think it is about. The first student to comment on a poem in this unit also reads it aloud, but since this poem is so powerful, sometimes a student anxious to talk about it will ask a better reader or a volunteer to read. This poem, with its rhythms and rhymes, stands out. Whatever the poem says about the daddy, the images have to fascinate: living in daddy's black boot, having one's tongue "stuck in a barb wire snare," having one's heart bitten in two, and driving a stake through the "fat black heart" of a vampire.

Mari Evans and June Jordan both touch on racial prejudice. Evans, who wants blacks to establish their own standards and follow their own paths since their heritage is inescapable, also sings of racial pride and woman pride in "I Am a Black Woman." Although she hums in a minor key as she reviews the history of her people, from their jumping slave ships to dying in Vietnam, at the end she stands like a cypress, defiant and undefeated, inviting people to look at her and be strengthened, reinvigorated. She finds it jolting to be confronted with the white system. For example, in "Coventry" she describes "the Veil that hung between [blacks] and Opportunity" that DuBois wrote of in his essay on the meaning of progress: a "gossamer" web, a clear, but impervious wall to bruise people who have dreams. "The Alarm Clock" concludes that it's dangerous for her to have something wake her up too quickly. A small blond girl has just reminded her that her people aren't served in this drug store—another jolt. "Status Symbol," with its lowercase *i*'s and upper case *They*'s, is heavy with sarcasm as the speaker records his or her arrival as the New Negro, earning the status symbol of a key to the locked john for whites only.

June Jordan's political poems remind students of Levertov. She advocates a New World, a non-European one, big, free, wild, and void of privilege and the violence of power. She laments government policies on the environment and inner cities in a poem called "Poem Towards a Final Solution," using that horrid phrase from Nazi Germany. In the poem's fictitious report, the government plans to count food stamps as income and place nuclear reactors in low-growth areas of inner cities in order to stimulate the relocation of poor people. In "A Song for Soweto" she traces the wishes of a young girl turned sour; she would "say water" but she learns to "cry blood." In a rapid-fire, phrases-only poem, "In Memoriam: Martin Luther King, Jr.," she characterizes America's killing, deforming, and terrorizing as too ubiquitous for anyone to stop. Her "Poem for Guatemala" builds upon an actual news account of soldiers invading an Indian village and, among other atrocities, cutting off the arms of a girl. Another political poem is "March Song" where apparently beautiful things, from snow piles in March to bread and honey, rest alongside of "pieces of children." Why? Because of the game nations and factions play in places "like Beirut." And, she adds, we who follow the leaders are responsible, too: although we may stand secure, holding each other's hands, we also hold the "pieces of children." Her poems are dynamite. Sometimes we read to students her "Poem about My Rights." It is so graphic and passionate, we don't expect verbal responses. When we heard Jordan read this poem in the mid-1980s, the audience was struck silent; our students are, too, so we read it at the end of class and just wait for the bell to ring.

Our text includes Cathy Song's "Lost Sister" poem. It's about the Chinese girl who escapes the stolen freedom of women with bound feet in China by coming to America, where men and women walk freely, stride for stride, together. But she finds another kind of strangulation here: loneliness and "dough faced landlords" who spy on her. In the end she leaves "no footprints" either and she discovers she needs China.

One poem by a Latina is Teresa Palomo Acosta's "My Mother Pieced Quilts." Acosta grew up in Texas, listening to her grandfather's stories of his childhood in Mexico. The mother's quilts in the poem are her love as well as weapons and armor to protect the children from whatever life throws against them, they are scrapbooks of lives, they are the mother's artwork, and like her, they withstand "the thrashings of twenty-five years."

Finally we read three Native American poets: Leslie Marmon Silko, Joy Harjo, and Roberta Hill. Silko's "Where Mountain Lion Lay Down with Deer" takes the speaker back to her beginnings, a mountain top, where the deer and mountain lion lie together. But she must swim away, down and out into the world. Time flows back and forth in the poem, not an easy concept for students. "Story from Bear Country" intrigues them: someone goes into bear country and apparently becomes a bear, "dark" and "shaggy" with bear prints instead of footprints. Several images from other stories and poems come together in this poem: Faulkner's story "The Bear" is one; Momaday's poem "The Bear" is another; and, of course, the idea of footprints. What does it mean to become a bear? It seems that the bears are the speakers in this poem. Silko's "Deer Song" unites the wolf and the deer it kills as brothers in spite of the tide reddened by the deer's blood and the pain of its wounds. Unity of time and place and all of nature's beings runs through these poems and also Harjo's "Eagle Poem." In this poem the speaker prays by opening herself to the sky, the earth, the sun, the moon, and to the voice within. Watching an eagle circle and soar, "rounding out the morning," a memory inside her, the speaker seeks to do all things with kindness and "in beauty." The last work is Roberta Hill's poem "Dream of Rebirth," a three-stanza poem that examines the Native American's past, present, and future. Standing "on the edge of wounds, hugging canned meat," her people carry grief and hatred, but also hidden within them, songs stir, songs to heal. And she dreams of eagles (to "restore our prayers"), of forgetting the strange pity of whites, of waking up unashamed and able to "rise . . . like the swallows."

These women writers are like the lioness, knowing of those distant places to explore; they do not lie helpless before the irons of tradition; their works are, like quilts, meant to inspire, to gather us in, to celebrate.

Works Cited

ACOSTA, TERESA PALOMO. 1976. "My Mother Pieced Quilts." In *Festival De Flor Y Canto: An Anthology of Chicano Literature.* Los Angeles: University of Southern California Press. Also in James E. Miller, Jr., et al., eds. 1979. *United States in Literature.* Glenview, IL: Scott, Foresman.

BALDWIN, JAMES. 1984. "The Creative Dilemma." In Porter, Terrie, and Bennett.

DILLARD, ANNIE. 1974. "Seeing." In *Pilgrim at Tinker's Creek.* New York: Harper & Row. Also in Porter, Terrie, and Bennett.

EVANS, MARI. 1968. "Coventry." In Abraham Chapman, ed., *Black Voices: An Anthology of Afro-American Literature.* New York: Mentor. First appeared in *Negro Digest.*

————. 1970. "The Alarm Clock," "Status Symbol," and the title poem. In *I Am a Black Woman.* New York: Morrow. "I Am a Black Woman" also in Porter, Terrie, and Bennett.

FAULKNER, WILLIAM. 1984. "The Bear." In Porter, Terrie, and Bennett.

HARJO, JOY. 1990. "Eagle Poem." In *In Mad Love and War.* Middletown, CT: Wesleyan University Press.

HILL, ROBERTA. 1984. "Dream of Rebirth." In Porter, Terrie, and Bennett.

JORDAN, JUNE. 1977. "In Memoriam: Martin Luther King, Jr." In *Things That I Do in the Dark.* Boston: Beacon.

————. 1980. "Poem about My Rights." In *Passion: New Poems, 1977–1980.* Boston: Beacon.

————. 1985. "March Song," "Poem for Guatemala," "Poem Towards a Final Solution," and "A Song for Soweto." In *Living Room.* New York: Thunder's Mouth Press.

KING, MARTIN LUTHER, JR. 1984. "I Have a Dream." In Porter, Terrie, and Bennett.

LEVERTOV, DENISE. 1975. "Fragrance of Life, Odor of Death" and "May Our Right Hands Lose Their Cunning." In *The Freeing of the Dust.* New York: New Directions.

————. 1978. "Movement" and "Scornful Reprieve." In *Life in the Forest.* New York: New Directions.

————. 1984. "Thinking About El Salvador." In *Oblique Prayers.* New York: New Directions.

————. 1986. "From the Image-Flow—South Africa 1986" and "Urgent Whisper." In *Breathing the Water.* New York: New Directions

MEAD, MARGARET. 1972. "On Being a Granddaughter." In *Blackberry Winter.* New York: Morrow. Also in Porter, Terrie, and Bennett.

MOMADAY, N. SCOTT. 1984. "A Vision Beyond Time and Place." In Porter, Terrie, and Bennett.

————. 1988. "The Bear." In Duane Niatum, ed., *Harper's Anthology of 20th Century Native American Poetry.* San Francisco: Harper & Row.

MORRISON, TONI. 1970. *The Bluest Eye.* New York: Washington Square. The excerpt we refer to is in Porter, Terrie, and Bennett.

OLSEN, TILLIE. 1956. "I Stand Here Ironing." *Tell Me a Riddle.* New York: Dell. Also in Porter, Terrie, and Bennett.

PLATH, SYLVIA. 1961. "Cut," "Daddy," and "Kindness." In *Ariel.* New York: Harper & Row.

PORTER, ANDREW J., JR., HENRY L. TERRIE, JR., and ROBERT A. BENNETT, eds. 1984. *American Literature.* Lexington, MA: Ginn and Company.

RICH, ADRIENNE. 1978. "The Lioness." In *The Dream of a Common Language: Poems 1974–1977.* New York: Norton.

———. 1984. "Aunt Jennifer's Tigers," "A Woman Mourned by Daughters," "Prospective Immigrants Please Note," and "Song." In *The Fact of a Doorframe: Poems Selected and New, 1950–1984.* New York: Norton.

——— 1989. "Divisions of Labor." In *Time's Power: Poems, 1985–1988.* New York: Norton.

SILKO, LESLIE MARMON. 1981. "Deer Song" and "Story from Bear Country." In *Storyteller.* New York: Seaver Books. (Also by Silko: *Ceremony,* a novel about a Native American man's conflicts with Caucasian culture. Relatively difficult.)

———. 1984. "Where Mountain Lion Lay Down with Deer." In Porter, Terrie, and Bennett.

SONG, CATHY. 1984. "Lost Sister." In Porter, Terrie, and Bennett.

TAN, AMY. 1989. *The Joy Luck Club.* New York: Ivy Books.

———. 1991. *The Kitchen God's Wife.* New York: Ivy Books.

WALKER, ALICE. 1973. "Everyday Use." In *In Love and Trouble.* San Diego: Harvest/Harcourt Brace Jovanovich.

WEST, DOROTHY. 1992. "Rachel." In *African American Literature: Voices in a Tradition.* Orlando: Holt, Rinehart and Winston.

Suggested Books for Students

ANGELOU, MAYA. Any of her autobiographies or poetry collections.

BAMBARA, TONI CADE. 1972. *Gorilla My Love.* New York: Random. Stories about girls and their growing up.

BURNS, OLIVE ANN. 1984. *Cold Sassy Tree.* New York: Dell. Fourteen-year-old Will Tweedy tells the story of the effect of his grandfather's unexpected marriage within days of his first wife's death. Set in Cold Sassy, a Georgia town, from 1906 to 1914, the love, mischief, and and growing insight of Will and his grandfather evoke laughter and tears.

CHÁVEZ, DENISE. 1986. *The Last of the Menu Girls.* Houston: Arte Público. An ordinary Chicana's life depicted in seven interrelated stories.

CHILDRESS, ALICE. 1986. *Like One of the Family: Conversations from a Domestic's Life.* Boston: Beacon. Sixty-two sharp, honest, humorous, on-the-mark conversations between Mildred, a black domestic, and her friend Marge show what the life of a black working woman was like in New York City in the 1950s.

CISNEROS, SANDRA. 1989. *The House on Mango Street.* New York: Vintage. A series of vignettes chronicling the growing up of Esperanza, the Hispanic narrator. Her neighbors and run-down street and hopes for "a house all [her] own" come to life in colorful snapshots.

———. 1991. *Woman Hollering Creek and Other Stories.* New York: Vintage. These short and short-short stories bring the Chicana world to life. The young narrator in "My Lucy Friend Who Smells Like Corn" explains what she and Lucy are going to do: "We're going to run home backwards and we're going to run home frontwards, look twice under the house where the rats hide and I'll stick one foot in there because you dared me, sky so blue and heaven inside those white clouds. I'm going to peel a scab from my knee and eat it, sneeze on the cat, give you three M&M's I've been saving for you since yesterday, comb your hair with my fingers and braid it into teeny-tiny braids real pretty."

COFER, JUDITH ORTIZ. 1989. *The Line of the Sun.* Athens: University of Georgia Press. Set in the 1950s and 1960s, the novel follows members of a Puerto Rican family from their village in Puerto Rico to a tough immigrant housing project in New Jersey. Strong characters struggle to assimilate without losing their old culture.

DILLARD, ANNIE. 1987. *An American Childhood.* New York: Perennial. This autobiographical work is for mature students who appreciate fine but subtle, poetical writing. Pittsburgh takes on a new character as Dillard waltzes us through her growing up there.

ERDRICH, LOUISE. 1984. *Love Medicine.* New York: Holt, Rinehart and Winston. Two Native American families, in three generations, tell their stories. Set in contemporary times. Requires some sophisticated reading to keep the strands straight.

EVANS, MARI. 1992. *A Dark and Splendid Mass.* New York: Writers & Readers Press. More poems by Evans.

GODWIN, GAIL. 1984. *The Finishing School.* New York: Avon. Skillful weaving of past and present as Justin, a successful actress in her forties, looks back to her teen years, remembering the importance of an older woman mentor. Themes of friendship, loyalty, and betrayal mixed with suspense.

GREENE, MELISSA FAY. 1991. *Praying for Sheetrock.* New York: Fawcett Columbine. A nonfiction account of civil rights movement in rural McIntosh County, Georgia, in the 1970s, complete with interviews woven into the stories of the people on both sides of the struggle. A detailed, lively, unsentimental, poetic, historical narrative.

HERNÁNDEZ, IRENE BELTRÁN. 1989. *Across the Great River.* Houston: Arte Público. A young girl has to lead the family when her parents become separated, illegally crossing the border into the United States. Some suspense as they deal with smugglers and authorities.

KINGSOLVER, BARBARA. 1988. *The Bean Trees.* New York: Perennial. Delightful story of a young woman driving west to escape the ruts of her hometown and who becomes, quite unexpectedly, the parent of a Native American baby girl. Funny, disarming, easy to read, it raises serious issues for young people today.

LE GUIN, URSULA K. 1969. *The Left Hand of Darkness.* New York: Walker. A science fiction, issues novel.

LORDE, AUDRE. 1984. *Sister Outsider.* Trumansburg, NY: The Crossing Press. As she does in her other essays, Lorde writes vigorously, whether she's discussing black lesbianism, anger, or why "the master's tools will never dismantle the master's house." Requires an alert, open-minded reader.

———. 1988. *A Burst of Light*. Ithaca, NY: Firebrand Books. These essays range from "Apartheid U.S.A." to Lorde's struggle with cancer.

MARSHALL, PAULE. 1959. *Brown Girl, Brownstones*. New York: Feminist Press. Selina Boyce, daughter of Barbadian immigrants, grows up aware of the deep differences between her gentle, dreamy father and her fierce, strong mother. Interesting minor characters. Racism, relationships, and questions of assimilation confront Selina.

MERIWETHER, LOUISE. 1970. *Daddy Was a Number Runner*. New York: Feminist Press. Francie is twelve, growing up in Harlem in the 1930s, and her prospects aren't good: work in a laundry, be a whore, clean houses, run poker games, or have a baby every year. Students like Francie's spunk while hating the depression-wracked Harlem that's trying to squash her.

MINOT, SUSAN. 1986. *Monkeys*. New York: Washington Square. These nine short stories trace the life of the Vincent family from 1966 to 1979 with its seven children, an alcoholic father, and an interesting mother who dies somewhat unusually.

MORRISON, TONI. 1973. *Sula*. New York: Bantam. Nel and Sula are best friends, but Sula is different, magical perhaps, independent, free, tough, with deep laughter and passion. She's too much for Nel. Sula is unforgettable in a town where all the women are the same.

———. 1987. *Beloved*. New York: New American Library. For the most mature students. See Chapter 10 for discussion.

MOSS, THYLIAS. 1983. *Hosiery Seams on a Bowlegged Woman*. Cleveland, OH: Cleveland State University.

———. 1989. *Pyramid of Bone*. Charlottesville: University Press of Virginia.

———. 1990. *At Redbones*. Cleveland, OH: Cleveland State University.

———. 1991. *Rainbow Remnants in Rock Bottom Ghetto Sky*. New York: Persea. All four volumes of Moss's poetry are excellent and accessible to high school students. Young, outspoken, energetic, Moss writes her people and places into life.

OLSEN, TILLIE. 1974. *Yonnondio: From the Thirties*. New York: Dell. The Holbrook family fights a losing battle to escape their poverty. Some hope survives in their daughter Mazie. A compassionate look at the depression years.

PLATH, SYLVIA. 1971. *The Bell Jar*. New York: Bantam. This autobiographical novel traces the breakdown of a brilliant and talented writer.

RANCK, KATHERINE QUINTANA. 1982. *Portrait of Doña Elena*. Berkeley: Tonatiuh-Quinto Sol. A young woman journeys to an old New Mexican village to learn about her dead mother's people.

SHANGE, NTOZAKE. 1985. *Betsey Brown*. New York: St. Martin's. Betsey Brown is thirteen, living in St. Louis in 1959 when the schools were desegregated. Her family has to work hard to hold itself together during this stress-filled time.

SOUTHERLAND, ELLEASE. 1979. *Let the Lion Eat Straw*. New York: Signet. The novel begins with Abeba Williams's childhood in the rural South and traces her growing up in a ghetto of the North, her marriage, and death. She's heroic and amazing as she holds off despair and defeat. Abbreviated prose, tight, spare.

STAFFORD, JEAN. 1947. *The Mountain Lion*. New York: Dutton. A story about Molly and Ralph, brother and sister, who seem to be afraid of something, some place, or someone most of the time. Their pain is made very clear.

TRAMBLEY, ESTELA PORTILLO. 1986. *Trini*. United States Hispanic Creative Literature Series. Binghamton, NY: Bilingual. Illegal entry to the United States, the death of her mother, dreams of owning land, childbirth, and love for an Indian man all become part of the growing up of a thirteen-year-old Tarahumara girl.

TYLER, ANNE. 1975. *Searching for Caleb*. New York: Knopf. Justine searches through four generations of her family, the Pecks of Roland Park, to find her own best life and ways to adjust to her family's demands. Tyler, as usual, introduces us to an eccentric and writes crisp and lively prose.

WALKER, ALICE. 1980. *You Can't Keep a Good Woman Down*. San Diego: Harcourt Brace Jovanovich. Collection of short stories.

———. 1982. *The Color Purple*. New York: Washington Square. Students also enjoy *Meridian* and *The Third Life of Grange Copeland*; a few tackle *The Temple of My Familiar* and poetry collections.

————. 1983. *In Search of Our Mothers' Gardens: Womanist Prose.* San Diego: Harcourt Brace Jovanovich. Essays: autobiographical; on Zora Neale Hurston and Martin Luther King, Jr., and civil rights; on mothers.

Useful Works for Teachers

HONGO, GARRETT. 1993. *The Open Boat: Poems from Asian America.* New York: Anchor Books. Male and female poets; a dozen women, including Nellie Wong and Cathy Song, with several poems by each.

JORDAN, JUNE. 1981. *Civil Wars.* Boston: Beacon. A series of essays that read like an autobiography of Jordan's political thinking and vision, the book deals with issues from love to power, from violence to sisterhood.

————.1985. *On Call: Political Essays.* Boston: South End Press. More of Jordan's intense calls for action to address issues of the third world, the poor, and women. She wants justice, liberation, and peace.

NAYLOR, GLORIA. 1992. *Bailey's Cafe.* New York: Harcourt Brace Jovanovich.

OSTRIKER, ALICIA. 1983. *Writing Like a Woman.* Poets on Poetry Series. Ann Arbor: University of Michigan Press. Includes chapters on Hilda Doolittle, Sylvia Plath, Anne Sexton, May Swenson, and Adrienne Rich. Ostriker looks for diversity in women poets, no generalities.

POEY, DELIA, and VIRGIL SUAREZ, eds. 1992. *Iguana Dreams: New Latino Fiction.* New York: Perennial. Male and female authors; one story by each.

WALKER, ALICE. 1988. *Living by the Word: Selected Writings, 1973–1987.* San Diego: Harcourt Brace Jovanovich. These essays focus on Walker's "journey to find [her] old planet," what's still left, what battering of it needs to cease, how we can all live on it, and what she discovered.

————. 1992. *Possessing the Secret of Joy.* San Diego: Harcourt Brace Jovanovich. A harrowing but beautifully written account of Tashi (a character appearing in both *The Color Purple* and *The Temple of My Familiar*), who decides as an adult to undergo the ritual of female circumcision in order to truly belong to her Olinka people.

WASHINGTON, MARY HELEN, ed. 1975. *Black-Eyed Susans: Classic Stories by and About Black Women.* New York: Anchor. Excellent introduction by

Washington. Includes excerpts from *The Bluest Eye* and *Maud Martha* along with short stories by Jean Wheeler Smith, Louise Meriwether, Toni Cade Bambara, Alice Walker, and Paule Marshall.

———, ed. 1980. *Midnight Birds: Stories of Contemporary Black Women Writers.* New York: Anchor. Another helpful introduction by Washington and stories with a wide range of tones and themes. Authors include Paulette Childress White, Alexis Deveaux, Ntozake Shange, Frenchy Hodges, Gayl Jones, and Sherley Anne Williams.

EIGHT

English Literature
700–1850

Say Tyrant Custom, why must we obey,
The impositions of thy haughty Sway;
From the first dawn of Life, unto the Grave,
Poor Womankind's in every State, a Slave.

SARAH FYGE FIELD EGERTON
"The Emulation"

Egerton's satiric eighteenth-century poem rattles the cage of custom in the interest of middle- and upper-class women of her time who suffer under the hands of nurses, governesses, parents, swains, and finally husbands. She is not the first to protest; hers is not the first female voice in the many centuries of English literature. But hers is one of the few voices high school students may hear from these early years in our semester-long English Literature I course. Approximately one-third of the works we study are by women or from a woman's point of view. All along the way we investigate the lives of women and reflect on the images of women portrayed.

You may well be asking, "How can I fit even these few women into an already jam-packed English Lit course?" We wondered, too. Our solution was to quicken the pace, cut down on the introductory material, eliminate the second or third work by an author, and extend the students' responsibility for taking charge and for working on their own, independent of class discussion. Instead of giving tests on the

151

periods studied, we have students write papers (sometimes on topics of their own design, sometimes after brainstorming as a class, and sometimes on one topic among many we suggest), and we add a reading assignment of works we didn't get to in class, asking that at least one of these be included in their papers. This way we find out if they can apply what they've learned to unfamiliar material, how they think about and analyze what they've read, and how they connect the new material to the discussed material. A bonus is that students have a chance to read all the well-known authors *and* we can teach our favorites.

Years ago when we thought of the Anglo-Saxon period, we pictured brawny men with two-headed battle-axes, roaring into battle; heroes eating and drinking in the great mead halls a-glitter with women, fine ornaments, and tales; winter cold; and, of course, Grendel. No longer. When we study *Beowulf,* several students investigate and report to the class on each of several topics covering some significant aspects of the poem. One of these is a close look at Grendel's mother: how she compares and contrasts with Grendel, what kind of mother she is, how they feel about her and her battle with Beowulf. Right from the beginning of the course students need to think about the roles and personalities of the women. Someone in the class invariably asks what the women are doing and who Wealhtheow is. We speculate about women's roles, and students grow angry and disappointed when they hear that Wealhtheow marries Hrothgar as a peace offering between her brother's people and Hrothgar's.

Fortunately for students reading about the Anglo-Saxon period, our text, the Scott, Foresman anthology *England in Literature* (1985; we also use the 1982 edition), includes two poems from the *Exeter Book,* "The Wife's Lament" and "The Husband's Message." In the "Lament" a woman is exiled by her husband's family. She sings of "sorrow unceasing," rails against her banishment, and despairs at her grim cave, loneliness, and heavy woe. She's helpless, quite unlike the woman in "The Husband's Message"; he, exiled but now rich and powerful, still loves her and writes for her to join him in his new land. A Celtic poem in the anthology, "Eagle of Pengwern," rounds out the images of women of this period: a sister laments the honorable death of her brother who died defending his town. Groups of students work together on these shorter works (including some riddles and a selection from Bede's *Ecclesiastical History*) and share their conclusions and questions with their classmates. Even this early in the course, students write questions and tasks for group work, such as defining a lyric poem, listing details from everyday life revealed in the riddles, or finding Anglo-Saxon values in the work. Having students responsible for the instruction allows the teacher to take a back seat, serving as a resource or occasional questioner. Reading more than *Beowulf*, students discover that in addition to warring, the Anglo-Saxons delighted in fine craftsmanship and riddles, admired leaders for their gentleness and mildness, and recognized their women's lot.

We have found no works by women for students to read from the Medieval Period, but we look closely at the women we find in the ballads and Chaucer, and we encourage students to read Mary Stewart's books about King Arthur and Mordred for their position papers. We also suggest they read Christine de Pizan's *The Book of the City of Ladies,* an argument on behalf of the rights of women written in 1405. The ballads offer a variety of women: cruel, generous, independent and dependent, clever and foolish. Students see that stereotypes won't fit. When we read Chaucer's "Prologue," we assign one student to each of the main pilgrims, encouraging students to compare and contrast their character to other pilgrims and to historical or contemporary figures. Students act as experts, characterizing their pilgrim and drawing the class's attention to passages to support their interpretations; they invite classmates to join in; they explain passages or traits classmates ask about. After enjoying the satire in the sketches of the Nun and the Wife of Bath, we look at what these two women have in common and what Chaucer is implying about the roles of women. Both have some power and status, and Chaucer wouldn't be satirizing them if he didn't accept their legitimate places in society.

The Elizabethan/seventeenth-century period provides opportunities to read works by women. Our anthology offers one poem by Elizabeth I, "When I Was Fair and Young," which depicts a young, haughty, but coy, woman who comes to repent her disdain for her suitors. The poem uses fairly complex meter and rhyme. A poem about Elizabeth I by the modern British poet Sylvia Ashton Warner, "Gloriana Dying," also in our text, portrays the indomitable, stubborn, loyal queen in her last years, choosing to lie on the floor to review her people from a new perspective. With these contrasting views of Elizabeth for background, we work on two poems by Elizabeth I from *The Norton Anthology of Literature by Women,* (Gilbert and Gubar, 1985), "The Doubt of Future Foes," and "On Monsieur's Departure," and two shorter pieces from *The Penguin Book of Women Poets.* In "On Monsieur's Departure," a personal poem, the speaker laments that she dare not show her love for a man who clearly loves her. She wishes she were made of tougher stuff, incapable of evoking or returning love. She can no longer live in "sweet content" since she has turned her lover away. We speculate on Elizabeth I's choice to remain single, to be fully a monarch, fully political. The other poems are political in theme. "The Doubt of Future Foes" bluntly warns people who would turn against her that she will "employ" her "rusty sword . . . to poll their tops." She will not brook "seditious sects." The poem's twisted syntax makes it difficult, but the tone is unmistakable. The two shorter poems are quoted below.

Written in Her French Psalter

No crooked leg, no bleared eye,
   No part deformed out of kind,
Nor yet so ugly half can be
   As is the inward suspicious mind.

On Fortune

Never think you fortune can bear the sway
Where virtue's force can cause her to obey.

Both of these reinforce Elizabeth's image as a clever, willful, politically shrewd executive. We also read to the class the whole of her speech to her troops just before the 1588 defeat of the Armada (in *Norton*). These additional works fill out the complex character of the queen and help account for her status. By now she has taken on human characteristics, and students criticize her poetic techniques while appreciating her political wiles and power. Why just read *about* her when she can very well speak for herself?

Before getting to Shakespeare, we want to introduce Margaret Cavendish, Duchess of Newcastle. Some thought she was mad. (The background material in *Norton* on the seventeenth century provides an excellent context for Cavendish, and students read some of it.) Cavendish wrote poems, plays, essays, even a science fiction narrative. She admitted to being ambitious and an exception to the silly women around her; when accused of wearing outlandish clothes, she said that she *made* fashion, rather than followed it. The brief biographical note about her in *The Penguin Book of Women Poets* (Cosman, Keefe, and Weaver 1978) cites an early critic who said of her: "It is plain, from the uncommon turn of her compositions, that she possessed a wild native genius, which, if duly cultivated, might probably have shown itself to advantage in the higher sorts of poetry" (p. 133). The note goes on to say that Pepys called her "a mad, conceited, ridiculous woman," based on his reading of her biography of her husband, but that Charles Lamb described the same work "a jewel." *Norton* includes some of her prose that students enjoy reading. Her "Female Orations" protests the conditions of women. She says the men "possess all the ease, rest, pleasure, wealth, power, and fame," while the women "live like bats or owls, labour like beasts, and die like worms." In her poem "Nature's Cook," Death is the cook. The poem describes vividly (and in almost perfect rhyming couplets of iambic pentameter) the various ways he does us in, taking all the images from cooking. For example:

> Some Death doth roast with fevers hot,
> And some he boils with dropsies in a pot; . . .
> In sweat sometimes he stews with savory smell,
> An hodge-podge of diseases he likes well.

What else but cooking are women expected to know about? Students admire her skill, wit, and outspokenness while getting a bit squeamish at some of the images.

Another female author of the period is Aphra Behn, the first English woman to earn her living by writing: seventeen plays, twelve novels, poems, stories, and translations. Her play *The Rover* was produced in Washington, D.C., in the early 1980s to good reviews. We usually have one student choose to read *The Rover* for a position paper. The Rover, an amorous rascal, visits Naples to woo the ladies, but instead he and his companions become entangled in episodes of mistaken identity, duels, outraged honor (of both men and women), and bartered brides. One year the young man who read this play wrote his best paper of the quarter on it, partly because he found it so amusing. He examined the attitudes of men and women toward each other, including to what extent he agreed with them and why. Behn's works earned her a burial spot in Poets' Corner in Westminster Abbey. Two of her poems, "Song" and "Love's Witness," offer another seventeenth-century opinion about love to accompany those of Donne, Marvell, Ben Jonson, and Herrick. In "Song" Behn describes how a man and a woman have armed the god Love with characteristics from themselves, such as "sighs" and "languishments" from the woman and "fire" and "killing darts" from the man. She concludes that her heart is harmed while his, the victor's, is free. "Love's Witness" contrasts the qualities of spoken and written words of love. "Slight" spoken words "borne by every common Wind . . . die as soon as born, . . . breathing all Contraries" while billet-doux are "constant, . . . substantial records, . . . digested and resolv'd," upon which the lover may rely. Although Raleigh speaks for the woman's point of view in his "The Nymph's Reply to the Shepherd," he still speaks as a man thinks a woman would; how much better to let the women speak for themselves.

When students look at the excerpts from the King James Bible in the text, we ask them to notice the difference between the two creation stories in Genesis 1 and 3. They quickly see that in the first chapter man and woman are created simultaneously: "male and female created he them." But in Chapter 3 the woman is constructed from Adam's rib as a helpmate. Typical student reactions: "Which one should we believe?" and "Is that why in some marriage ceremonies the woman says 'cherish and obey' but the man doesn't?"

Many students, unfamiliar with the story of the serpent's temptation of Eve and all the implications of it for the status of women, shake their heads, especially after reading Milton's elaboration on it, which casts Eve as the wicked and weak creature dooming the human race. "That makes me mad!" said one student who had taken our Women's Literature course. Churchgoing students talk about the roles of women in their churches.

As the class studies the Elizabethan/seventeenth-century poets, individual students have the responsibility of formulating key questions or topics on their assigned poem for the class to discuss. As the discussion proceeds, the student leader asks follow-up questions while we teachers remain out of the discussion unless called upon or until we want to join in as just other readers. We try, but don't always succeed, to avoid taking over the discussion even after the student leader has exhausted her or his ideas. We assign female poets right along with male poets and encourage the students to accept women's place in the curriculum, which means that these writers are also subject to the students' criticism and skepticism.

Shakespeare. With him, Adrienne Rich's re-visioning comes into full play. ("Re-vision—the act of looking back, of seeing with fresh eyes, of entering an old text from a new critical direction—is for women more than a chapter in cultural history; it is an act of survival." Rich 1971, p. 35.) Along with having students discuss and explain such things in *Hamlet* as the deceptions, Hamlet's soliloquies, and the consequences of Polonius's death, they also discuss and explain Hamlet's treatment of his mother, Gertrude's character, and Ophelia's madness and death. Five of fifteen assigned topics deal with the women in the play. To open the discussion, students write a short paper on their topic to share with the class. They present passages for us to review and interpretations for us to consider. We say "us" because we want the students to manage the discussion. The question of why Gertrude marries Claudius in the first place raises questions about the options for women during those times as well as comparisons to contemporary conditions. Also, students speculate on different ways to act out the scenes with Ophelia: Would Hamlet throw her around? Would she be a rag doll, limp and obedient? What does

Hamlet see in her that he should claim to love her so much? Some students have seen Mel Gibson's portrayal of Hamlet, or Olivier's, and they have strong opinions on how Ophelia might be acted.

When we brainstorm some possible topics for a paper, in lieu of a test, on *Hamlet,* many responses include issues relating to the women, such as studying the consequences of being innocent in this play or discussing the events from Ophelia's or Gertrude's point of view. One paper showed the complexities of Gertrude. The student saw her as the most human of all the characters in her inconsistencies and double loyalties; she was honest, practical, and innocent, but a hindrance to both Claudius and Hamlet, who saw her as a "little glitch they had to remove before they could go after each other." Another student wrote about Ophelia's "patterned madness, . . . directed by a reserve of reason, but . . . unfeigned and out of her control." She concluded that her madness and Hamlet's brought them a kind of freedom to "cope with the unjust wrongs" they had suffered. The point is that students should be expected to discuss *all* the characters in the play, not just Hamlet and Claudius; in this play, the two women are deeply entwined in the motives and actions of the men.

More and more works written by women from the late 1700s on are appearing in print. Authors studied in the Age of Reason can be almost evenly divided between male and female. Usually we have four of each for whole-class discussion. After reading selections from Pepys's *Diary* and Defoe's *Journal of the Plague Year,* we investigate some poems of Anne Finch and Lady Mary Wortley Montague.

Anne Finch, Countess of Winchilsea, published a volume of poems in 1713. William Wordsworth said that the images in her "A Nocturnal Reverie" were the freshest since those in Milton's *Paradise Lost* on the same subject. Finch describes the kind of gentle night "when every louder Wind / Is to its distant Cavern safe confin'd," a night when "in some River, overhung with Green, / The waving Moon and trembling Leaves are seen." The speaker in the poem thinks such a night disarms "the elements of Rage," composing the soul. She stays "abroad" all night, knowing that with the morning "Our Cares, our Toils, our Clamours are renew'd, / Or Pleasures, seldom reach'd, again pursu'd." The pensiveness of this poem contrasts with the vigor of "On Myself." In this poem, Finch thanks heaven that, though she is made the weaker sex, she finds herself "rescued from the Love / Of all those Trifles" that move most women. Instead, she "on [herself] can Live," whether that means to display her wings in the sun or retire in the shade, blessing it. One young woman in my class immediately saw how this poem paralleled Denise Levertov's poem "Movement," which she had read a year and half earlier. Levertov speaks of love as not bending over toward someone else but feeling "a flexible steel upright" running vertically inside oneself "from which to stretch." In "A Song" Finch chastises herself for depending on another's, presumably a man's, good will and affection for her heart's peace:

> 'Tis strange, this Heart within my breast,
>   Reason opposing, and her Powers,
> Cannot one gentle Moment rest,
>   Unless it knows what's done in Yours.

Finch ends the poem declaring that she will no longer inquire of the man what he thinks of her. Students find the poem quite contemporary in its theme. A fourth poem by Finch, "The Introduction," laments the scorn heaped upon women who attempt to publish, especially when much of what they write has more wit than the work of dull and untaught men. A twentieth-century American poet, Dilys Laing, in "Sonnet to a Sister in Error" addressed Finch: "Staunch Anne! I know your trouble. The same tether / galls us." Some students are impressed that women protested "way back then" and that some things haven't changed.

Lady Mary Wortley Montague, unlike Anne Finch, led an unusual life: she eloped, inoculated her children against smallpox, left her husband, and was sent letters of admiration from Alexander Pope (until they quarreled; his later letters attacked her). Students read and puzzle over the following poem by her. They look up *harshorn* tea, don't find it, but fail to look up *receipt*, *vapours*, and *spleen*, thinking they know these words. In spite of many reminders that meanings of words change over time, they still forget to check out the archaic meanings.

Receipt for the Vapours
Written to Lady J—n

Why will *Delia* thus retire,
And languish life away?
While the sighing crowd admire,
'Tis too soon for harshorn tea.

All those dismal looks and fretting
Cannot *Damon's* life restore;
Long ago the worms have eat him,
You can never see him more.

Once again consult your toilet,
In the glass your face review:
So much weeping soon will spoil it,
And no spring your charms renew.

I, like you, was born a woman,
Well I know what vapours mean:
The disease, alas! is common,
Single, we have all the spleen.

All the morals that they tell us
Never cur'd the sorrow yet:
Choose, among the pretty fellows,
One of humour, youth, and wit.

Prithee hear him every morning,
At the least an hour or two;
Once again at night returning,
I believe the dose will do.

Students don't know quite what to make of this poem until they discover it is a prescription for curing melancholy. "Who is Lady J—n?" "What are the 'vapours'?" The unabridged dictionary resolves the confusion. Usually one or two students detect some sarcasm, even satire. Even those who take the poem as serious see that women are trapped into believing that appearance and husbands are to be depended upon for all happiness.

The Age of Reason finds the satirists in full bloom, but how often do we think of Lady Chudleigh and Sarah Egerton along with Pope and Swift? As this chapter's opening quote from Egerton's "The Emulation" suggests, these two authors attacked traditions of male dominance in education, the arts, and marriage with the same intensity and sharp satire Pope and Swift used. We use two works by Chudleigh: an excerpt from "The Ladies Defence" and "To the Ladies." The "Defence" is a response to a sermon preached by John Sprint, in which he advocated women's total subjection to their husbands. Her anger against the church for making it a duty for wives to be silent, abjectly obedient, and tolerant of abuse shines strongly in this work. She points out how men cover their every failure and vice by giving each "some specious Name," such as calling cowards "wary," fops "genteel," and avarice "frugality." She goes on to ask why women alone must obey and drudge while the men command and hold arbitrary sway. In her poem "To the Ladies" she says that once the "fatal knot" of marriage is tied, a wife "like mutes . . . signs alone must make, / And never any freedom take: / But still be governed by a nod, / And fear her husband as her God." "Value your selves . . . You must be proud, if you'll be wise," she says, even if that means shunning the "wretched state" of marriage. Strong stuff, echoing Cavendish's outcries.

Egerton laments the exclusion of women from education, from the study of philosophy, science, the arts, and religion in "The Emulation," first published in her *Poems on Several Occasions* in 1703.

Say Tyrant Custom, why must we obey,
The impositions of thy haughty Sway,
From the first dawn of Life, unto the Grave,
Poor Womankind's in every State, a Slave.
The Nurse, the Mistress, Parent and the Swain,
For Love she must, there's none escape that Pain;
Then comes the last, the fatal Slavery,
The Husband with insulting Tyranny
Can have ill Manners justify'd by Law;
For Men all join to keep the Wife in awe.

Moses who first our Freedom did rebuke,
Was Marry'd when he writ the Pentateuch,
They're Wise to keep us Slaves, for well they know,
If we were loose, we soon should make them, so.
We yield like vanquish'd Kings whom Fetters bind,
When chance of War is to Usurpers kind;
Submit in Form; but they'd our Thoughts controul,
And lay restraints on the impassive Soul:
They fear we should excel their sluggish Parts,
Should we attempt the Sciences and Arts.
Pretend they were design'd for them alone,
So keep us Fools to raise their own Renown;
Thus Priests of old their Grandeur to maintain,
Cry'd vulgar Eyes would sacred Laws Prophane.
So kept the Mysteries behind a Screen.
There Homage and the Name were lost had they been seen:
But in this blessed Age, such Freedom's given,
That every Man explains the Will of Heaven;
And shall we Women now sit tamely by,
Make no excursions in Philosophy,
Or grace our Thoughts in tuneful Poetry?
We will our Rights in Learning's World maintain,
Wit's Empire, now, shall know a Female Reign;
Come all ye Fair, the great Attempt improve,
Divinely imitate the Realms above:
There's ten celestial Females govern Wit,
And but two Gods that dare pretend to it;
And shall these finite Males reverse their Rules,
No, we'll be Wits, and then Men must be Fools.

Students react with "I don't believe this!" Egerton's idea that
Custom says women needn't be educated raises the current issue of
girls doing less well in science and math than boys, especially at the
high school level. Her idea that the vulgar eyes of women would
profane the sacred laws connects to the present as well, for instance
in our uneasiness with female priests. Students note the threatening
tone at the poem's end, but usually don't see why men and women
can't both learn, both be wits and neither fools. In discussing the

162

general conditions of the 1700s, students see that the enforced idleness, servitude, and ignorance of married upper-class women were not universal: in the poorer classes the women worked right alongside the men to provide for their families, often taking over their husbands' businesses when they died or disappeared.

The semester ends with the Romantics: Blake (with some Burns in our introduction), Wordsworth, Mary Wollstonecraft, Mary Wollstonecraft Shelley, Percy Bysshe Shelley, and Keats. Students lead the discussion on most of the works by these authors. Fortunately, our school kept class sets of the 1982 edition of the Scott, Foresman *England in Literature*. Why? Because when the 1985 edition came out, it replaced the Wollstonecraft selection with a long excerpt from Mary Shelley's *Frankenstein*. (What the one edition gives, the other takes away. Why not include both authors?)

In introducing the Romantics, we ask students what they know about Jean-Jacques Rousseau's philosophy. We discuss his theory of the noble savage and then his dictates for women: to be useful to men, serve them, raise the children, be agreeable, manage their households. Their formal education would include some foreign languages, music, embroidery, watercoloring, and strict training in propriety. With Rousseau begin the Victorian ideals for well-off women: selfless angels or serene queens.

Needless to say, class conversation grows lively over the selections from Chapters 2 and 9 of Wollstonecraft's *A Vindication of the Rights of Woman*, clearly a document opposing Rousseau's views. Students work hard to determine the reasoning underlying the long sentences, but they soon recognize the complaints and see that in some ways Wollstonecraft could be speaking about men and women today: "If then women are not a swarm of ephemeron triflers, why should they be kept in ignorance under the specious name of innocence?" Good question. Wollstonecraft adds that the perfect education "is such an exercise of the understanding as is best calculated to strengthen the body and form the heart. Or, in other words, to enable the individual to attain such habits of virtue as will render it independent." Students are delighted to find that she knows full well that a woman's beauty will keep her protected for about twenty years only and that one way or another woman's cunning will come out: the more obedient men insist their women be, the more deceitful the women will become. What a waste, she says; "the rational fellowship" of a woman would be much more satisfactory for the husband because, for one thing, his peace of mind "would not be interrupted by the idle vanity of his wife."

In our text, right after the Wollstonecraft selections comes an essay on Wollstonecraft by Virginia Woolf. Student leaders are asked to digest this piece and convey to the class the conflicting elements Woolf finds in Wollstonecraft's nature and thinking as well as the qualities Woolf obviously admires. Wollstonecraft's marriage arrangements with William Godwin amuse the students at first, but then they get to thinking about them as a more serious possibility. Wollstonecraft wanted to be necessary to the man she loved but not worshipped. She and Godwin maintained separate households; and even though she was a reformer, she married so their child would not be a bastard. Godwin, every bit as radical as she when it came to relations between the sexes, finally agreed with her that they should live under the same roof, with his having separate working quarters and both feeling free to dine and make friends with whomever they chose, and separately if they wished. They sought the best of both worlds: independence and security. Wollstonecraft died shortly after their daughter, Mary, was born.

At sixteen, Mary Godwin eloped with Percy Shelley. After his wife's suicide, she married him, bore him four children, three of whom died, and was left a widow at age twenty-four. Although she wrote a number of pieces to help earn her living, she is best known for her short novel *Frankenstein.* Students are surprised to find that Frankenstein is the name of the scientist, not the creation. (One student reported that her mother's teacher in a women's literature course at the University of New Hampshire said that Frankenstein's creature was actually a metaphor for women. Now there's something to think about!) They also love discussing the issues of ethics in science and general human morality raised by the story. The abridged version in our text covers some material from each section of the novel. Since several students read the whole book for position papers, the class can burrow pretty deeply. So far students have not commented on its having been written by a woman; they simply praise it. (Besides, since so much of the course has been poetry, they thoroughly enjoy the prose of these female authors.)

Along the way students read two novels: *Pride and Prejudice* by Jane Austen and *Wuthering Heights* by Emily Brontë. We work these in by assigning approximately one-third of a novel for Mondays, giving students the weekends to read these sizable chunks. (Sometimes the discussion carries over to Tuesday.) Students have responsibility for talking about certain characters, choosing words to describe their personalities, passages they found particularly revealing, and questions about their roles, relationships, motives, or whatever. A quiz on some quotes may begin the discussion the first week. Instead of a test on the novels, students write analytical/response papers of five to seven hundred words. (These often run longer.) Students choose to explore the various kinds of marriages and compare and contrast some of the leading women in *Pride and Prejudice* more often than they depict the follies of Mr. Collins or the satire of Mr. Bennet. One student wrote wittily about the intellectual match between Lady Catherine and Elizabeth, speculating that perhaps Lady Catherine is finally drawn to Pemberley lest she succumb to sheer boredom. And despite *Wuthering Heights* being written by a woman, they find Heathcliff irresistible as a romantic figure or demonic avenger, rarely questioning how he or the whole story could be created by a woman. Many of the young women in the class choose novels by Jane Austen and Charlotte Brontë to read for their position papers.

On the down side, many students find *Pride and Prejudice* boring; they simply don't like it. Their classmates point out the satire, how funny and foolish the whole premise of the book is, how laughable and ugly Lady Catherine is, and how much they can expand their vocabulary and knowledge of the early-nineteenth-century English upper classes. If they are not won over, the last day's attempt to rank the characters from most to least proud and narrow-minded usually draws the resisters in. Students have been assigned a character to rank. The debate not only reviews the characters but creates some passion and hilarity as we remember their wickedness or officiousness or refreshing good sense.

Since the students have done much of the teaching—have conducted the discussions—during the semester and have written papers (too many, they say) on the units and novels, we struggle with what kind of final exam to give. A few years ago we heard about an oral final exam for an American literature class. "What a great idea!" we thought. We've tried it twice since, when the general level of maturity and cohesiveness of the class augured well. Here's how the oral exam works. Students read four or five unfamiliar works, some by authors we've studied, covering the range of the course (another way to add more authors and works to the course without removing the old favorites). Each student is expected to come in with two important things to say about each piece; they are also to be aware that every member of the class must have a chance to talk, that the give and take must be more or less balanced. We sit at our desk, silent, making notes for each student as they contribute to the discussion. We have symbols for different kinds of contributions: responding to someone else's remark, making a connection to other works, making a personal connection, asking a question, doing some analysis, and drawing someone else in. A vertical line between marks indicates the discussion has moved to another work. By totaling the contributions and checking the kind of contribution as soon as possible after the exam, we have little trouble determining grades, which range from D to A. A student who only asks questions or who speaks only at the very beginning of the conversation on a work scores poorly; a student who invites the quiet ones to speak, who comments and makes connections, and who raises questions about style earns a high grade. The students love it; so do we. They can discuss a work as fully as they want; others' comments extend their thinking; they work hard to understand the new pieces in relation to the periods they came from; and they are more sensitive than usual to including the quieter members. Several report that it was the best discussion they've ever had in a literature class. They discover that they can indeed read, understand, and appreciate literature on their own. That's one of our main goals: to help students speak from their own authority, trust their own abilities, and know that everyone's perceptions contribute in some measure to their understanding—that cooperation extends their learning more than competition. Not having to read yet another paper pleases us, but students are even more pleased to escape having to write one. But the method isn't perfect. Only four works can be discussed in the allotted time, three in depth; and once in spite of one young woman's vigorous requests to discuss "Wit's Abuse" by Anne Wharton each time the class decided to switch authors, they refused to look at it. From now on we'll include two works by women and two by men.

New books keep coming out with newly discovered female authors from the 1600s on. The writers mentioned in this chapter are only some. We're looking forward to finding new ones to bring in. We think the young women in the class appreciate having women writers to talk about when it's their turn to be in charge of the discussion. Besides, England was and is populated by women as well as men, and women's point of view must be included if we are to say we are offering a course in English literature.

Works Cited

AUSTEN, JANE. 1980. *Pride and Prejudice.* New York: Signet.

BEHN, APHRA. 1974. "Song." In Goulianos.

———. 1988. *The Rover.* Portsmouth, NH: Heinemann.

———. 1992. "Love's Witness." In Aliki Barnstone and Willis Barnstone, eds., *A Book of Women Poets from Antiquity to Now.* New York: Schocken Books. International, grouped by country, smooth translations; many, many poems appropriate for high school students.

BRONTË, EMILY. 1959. *Wuthering Heights.* New York: Signet.

CAVENDISH, MARGARET. 1985. "Female Orations" and "Nature's Cook." In Gilbert and Gubar.

CHUDLEIGH, LADY MARY LEE. 1985a. "The Ladies Defence." In Moira Ferguson, ed., *First Feminists: British Women Writers, 1578–1799.* Bloomington: Indiana University Press. Strong biographical information, ample selections; Behn, Cavendish, Egerton, Finch, Montagu, Wollstonecraft, along with some twenty others.

———. 1985b. "To the Ladies." In Gilbert and Gubar.

COSMAN, CAROL, JOAN KEEFE, and KATHLEEN WEAVER, eds. 1978. *The Penguin Book of Women Poets*. New York: Penguin. Brief but helpful biographical notes; international from ancient Egyptian to middle twentieth century authors.

DE PIZAN, CHRISTINE. 1982. *The Book of the City of Ladies*. New York: Persea. This fifteenth-century work has limited appeal to students because it is so philosophical and theological. Argues for such things as equal access to education for women, equality in marriage for women, and protection for women against rape.

"Eagle of Pengwern." 1985. Trans. Gwyn Williams. In McDonnell, Pfordresher, and Veidemanis.

EGERTON, SARAH FYGE FIELD. 1989. "The Emulation." In Roger Lonsdale, ed., *Eighteenth-Century Women Poets: An Oxford Anthology*. New York: Oxford University Press. A rich collection for your enjoyment with fewer choices for high school students.

ELIZABETH I. 1978. "On Fortune" and "Written in Her French Psalter." In Cosman, Keefe, and Weaver.

———. 1985a. "On Monsieur's Departure" and "The Doubt of Future Foes." In Gilbert and Gubar.

———. 1985b. "When I Was Fair and Young." In McDonnell, Pfordresher, and Veidemanis.

FINCH, ANNE. 1974. "A Nocturnal Reverie," "A Song," "On Myself," and "The Introduction." In Goulianos.

GILBERT, SANDRA M., and SUSAN GUBAR, eds. 1985. *The Norton Anthology of Literature by Women*. New York: Norton. A must for every high school. American and English writers, prose and poetry, including Toni Morrison's *The Bluest Eye*; extensive biographies and full introductions to the six literary periods included.

GOULIANOS, JOAN, ed. 1974. *by a Woman writt: Literature from Six Centuries by and About Women*. London: New English Library. Twenty authors from Margery Kempe to Muriel Rukeyser, many poems or long prose selections to become well acquainted with each author.

GREER, GERMAINE, SUSAN HASTINGS, JESLUN MEDOFF, and MELINDA SANSONE, eds. 1988. *Kissing the Rod: An Anthology of Seventeenth-Century Women's Verse.* New York: Noonday Press. Long and interesting biographies, extensive selections, and scholarly notes. Little for high school students.

"The Husband's Message." 1985. Trans. Burton Raffel. In McDonnell, Pfordresher, and Veideman

LAING, DILYS. 1974. "Sonnet to a Sister in Error." In Goulianos.

LEVERTOV, DENISE. 1978. "Movement." In *Life in the Forest.* New York: New Directions.

MCDONNELL, HELEN, NEIL E. NAKADATE, JOHN PFORDRESHER, and THOMAS E. SHOEMATE, eds. 1982. *England in Literature.* Glenview, IL: Scott, Foresman.

MCDONNELL, HELEN, JOHN PFORDRESHER, and GLADYS V. VEIDEMANIS, eds. 1985. *England in Literature.* Glenview, IL: Scott, Foresman.

MONTAGU, LADY MARY WORTLEY. 1978. "Receipt for the Vapours." In Cosman, Keefe, and Weaver.

RALEIGH, SIR WALTER. 1985. "The Nymph's Reply to the Shepherd." In McDonnell, Pfordresher, and Veidemanis.

RICH, ADRIENNE. 1979. "When We Dead Awaken: Writing as Re-Visioning." In *On Lies, Secrets, and Silence: Selected Prose, 1966–1978.* New York: Norton.

SHELLEY, MARY WOLLSTONECRAFT. 1985. *Frankenstein.* Excerpted in McDonnell, Pfordresher, and Veidemanis.

WARNER, SYLVIA ASHTON. 1985. "Gloriana Dying." In McDonnell, Pfordresher, and Veidemanis.

WHARTON, ANNE. 1988. "Wit's Abuse." In Greer et al.

"The Wife's Lament." 1985. Trans. Charles W. Kennedy. In McDonnell, Pfordresher, and Veidemanis.

WOLLSTONECRAFT, MARY. 1982. *A Vindication of the Rights of Woman.* In McDonnell, Nakadate, Pfordresher, and Shoemate.

WOOLF, VIRGINIA. 1982. "Mary Wollstonecraft." In McDonnell, Nakadate, Pfordresher, and Shoemate.

Suggested Books for Students

AUSTEN, JANE. 1981a. *Emma.* New York: Bantam Classic.

————. 1981b. *Persuasion.* New York: Penguin. Both in several other paperback editions.

BRADLEY, MARION ZIMMER. 1984. *The Mists of Avalon.* New York: Ballantine. The story of King Arthur from Morgan Le Fay's point of view. Long, detailed, different. For students familiar with the Arthur story.

COLLIS, LOUISE. 1964. *Memoirs of a Medieval Woman.* New York: Perennial. A biography of Margery Kempe of the fifteenth century. She traveled widely in Europe and to the Holy Land where she sought expiation for some secret sin. Colorful picture of these times and its people. Incidentally, Kempe had fourteen children.

GATES, BARBARA TIMM, ed. 1991. *Journal of Emily Shore.* Charlottesville: University Press of Virginia. Diary covers period from July 5, 1831, when the author was eleven, to June 24, 1839, two weeks before her death of consumption. An example of her writing, on *Hamlet*: "This is my favourite play. . . . The whole interest, indeed, is swallowed up in Hamlet, but how deep, how absorbing is that interest! His profound melancholy, the struggles and conflicting passions in his noble mind, his painful sense of his own want of resolution, unite informing one of the grandest conceptions and creations of even Shakespeare's mighty genius."

WELDON, FAY. 1984. *Letters to Alice: On First Reading Jane Austen.* New York: Taplinger. Witty comments to punk niece about why she should be patient with Austen. Mature students would enjoy it.

WOLLSTONECRAFT, MARY. 1975. *Maria, or the Wrongs of Woman.* New York: Norton. Somewhat bleak tale of Maria's struggles, laced with Wollstonecraft's ideas about independence for women.

Useful Works for Teachers

GOREAU, ANGELINE, ed. 1985. *The Whole Duty of a Woman: Female Writers in Seventeenth Century England.* Garden City, NY: Dial. Prose and poetry 175 years before Wollstonecraft. Feminist women argue vigorously for their right to publish and respond to antifeminist diatribes from male authors. Helpful social background for these writers; modernized spelling and punctuation.

MAHL, MARY R., and HELENE KOON. 1977. *The Female Spectator: English Women Writers Before 1800.* New York: Feminist Press. One fascinating section is Eliza Haywood and *The Female Spectator,* a magazine published between 1722 and 1746, the first magazine by and for women. Written almost entirely by Haywood, it dealt with questions of female education, literature, the arts, and philosophy. Helpful introductions to all the writers.

ROGERS, KATHARINE M. 1979. *Before Their Time: Six Women Writers of the Eighteenth Century.* New York: Ungar. Includes a valuable introduction and a chronology with important historical events; places publications of female authors next to those of male authors.

ROGERS, KATHARINE M., and WILLIAM MCCARTHY, eds. 1987. *The Meridian Anthology of Early Women Writers: British Literary Women from Aphra Behn to Maria Edgeworth, 1660–1800.* New York: Meridian. Includes all of *Oroonoko,* Behn's short novel about slavery; many Finch poems; letters from Lady Montagu. Also others, such as Mary Astell, who writes in "A Serious Proposal to the Ladies": "Let us learn to pride ourselves in something more excellent than the invention of a fashion, and not entertain such a degrading thought of our own *worth,* as to imagine that our souls were given us only for the service of our bodies, and that the best improvement we can make of these, is to attract the eyes of men."

NINE

English Literature
1850 to the Present

*Literature is not an aerobics class or a session at the
therapist's. But then I think of myself as a child, leafing
through anthologies of poetry for the names of women.
I never would have admitted that I needed a role model,
. . . but why was I so excited to find a female name,
even when, as was often the case, it was attached to a
poem of no interest to me whatsoever? . . . I have to
admit it, just by their presence . . . they did something
for me.*

KATHA POLLITT
"Canon to the Right of Me . . ."

In her article in *The Nation*, Katha Pollitt (1991) points out that in
a nation of readers, the idea of a canon should be unnecessary, as we
would all be reading all sorts of books, one leading to another. But in
our nation, she says, we assume that the only books young people will
read are the ones on a list for some school course. Lamentably, it may
be true. Moreover, people without independent reading lives "won't
like reading the books on the list and will forget them the minute
[they've] finished them" (p. 330). Pollitt concludes her essay by saying no batch of books can work magic for good or ill; there is no
"one-on-one correlation between books and behavior. . . . Books do
not shape character in any simple way" (p. 330, 332). And so the

claims of the canon supporters are specious: no handful of books can do so much. Agreed: relying on the canonical anthologies won't do it. Then whom should we read in a high school literature course? Why not work toward two goals: including many women authors (to "do something" for the young women in the class) and including a large number of authors. Aim for extensive coverage, rather than an intensive examination of fewer works, in hopes of raising the chances for developing lifelong readers.

In teaching English Literature II, a semester-long course on works from 1850 to the present, we have to remind ourselves that our students are not college English majors: we cannot expect them to grasp all the finer points of style or the many slots in the class system of England. They struggle enough with the vocabulary, so we offer a variety of opportunities for them to discover points of interest in the readings and to make sense on their own terms of what they read. We hope that some generalizations (admittedly oversimplified) about English literary periods and biographical facts about authors will create a context students will remember. But whatever else, with Pollitt in mind, we can make sure that almost half of the authors in English Literature II are female.

Since we use many of the techniques mentioned in Chapter 8 in teaching this course, we needn't repeat them here. Instead, this chapter will concentrate on describing works by women.

One way to bring in more women is to have an introductory packet for study before doing the chronological survey. One such packet we use has six prose passages—the opening paragraph or two from novels by Dickens, Eliot, Hardy, Conrad, Woolf, and Atwood. (Another way to extend the available literature is to include authors from Commonwealth nations.) In examining these selections, students review sentence structure, use of metaphor, tone, characterization, and diction, and they see changes in these elements over time and, perhaps, some differences between male and female points of view. Having equal numbers of male and female authors sets the pattern for the course and prepares students for the kind of writing they will find in books they read on their own for position papers.

The semester begins with the Victorians. Using both the 1982 and 1985 editions of Scott, Foresman's *England in Literature,* we teach works by Elizabeth Barrett Browning, Emily Brontë, Christina Rossetti, and George Eliot; in addition, we study John Stuart Mill's essay "On the Subjection of Women."

Elizabeth Barrett Browning's selections from "Sonnets from the Portuguese" in the older edition have less than pleasant themes. Sonnet 3, beginning "Unlike are we, unlike, O princely Heart!/ Unlike our uses and our destinies," points out how he, a chief musician, is consecrated a prince while she, annointed only with dew, languishes, a wandering singer; the two of them may be made level only by Death. Sonnet 22 speaks of two lovers standing face to face in a space cleared for them "with darkness and the death-hour rounding it." But in the three sonnets in the 1985 edition, students see the power and richness of her growing love for Robert Browning.

Browning didn't write just love sonnets; she wrote on a variety of topics in a number of poetic forms. One student in a poetry class found several poems to share with the class for her independent project on a poet. In "The Best Thing in the World" the speaker asks, "What's the best thing in the world?" After listing such things as "Truth, not cruel to a friend" and "Light, that never makes you wink," she concludes, "Something out of it [the world], I think." Melancholy, yes, but students recognized the mood. They also recognized the "dreary life" and "strife" and "struggle" in "Patience Taught by Nature." At the end of this poem, the speaker asks God for "so much patience as a blade of grass / Grows by, contented through the heat and cold." *The Norton Anthology of Literature by Women* carries two of Browning's poems to George Sand: "A Desire" and "A Recognition," both dense but worth investigating. Browning is a far more complex person than sonnets from her series on falling in love with Robert Browning reveal.

Emily Brontë's poems deserve study. They are particularly helpful for students who read *Wuthering Heights,* partly because they provide some context for the novel, some glimpse into her life. One student read a collection of her poems for a position paper. In "Ah, Why,

Because the Dazzling Sun" the poet longs for Night, concluding the poem with:

> O Stars and Dreams and Gentle Night;
> O Night and Stars return!
> And hide me from the hostile light
> That does not warm, but burn—
>
> That drains the blood of suffering men;
> Drinks tears, instead of dew:
> Let me sleep through his blinding reign,
> And only wake with you!

Brontë appears to find peace in the darkness and pain in the light and on the earth. In fact, in "I'll Not Weep" she says she is "weary of the anguish" and "sick to see the spirit languish" as she tends a dying sibling or friend. "There is nothing lovely here" (on earth), so if she should cry, it will be because her "soul is sighing / To go and rest with" him or her. Seeing her pensive mood in these two poems as well as her prayer for "a chainless soul with courage to endure" (from "Riches I hold in light esteem") and her reaction to the night wind in "The Night Wind" helps students understand, perhaps, Catherine and Heathcliff's welcoming death and their later ghostly wanderings. Students should know that Brontë wrote poems, and *Norton* includes at least two other poems high school students might find interesting: "No coward soul is mine" and "Stanzas." The former reveals a great faith, arming the speaker who does not tremble "in the world's storm-troubled sphere." She knows that "there is not room for Death" because even if the "earth . . . and suns and universes ceased to be," she would exist in God, who "may never be destroyed." In "Stanzas" she "walks where [her] own nature would be leading." She wants no other guide. The poem ends:

> What have those lonely mountains worth revealing?
>   More glory and more grief than I can tell:
> The earth that wakes one human heart to feeling
>   Can centre both the worlds of Heaven and Hell.

We think of the young Catherine and Heathcliff roaming the heath on a wild night, centering their Heaven and Hell.

A third woman poet to balance Tennyson, Robert Browning, and Arnold could be Christina Rossetti. Both of her poems in our text involve blindness: blindness to the importance of a meeting and blindness from being shut out. "Shut Out" gets students to wondering what the garden (once hers) represents, who shuts her out, and why she has lost it. In "Song" she says, "When I am dead . . . sing no sad songs for me," for dead, "haply I may remember, / And haply may forget." Her soul in the poem "A Soul" stands like Cleopatra's: "alone, . . . patient nerved with inner might, / Indomitable in her feebleness, / Her face and will athirst against the light." In "Cobwebs" she adds that after death there is "no future hope, no fear for evermore." Gloom and peace are mixed. In "Up-hill" she asks, "Does the road wind up-hill all the way? / Yes, to the very end." But there are "beds for all who come." When Rossetti looks into the very bottom of herself in "Enrica, 1865," she finds herself like other English women: "trim, correct . . . at our deepest, strong and free." Surely these words should stand next to Tennyson's "To strive, to seek, to find, and not to yield" ("Ulysses").

To encourage students to let the poems speak to them in their own ways, we have them work on the Rossetti and the Brontë poems in small groups. They look for ways to explain their interpretations and reactions to their classmates and for connections between the poems by each author. We don't always agree; we admit to several possibilities; we point out that well-established interpretations (such as those that published critics have for the more famous authors' works) aren't necessarily the ones that must be reached.

Enough about poets; on to prose. "The Lifted Veil" by George Eliot is otherworldly and pairs well with the abridged version we read of Lewis Carroll's *Alice's Adventures Under Ground*: both stories go beyond science and logic; both provide interesting female characters. (What would the Carroll stories be like if Alice were an Arthur?) The excerpt we read from Eliot's *The Mill on the Floss* (portions of Chapters 3 and 4 of Book One) provokes interesting discussion and an appropriate follow-up to Wollstonecraft. Maggie Tulliver, in this early chapter, shows atypical female behavior and interests, things like a love of learning, rebellion, and passion, all quite unladylike; they doom Maggie in the end. The excerpt also implies two damaging male attitudes of the time; both become explicit later in the book. The first is expressed by the father of a man who loves Maggie: "We don't ask what a woman does—we ask whom she belongs to." The second comes from Maggie's brother (whom she adores). He explains to her how he shows his feelings quite differently from the ways Maggie shows hers. She accounts for the major difference between them: "Because you are a man, Tom, and have power, and can do something in the world." Tom replies, "Then, if you can do nothing, submit to those that can." Submission is not for Maggie, both in this excerpt and later in the book. Nor does the idea of the subjection of women please John Stuart Mill who opposed tyranny of all kinds. "The legal subordination of one sex to the other . . . is wrong in itself, and now one of the chief hindrances to human improvement." His arguments in "On the Subjection of Women" take on history, psychology, and education. He claims that natural differences between men and women can be the subject of conjecture only. He decries women's dependent position in such statements as "It may be asserted without scruple, that no other class of dependents have had their character so entirely distorted from its natural proportions by their relation with their masters." Published in 1869, 166 years after Sarah Egerton's "The Emulation" protested the tyranny of men over women, and 100 years after Wollstonecraft's *Vindication*, this essay offers support for their arguments. It, too, was very unpopular.

Browning and Eliot both wrote many letters, now available: *The Letters of Elizabeth Barrett Browning to Mary Russell Mitford, 1836–1854* and *Selections from George Eliot's Letters*. Why not try some of these in class?

Yet another way to bring women's lot into perspective is to compare and contrast Dickens and Eliot passages that describe schooling. A scene in Chapter 2 of Dickens's *Hard Times* of Mr. Gradgrind's classroom shows a girl being addressed as "girl number twenty-seven" and all of the students being stuffed with facts, facts, facts. Chapter 1 of Book III in *The Mill on the Floss* describes Tom's schooling under Mr. Stelling and exposes Maggie's unacceptable intelligence and interest in book learning. Students love this opportunity to talk about their own schooling.

The next group of authors in our text, from around the turn of the century to the first world war, includes no women. Shaw's *Pygmalion* raises many class, ethical, and gender issues, and it does so with such good humor that even students grouching about "the woman thing" can enjoy the discussion. In looking for women poets to balance Hardy, Hopkins, and Housman, we found two in *Norton*: Mary Elizabeth Coleridge (the great-great-niece of Samuel Taylor Coleridge) and Charlotte Mew.

Coleridge strikes a familiar note in "The Other Side of a Mirror" where she sees in the glass "a woman, wild with more than womanly despair." This woman in the glass hides behind the comfortable and apparently serene life of an English literature teacher at a working women's college. Haven't we all seen another self in a mirror? Food for thought and discussion here. Coleridge also writes about the devil and witches. "The Devil's Funeral" rejoices that the devil is dead, but ends with his transformation into an angel of light who may "work more utter woe / Than ever he worked when he dwelt below." Her doubts and strange confounding of the living and the dead harmonize well with the dark notes of Hardy.

Charlotte Mew was known and admired by Hardy, and the bleakness of some of her works is echoed in his. She, like Coleridge, may have secretly revolted against the "veneer of docility" expected of women. Never able to earn quite enough money, she committed suicide, alone and impoverished. In "The Farmer's Bride," the farmer's wife, too young married, runs away from her husband's touch but lives on at the farm, a furtive thing, sleeping in the attic. In "The Quiet House," bleakness creeps through the poem and ends with the speaker seeing the misty rain and streetlights; not one is lit for her. She thinks, "It is myself I go to meet," but she doesn't care because "some day I shall not think; I shall not be." The melancholy is not unlike that of Hardy and Housman; our female students have the right to hear a woman poet voice it.

Most of us are fairly familiar with twentieth-century English writers. We think teachers ought to teach works they like regardless of what the anthologies may have to offer, and with more and more books coming out, finding women authors gets easier. A useful paperback anthology is *Scars upon My Heart,* edited by Catherine Reilly and published by Virago, an English press. The title comes from a Vera Brittain poem about World War I, "To My Brother," written four days before his death. She calls his wounds "scars upon my heart," and she calls the war a "grand and tragic 'show'." All the poems in this collection are by women, both English and American, and about war, specifically World War I. These poets match Wilfred Owen and Seigfried Sassoon, protesting war, reflecting on experiences nursing the wounded, and recounting the pain of soldiers and loss. Maud Anna Bell in "From a Trench" writes about "the dogs of war [running] loose," in fields where once "the living corn" grew. Eva Dobell in "Pluck" writes of a seventeen-year-old boy "crippled for life." As he looks at his smashed legs, his "eyes seem to question why." And in "The Dancers" Edith Sitwell writes of a dance floor in 1916, "slippery with blood" where dancers dance and carrion flies grow fat and God dies, "mad from the horror." Even the light is "flecked with blood." Charlotte Mew has three poems in this collection.

Vera Brittain wrote two books accessible to high school students: *Testament of Friendship* and *Testament of Youth.* The latter recounts Brittain's experiences during the war years: her education, her engagement, her work as a Red Cross nurse, her anguish at her fiancé's death "of wounds at a Casualty Clearing Station," and her continuing work at hospitals, enduring in spite of the deaths of her brother and friends to add to her grief. This autobiography and the Reilly collection of poems show us the war the women knew. Can we see what this war, or any war, is truly like without women's experience of it? Their works expose a wasteland as surely as T.S. Eliot's poems do.

To include an equal number of works by women in the modern period, we use a splendid paperback to supplement our text: *British Motifs* (Miller, Hayden, and O'Neal 1973). The collection includes short stories by men and women from most of the Commonwealth nations. Students like short stories, so we usually have two units of stories, with a unit of poetry in between. We don't think it matters much which authors we use, so long as the men and women are equally represented. Following are brief notes on some stories by women most students have enjoyed or found interesting from both *Motifs* and our main texts.

"The Legacy" by Virginia Woolf finds Gilbert Clandon reading through his dead wife's diaries, discovering that she was not the person he had thought, nor did her depiction of him match his depiction of himself. The story ends: "She had stepped off the kerb to rejoin her lover. She had stepped off the kerb to escape from him."

In Sylvia Ashton Warner's "The Phoenix," Lord Strawberry brings home from Arabia a "remarkably fine phoenix, with a charming character—affable to the other birds in the aviary and much attached to Lord Strawberry." When Lord Strawberry dies penniless (it costs a good deal to run an aviary), the phoenix is sold to Mr. Poldero, owner of Poldero's Wizard Wonderland, but the amiable bird attracts few visitors to pay for his bird seed. Mr. Poldero and Mr. Ramkin, his manager, think to age the bird (by halving its food and turning down the heat) so it will build its pyre, burn up, and be reborn, all to the flash cameras and delight of the paying public. The polite, civil bird finally weakens and appears to fall asleep on its pyre. "Some thousand people, including Mr. Poldero, perished in the blaze."

Katherine Mansfield's "The Doll's House" is as sensitive as Warner's is witty and clever. Class prejudice reaches out its ugly hand to harm the poor, fatherless Kelvey sisters, Lil and Else. One day at school, two of the wealthy Burnell sisters brag of their large, new, exquisitely detailed doll's house. While Kezia, the kind-hearted sister, shows it to Lil and Else, her Aunt Beryl chases off the "little rats of Kelveys," but not before Else's eyes and heart are filled by the lovely little lamp Kezia so loves.

Elizabeth Bowen's "The Cat Jumps," a story about people at a weekend housewarming, includes details from a grisly murder some years earlier at the house and its effects, both negative and humorous, on these guests.

"The Story of the Widow's Son" by Mary Lavin has two endings. The widow makes plans for her son, Packy; she lives for him, and "his character was strengthening . . . under his mother's sharp tongue." The two endings have to do with the consequences of Packy's reaction when a distracted old hen flutters into the road in front of him as he flies down the hill toward home on his bike. In both endings the widow loses her son.

In Joyce Marshall's story "The Old Woman" as Molly finds fulfillment serving as a nurse/midwife for the people of northern, barren Quebec, her husband, Toddy, falls in love with the turbines and generators of his power plant— "bushed," they call his kind of obsessive withdrawal from reality.

Groups of students take on the responsibility for teaching the short stories. They consider how they want to run the class and what they want their classmates to do; they may even include a writing assignment. We suggest five areas students may want to cover, but they are not limited to these: characters (What are the people like? What do they value? What are their motives? How do you feel about them?); style (sentence structure, use of dialogue, diction, structure of the story); issues (What problems or issues are raised in the story? What solutions, resolutions? How do they connect with current affairs or student lives?); key passages (attention is directed to them, probably as the above issues come up); and overall considerations (How successful or meaningful was the story for you? What makes it work or not work for you?). Comparisons and contrasts abound once we get past the first story. A colleague has each group write a paper after they have dealt with all the stories. They talk and create notes. Then one member writes the first draft; a second writes the revision after more group work; another edits; and another writes the final copy.

One novel we have used with some success (it depends on the class) is Muriel Spark's *The Prime of Miss Jean Brodie.* It's puzzling, a bit like a mystery story, but it raises questions about education, teaching, power, religion, politics (fascism, for example), loyalty, and betrayal. Miss Brodie has a select group of young female students, whom she teaches both in and out of the classroom. Fascinated by her and their own eliteness, they look at the world through her eyes and later through their own as they begin to question what they've been taught by her. We see all six members of the group grow up; we see Miss Brodie die; we see her legacy, and we are left with unresolved questions, questions worth asking. This short book (which is full of references that may need explaining) also deals with emerging sexuality.

Doris Lessing's *The Memoirs of a Survivor* is a strange and somewhat depressing book. The narrator, an older woman, watches the degeneration of her society while listening in on another society just on the other side of her apartment wall. The book includes a warning about love: beware of love, for if you have goals and purposes for your life, love can derail you. The end of the book implies that a woman will lead the survivors into a better world.

Who are some female British poets of the later twentieth century to read? One is Stevie Smith. Her poems are short, witty, spare. She says flat out she has no respect for a person with "a coward's soul" ("No Respect"). And the reason a person in her poem "The Reason" cannot vote for suicide in the face of a "vile" life is that he or she cannot decide about God: is He "good, impotent or unkind"? She offers another view of the frog prince in her poem of that title: he is quite happy until he realizes that part of the spell is to feel happy and fear disenchantment; he thinks it would be heavenly to be set free; he says he can be happy until then, but he cannot be heavenly. Whether her speakers are moving more and more quickly in the "wrong direction" ("Alone in the Woods") or being "much too far out" all their lives and, in fact, drowning ("Not Waving But Drowning"), they offer views students can relate to.

Her clear, simple style contrasts with Margaret Atwood's richer, longer poems. Try Atwood's "This Is a Photograph of Me," "Eden Is a Zoo," "Postcard," "The Landlady," or "Procedures for Underground," all full of images, anger, and issues. (For example, the landlady is a swollen knot, "a raucous fact, . . . immutable, . . . solid.") In "Eden Is a Zoo," her parents are kept in a garden inside a "hedge of spikes" where they stomp around in old-fashioned clothes that look as "innocent as plain skin." The narrator questions who she is in "This Is a Photograph of Me." The photo was taken one day after she drowned.

A third poet to try would be Elizabeth Jennings. In "The Climbers," she describes the hikers "without their women" becoming small at the top, no longer possessing the mountain, and resentful. Students relate quickly to this experience, especially the track and field athletes, the hikers, and the hunters. She praises the simple life of insignificance in "Not in the Guide-Books." Tourists don't stay in this place with no "marvelous death or battle" to hold them.

A host of modern and contemporary women authors from England and the Commonwealth countries could be made a part of this course. (See the Suggested Books for Students list at the end of this chapter.) But adding just the women described in this chapter can fill up the semester.

One final suggestion: show the Australian movie *My Brilliant Career* (available in video), based on the book by Miles Franklin. It offers a look at poor farmers as well as the upper classes, but best of all it tells about a young outback woman, Sybylla, who puts her ambition to write, to write about her people with love and pity, above the comforts of marrying into a socially distinguished family. Sybylla's grandmother explains that an unmarried woman is a burden to her family and has no status; besides, she says, marriage will give her respectability. Harry truly loves her and waits for two years while she tries to decide who she is and what the world is all about; he promises not to interfere with her writing. But Sybylla turns Harry down (much to the discomfort, even anger, of some students) because she feels she would destroy him. "I cannot lose myself in somebody else's life when I haven't even lived my own yet. I want to be a writer . . . but I've got to do it now, and I've got to do it alone." She's spontaneous, unaffected, perceptive, refreshing, and most improper, dancing with the servants, tipping over the boat Harry has taken her for a ride in, and leaving Frank, another suitor, to walk home and to walk out of a sheep pen the two times he makes passes at her. Sybylla sees that marriage will curtail, if not kill, her career. The movie ends with her sending off her manuscript for publication. Students divide about half and half on whether or not she should marry Harry, a very likable young man. Although the movie takes place in the nineteenth century, students react vigorously and speak passionately about their own ambitions and how these fit into marriage, and if they do, what kind of marriage.

Sybylla will not suffer subjection, but she will testify. In "On the Subjection of Women" Mill wrote, "It [the mental characteristics of women] is a subject on which nothing final can be known, so long as those who alone can really know it, women themselves, have given but little testimony, and that little, mostly suborned." We have greater access to women's testimonies today, so we have no excuse not to include this half of the human race in our courses. Besides, we never know but that "just by their presence . . . they [may do] something for" our female students as they did for Katha Pollitt.

Works Cited

ATWOOD, MARGARET. 1985. "Eden is a Zoo," "Postcard," "Procedures for Underground," "The Landlady," and "This Is a Photograph of Me." In Gilbert and Gubar.

BELL, MAUD ANNA. 1981. "From a Trench." In Reilly.

BOWEN, ELIZABETH. 1973. "The Cat Jumps." In Miller, Hayden, and O'Neal.

BRITTAIN, VERA. 1978. *Testament of Youth: An Autobiographical Study of the Years 1900–1925*. New York: Penguin.

———. 1981. "To My Brother." In Reilly.

———. 1988. *Testament of Friendship: The Story of Winifred Holtby*. London: Virago.

BRONTË, EMILY. 1982. "Ah, Why, Because the Dazzling Sun," "I'll Not Weep," and "The Night Wind." In McDonnell, Nakadate, Pfordresher, and Shoemate.

———. 1985. "No coward soul is mine," "Riches I hold in light esteem," and "Stanzas." In Gilbert and Gubar.

BROWNING, ELIZABETH BARRETT. 1974. "The Best Thing in the World" and "Patience Taught by Nature." In *The Poetical Works of Elizabeth Barrett Browning*. Boston: Houghton Mifflin.

————. 1982. "Sonnets from the Portuguese: 3, 22." In McDonnell, Nakadate, Pfordresher, and Shoemate.

————. 1983. *The Letters of Elizabeth Barrett Browning to Mary Russell Mitford, 1836–1854.* 3 vols. Winfield, KS: Wedgestone Press.

————. 1985a. "A Desire" and "A Recognition." In Gilbert and Gubar.

————. 1985b. "Sonnets from the Portuguese: 1, 28, 43." In McDonnell, Pfordresher, and Veidemanis.

CARROLL, LEWIS. 1982. *Alice's Adventures Under Ground.* Abridged in McDonnell, Nakadate, Pfordresher, and Shoemate.

COLERIDGE, MARY ELIZABETH. 1985. "The Devil's Funeral" and "The Other Side of a Mirror." In Gilbert and Gubar.

DICKENS, CHARLES. 1981. *Hard Times.* New York: Bantam.

DOBELL, EVA. 1981. "Pluck." In Reilly.

ELIOT, GEORGE. 1982. "The Lifted Veil." In McDonnell, Nakadate, Pfordresher, and Shoemate.

————. 1985a. *The Mill on the Floss.* Excerpted in MacDonnell, Pfordresher, and Veidemanis.

————. 1985b. *Selections from George Eliot's Letters.* Ed. Gordon S. Haight. New Haven: Yale University Press.

FRANKLIN, MILES. 1984. *My Brilliant Career.* New York: Washington Square.

GILBERT, SANDRA M., and SUSAN GUBAR, eds. 1985. *The Norton Anthology of Literature by Women.* New York: Norton.

JENNINGS, ELIZABETH. 1982. "Not in the Guide-Books" and "The Climbers." In McDonnell, Nakadate, Pfordresher, and Shoemate.

LAVIN, MARY. 1973. "The Story of the Widow's Son." In Miller, Hayden, and O'Neal.

LESSING, DORIS. 1974. *The Memoirs of a Survivor.* New York: Bantam.

MCDONNELL, HELEN, NEIL E. NAKADATE, JOHN PFORDRESHER, and THOMAS E. SHOEMATE, eds. 1982. *England in Literature.* Glenview, IL: Scott, Foresman.

McDonnell, Helen, John Pfordresher, and Gladys V. Veidemanis, eds. 1985. *England in Literature.* Glenview, IL: Scott, Foresman.

Mansfield, Katherine. 1985. "The Doll's House." In McDonnell, Pfordresher, and Veidemanis.

Marshall, Joyce. 1973. "The Old Woman." In Miller, Hayden, and O'Neal.

Mew, Charlotte. 1985. "The Farmer's Bride" and "The Quiet House." In Gilbert and Gubar. She also has poems in Reilly.

Mill, John Stuart. 1982. "On the Subjection of Women." In McDonnell, Nakadate, Pfordresher, and Shoemate.

Miller, James E. Jr., Robert Hayden, Robert O'Neal, eds. 1973. *British Motifs: A Collection of Modern Stories.* Glenview, IL: Scott, Foresman.

Pollitt, Katha. 1991. "Canon to the Right of Me . . ." *The Nation.* September 23.

Reilly, Catherine, ed. 1981. *Scars upon My Heart.* London: Virago.

Rossetti, Christina. 1982. "Monna Innominata, Sonnet 2" and "Shut Out." In McDonnell, Nakadate, Pfordresher, and Shoemate.

———. 1985. "A Soul," "Cobwebs," "Enrica, 1865," "Song," and "Uphill." In Gilbert and Gubar.

Shaw, George Bernard. 1985. *Pygmalion.* In McDonnell, Pfordresher, and Veidemanis.

Sitwell, Edith. 1981. "The Dancers." In Reilly.

Smith, Stevie. 1976. "Alone in the Woods," "Frog Prince," "No Respect," "Not Waving But Drowning," and "The Reason." In *Collected Poems.* New York: New Directions.

Spark, Muriel. 1966. *The Prime of Miss Jean Brodie.* New York: Dell.

Tennyson, Alfred. 1985. "Ulysses." In McDonnell, Pfordresher, and Veidemanis.

Warner, Sylvia Ashton. 1985. "The Phoenix." In McDonnell, Pfordresher, and Veidemanis.

Woolf, Virginia. 1982. "The Legacy." In McDonnell, Nakadate, Pfordresher, and Shoemate.

Suggested Books for Students

CONWAY, JILL KER. 1989. *The Road From Coorain*. New York: Knopf. Conway was president of Smith College for ten years during the 1970s and 1980s. The book is the beautifully written story of Conway's growing up in the Australian outback and moving to Sydney before coming to America.

DAVIES, STEVIE, ed. 1976. *The Brontë Sisters: Selected Poems*. Guilford, England: Carcanet. An inclusive selection with an informative, brief introduction by the editor, a lecturer in English Literature at the University of Manchester, England.

FRANKLIN, MILES. 1981. *The End of My Career*. New York: Washington Square.

GODDEN, RUMER. 1958. *The Greengage Summer*. New York: Viking. Also *As Kingfishers Catch Fire* and *An Episode of Sparrows*. The third book is set during World War II.

GORDIMER, NADINE. 1979. *Burger's Daughter*. New York: Penguin. A young woman in South Africa develops a political consciousness.

———. 1981. *July's People*. New York: Penguin. What happens to a liberal white family in South Africa when they are rescued by their black servant, July, and taken to his village during an uprising in the city.

HULME, KERI. 1983. *The Bone People*. New York: Viking. Australian. A complex, somewhat mystifying, long tale about the author and her involvement with an abused boy, overlaid by Maori myths and practices.

JAMES, P. D. Any of her mystery novels. More complex than Agatha Christie's; they deal with moral issues.

JENNINGS, ELIZABETH. 1986. *Collected Poems*. New York: Carcanet.

MARKHAM, BERYL. 1942. *West with the Night*. San Francisco: North Point Press. The adventures of Markham, raised in East Africa in the early twentieth century; she trained horses, learned to fly, and transported passengers and mail in her small plane.

MUNRO, ALICE. 1971. *Lives of Girls and Women*. New York: Plume. Del's coming of age from age nine to nineteen during the 1940s in Canada under an unforgetable mother's influence. For mature readers. The novel explores the role of sex in this adolescent's life.

————. 1979. *The Beggar Maid: Stories of Flo and Rose.* New York: Penguin. About two delightful women.

————. 1984. *The Moons of Jupiter.* New York: Penguin. A Canadian, Munro writes short stories in spare prose about remarkable characters. Realistic, sometimes funny, her women puzzle out their lives.

WOOLF, VIRGINIA. 1925. *Mrs. Dalloway.* San Diego: Harvest/Harcourt Brace Jovanovich.

————. 1927. *To the Lighthouse.* San Diego: Harvest/HarcourtBrace Jovanovich.

Useful Works for Teachers

BAKER, DENYS VAL. 1979. *Women Writing: An Anthology.* New York: St. Martin's. Brief introduction and biographical entries for the twelve contemporary British women writers included.

DINESEN, BETZY. 1982. *Rediscovery: 300 Years of Stories by and About Women.* New York: Avon. English and American authors; stories cover women's experiences from childhood to old age.

FRASER, REBECCA. 1988. *The Brontës: Charlotte Brontë and Her Family.* New York: Crown. Fraser concentrates on Charlotte but shows how all three surviving Brontë women were strong and assertive, often going against the grain of the circumscribed expectations of their times. A good index makes it possible to find easily Charlotte and the writing of *Jane Eyre,* for example.

KENYON, OLGA. 1989. *Women Writers Talk: Interviews with Ten Women Writers.* New York: Carroll & Graf. Lively conversations with ten contemporary British women writers: Anita Brookner, Margaret Drabble, Alice Thomas Ellis, Eva Figes, Nadine Gordimer, P. D. James, Iris Murdoch, Michele Roberts, Emma Tennant, and Fay Weldon.

SCOTT, DIANA, ed. 1982. *Bread and Roses: An Anthology of Nineteenth- and Twentieth-Century Poetry by Women Writers.* London: Virago. Divided into sections, such as "We Who Bleed: Women's Poetry 1820–1860" and "The Renaming: Poetry Coming from the Women's Liberation Movement, 1970–1980."

SHOWALTER, ELAINE. 1977. *A Literature of Their Own: British Women Novelists from Brontë to Lessing.* Princeton: Princeton University Press. The book explores the achievements of English women novelists. Chapters on female traditions, feminine heroines and heroes, feminists, and contemporary authors. List of authors with a few facts and titles for each.

Women and Literature: An Annotated Bibliography of Women Writers. 3rd ed. 1976. Cambridge, MA: Women and Literature Collective. Lists American, English, and international authors with paragraph-length plot summaries and some critical comments and biographical information.

TEN

Teaching Novels

I wrote about a victim who is a child, and adults don't write about children. The novel is about a passive kind of person and the people around her who create the kind of situation that she is in. I did not think that it would be widely distributed because it was about things that probably nobody was interested in except me. I was interested in reading a kind of book that I had never read before. I didn't know if such a book existed, but I had just never read it in 1964 when I started writing The Bluest Eye.

TONI MORRISON
"Complexity"

When we were growing up in the 1940s, the novels we read were written primarily by men: Hemingway's *For Whom the Bell Tolls*, Norman Mailer's *The Naked and the Dead*, other best sellers. Older novels included those by William Faulkner and F. Scott Fitzgerald. Our ideas of romantic love, what women should be like, their roles in marriage and work all came from male authors. For the most part, men wrote about women as male-imagined fantasy figures. For example, many girls or women reading these books and later experiencing sex were disappointed at the terrible gap between fantasy and reality. Not until women began to write honestly about their sexual experiences and publishers were willing to print and promote these novels did women begin to recognize themselves—their true selves—in books.

One woman in fiction who certainly cannot be read about today without snickering (by both men and women) is Catherine Barkley in Hemingway's *A Farewell to Arms*. Catherine is Woman as Doormat carried to the nth degree. She has little personality of her own; she exists to please Frederick Henry, and ultimately she and her child die to make his "farewell to arms" a double goodbye to war and love. We can rightly praise Hemingway for many feats as a writer, but creating believable fictional women is not one of them.

This point raises the larger issue of what to do with fictional women who do not make sense, to us today. We think we have an obligation and a responsiblity to get students to look critically at the characters authors create, both male and female, of course, but especially, for our purposes in this book, female characters. And so one would have to fault Fitzgerald and Faulkner along with Hemingway. Daisy Buchanan in *The Great Gatsby* is too limited; Nicole Diver in *Tender Is the Night* is also. Joanna Burden in *Light in August* becomes a caricature, as does Lena Grove in that novel. Not too many high school students will wrestle with Faulkner's *The Sound and the Fury*, perhaps, but they should approach Caddy with a critical sensibility if they do tackle this novel.

When we look at some novels with strong female characters written by women early in the twentieth century, what do we find? Consider Edith Wharton's *Ethan Frome*; Willa Cather's *O Pioneers!*, *My Ántonia*, and *A Lost Lady*; and Anzia Yezierska's *Bread Givers*.

Ethan Frome can be seen as the least feminist of these. Mattie is long-suffering, good-hearted, self-sacrificing, generous. Where is her core? What is her personality? Zeena appears to be a woman of unmitigated cruelty, jealousy, meanness. Edith Wharton has written other novels in which women struggle to overcome the barriers of their times (*The House of Mirth* and *The Age of Innocence*), but *Ethan Frome* is the novel most often assigned to classes in American Literature courses. The focus is on the tragedy of the male protagonist's life, as he is drawn inexorably into the lives of the two women. What keeps Ethan Frome from finding happiness—his own undue kindness and compassion? his misguided integrity? his overworked sense of guilt? bad luck? The short novel bears close reading and close analysis. One important challenge for the teacher is to help students view Zeena sympathetically. Just to let students scoff at her is to allow them to misread the book. Point out, for example, how, at the end of the novel, Mattie and Zeena have changed places; what does that suggest? What about Zeena's special attachment to the pickle dish that gets broken?

The three Cather novels mentioned all offer strong and interesting women. One can certainly make the case that in *O Pioneers!* and *My Ántonia* Cather idealizes her protagonists into romantic, larger-than-life figures. Not quite credible women, perhaps, but they embody strong values—vitality, endurance, and stability—nourished by the land. *O Pioneers!* is especially suitable for ninth and tenth graders. *My Ántonia* is very accessible to juniors and seniors. And *A Lost Lady* fits well into American literature of the early twentieth century (see Chapter 6). It could also be used in other courses with juniors and seniors.

In Anzia Yezierska's *Bread Givers* (which we use in an American studies course on social and cultural history from 1890 to 1970), we have a strong female protagonist. The fictional Sara Smolinsky is an excellent young woman for high school students to encounter. She decries her "lazy" father, who spends all his time studying the Talmud while his wife and four daughters slave to earn money to keep food on the table. His wife reveres him as a scholar; scholars are not expected to earn money. This novel thus poses all sorts of questions about problems of immigrants to this country as they try to integrate differing religious beliefs, differing expectations for men and women, and differing expectations for daughters. Autobiographical to a large extent, the book follows the real life of Anzia Yezierska, though not entirely, for Sara does find a congenial husband in the end and manages to take her complaining and curmudgeonly father into her home.

What about the great male and female nineteenth-century English novelists? How might we approach their fictional female protagonists, or their female characters in general? In teaching the novels of Charles Dickens in an English Literature course, we think it not inappropriate to use the chapter in Phyllis Rose's *Parallel Lives* in which she shows how egregiously Dickens treated his wife when, in midlife, he fell in love with a young actress. Early love letters to Catherine, his wife, attested to his great love for her; later he tried to destroy that evidence and claim the marriage had never been happy. This all-or-nothing view of his seems to be recreated in his one-sided female characters—for example, Dora, the poor, helpless child-wife, or the pure and too-good-to-be-true Agnes Wickfield, both in *David Copperfield.* Estella of *Great Expectations* exemplifies another type. She is cruelty personified, a woman who would torment poor Pip and lead him to pursue her with no hope of ever reaching the "star," which her name means. Other characters in the novel, like Miss Havisham and the woman who worked for Jaggers, are little more than caricatures; in *David Copperfield* we meet Aunt Betsy Trotwood and Mrs. Micawber, again more caricatures than real people. Certainly many of Dickens's male characters are also caricatures; however, too many of the females are negative. Think, for example, of that child abuser, Mrs. Joe Gargery, in *Great Expectations,* who brought Pip up "by hand."

Pairing novels in English literature can also be useful: *David Copperfield* or *Great Expectations* with either *Jane Eyre* or George Eliot's *The Mill on the Floss.* We teach *Jane Eyre* in a women's literature course, but for those who don't have such a course, this novel of Charlotte Brontë's could be used in a classic novel course or a British literature course. When teaching it in tandem with Dickens's *Great Expectations,* it may be useful to set up chronological benchmarks and see how Pip and Jane fare at similar ages in their lives. One could also look at their clashes with class, their money problems, their love lives, their familes, and their friends. The same measures of comparison could be used if *The Mill on the Floss* were substituted for *Jane Eyre.*

As for American literature of the late-nineteenth and early-twentieth centuries, Sarah Orne Jewett's *A Country Doctor* is a relatively short novel we have used with individual students with great success. It concerns Nan Prince, a young orphan who wants to be a doctor. Her mentor and friend, Dr. Leslie, encourages her to read and study and allows her to accompany him on his medical visits. The novel is autobiographical to this extent: the young Jewett followed her father on his medical rounds to local people; she wanted to become a doctor, but her fragile health and general frailty prevented it. Jewett deals with the roadblocks women faced when they aspired to a male career such as medicine. Even though the book sometimes seems old-fashioned to today's teenagers, they still enjoy it. A second novel of the period, more difficult but one individual students still read and appreciate, is *The Story of Avis* by Elizabeth Stuart Phelps. Avis, a nineteenth-century woman with artistic talent, vows to let nothing stand in the way of her pursuing her art. However, Philip Ostrander overcomes this ambition and persuades her to marry him, telling her that she can still be an artist while married to him. Philip proves to be both a physical and emotional drain on Avis; her downfall as an artist is assured.

If you are looking for a novel depicting American life in the 1920s, we particularly recommend a powerful novel written in 1987, *Storming Heaven* by Denise Giardina, about the coal wars in West Virginia. We have used it as our novel for that epoch in our American studies course described earlier. The novel most teenagers think of when asked to name an important book of the 1920s is Fitzgerald's *The Great Gatsby*. We see *Storming Heaven* as a necessary antidote to *Gatsby* and its relentless pursuit of that mythical great American dream. Four distinct voices tell the story of *Storming Heaven*: C. J. Marcum, an activist for the miners; Rondal Lloyd, a tempestuous loner and union man; Carrie Bishop, the independent, feisty nurse who loves Rondal; and Rose Angelelli, a lonely Sicilian immigrant who loses four sons to the mines. The interlocking sections with the differing points of view may be a little confusing at first to students, but with a firm, directed reading and explanation by the teacher early on, students come to appreciate the tale being told. It is an eye-opener for most students who haven't been exposed to the coal wars in United States history courses. In addition, we take this opportunity to tie in the coal miners' plight in 1921 with coal miners' issues today, since strikes and cave-ins continue.

When we teach American studies, we offer a choice for a book of the 1930 to 1945 epoch, either Richard Wright's autobiography *Black Boy* or Zora Neale Hurston's novel *Their Eyes Were Watching God*. Hurston gives us the spirited Janie Crawford, who hopes to reach greater heights than her grandmother has prescribed for her. As her grandmother puts it:

> Honey, de white man is de ruler of everything as fur as Ah been able tuh find out. Maybe it's some place way off in de ocean where de black man is in power, but we don't know nothin' but what we see. So de white man throw down de load and tell the nigger man tuh pick it up. He pick it up because he have to, but he don't tote it. He hand it to his womenfolks. De nigger woman is de mule uh de world so fur as Ah can see.

Although her life is somewhat defined in terms of the men Janie marries, she grows in each marriage to become decidedly her own person, and in Teacake, husband number three, she finds her equal, a man who treats her with love and respect.

Since *Their Eyes Were Watching God* was not like the angry novels decrying white racism white publishers were looking for from black authors in the 1930s, it didn't get the exposure and promotion it should have. Also, black men did not see it as polemical enough. But the novel has been retrieved since the late 1970s and is now widely read. It deserves a place in any high school English curriculum with its strong, bright, positive, affirmative female protagonist and its exquisite combination of lyrical imagery and authentic black dialect:

> Then you must tell 'em dat love ain't somethin' lak uh grindstone dat's de same thing everywhere and do de same thing tuh everything it touch. Love is lak de sea. It's uh movin' thing, but still and all, it takes its shape from de shore it meets, and it's different with every shore.

The Street by Ann Petry, written in the 1940s, has been a favorite of our students for the last five or six years. Ann Petry grew up in one of the few black families in Old Saybrook, Connecticut, where her father was a pharmacist. She, too, became a pharmacist as well as a writer. This novel paints a powerful portrait of Lutie Johnson and all her efforts to beat the system and insure that her son have a better chance than she. Graphic and painful, *The Street* portrays a black woman who cannot climb out of the endless cycle of poverty, crime, and degradation that the dominant culture has carved for blacks. Tragic, poignant, and forcefully rendered with telling details and sharply defined characters, the novel is as pertinent today as it was when first published.

A novel of the 1950s, *The Dollmaker* by Harriette Arnow, compares favorably with Steinbeck's *The Grapes of Wrath*. Because it is over six hundred pages long, one year we gave students summaries of some chapters to cut down on the reading. Individual students use it for extended essays. Arnow transplants a rural, poor Kentucky family to a crowded neighborhood near the defense plants of Detroit during World War II. Gertie Nevels, the mother and the dollmaker of the title, is one of the great heroines in literature, much more fully realized than Ma Joad in the Steinbeck novel, for example. Compelling and tragic, the novel delineates the stories of Gertie and various members of her family and how they survive or do not survive their move to Detroit. Gertie reluctantly follows her husband, Clovis, to Detroit; a son runs away home to Kentucky; a child dies horribly. Gertie helps her neighbors, and she carves dolls for money. But even more important, she carves a Christ figure out of an exquisite piece of wood. The carving expresses her character, which has been as cramped by the polluted, mechanical, cold city atmosphere of Detroit as her six-foot frame has been cramped by their tiny tenement apartment. At the beginning of the novel she saves her baby son by performing a rude tracheotomy, but at the end, we are left to wonder whom she can save. Gertie and her neighbors in their tenements in Detroit provide a microcosm of society, and although Arnow spends perhaps too much time with these various neighbors and creates too many of them, she offers the patient reader a deep look at World War II on the home front in working-class Detroit.

Moving into the 1960s, we find Toni Morrison, who has written several novels highly accessible to secondary school students. *The Bluest Eye* is a bleak evocation of the life and tragedy of Pecola Breedlove. Treated badly by her parents and peers, eleven-year-old Pecola feels neglected and unnoticed; she dreams of having blue eyes, thinking such an acquisition will win her acceptance and love. We prepare students for the austerity and grimness, but at the same time the exquisite artistry, of this novel. It is a short book, but as with all of Morrison's novels, it demands attentive reading and thoughtful engagement.

Another Morrison novel we have used with students is her short but enigmatic, demanding *Sula*, a tour de force. One must spend some time dealing with Morrison's magical realism and her use of the supernatural and the myths and folklore of Africa. Striking and rich, *Sula* portrays the friendship between Nell and Sula, which Nell can appreciate only after Sula's death. We think it is very important to offer students a novel about a strong friendship between women.

One year in Women's Literature we decided that perhaps we should use a novel with a male protagonist, though of course the author had to be female. We chose Morrison's *Song of Solomon*. We have used it also in American Literature II. Milkman Dead's evolution through the nurturing of Pilate is a journey worth taking. This novel has strong and varied characters and a plot that is almost a mystery (there is plenty of suspense), which high school students love. We do not know what Milkman will discover as he leaves Ohio and journeys south to find out about his name and his roots. Guitar, his friend, plays a rich and complex foil to Milkman; the women Reba and Hagar; his sisters, Magdalene called Lena and First Corinthians; and his mother, Ruth, all are fascinating people. Above all there is Pilate, Milkman's aunt, who says near the very end of the novel, "I wish I'd a knowed more people, I would of loved 'em all. If I'd a knowed more, I would a loved more." Through her nurturing and teaching, Milkman is encouraged to learn his name and discover his past, his heritage. Pilate, one "who had one earring, no navel, and looked like a tall black tree," was so magical, so strong that "without ever leaving the ground, she could fly." The whole pervasive metaphor of flying is handled with ease, precision, and eloquence. The importance of learning one's name, of naming one's self, of accepting one's heritage and legacy—all are underscored in a novel rich in symbolism and extended images. *Song of Solomon* allows students to easily find a passage, place it in context, respond to it viscerally and intellectually, and then show how it relates to the entire novel (see the explanation of our generic writing assignment in Chapter 6).

We think Morrison's novel *Beloved* is too difficult for whole-class study. However, many of our students have read the book on their own for extended essays. As explained in Chapter 5, our use of Harriet Jacobs's *Incidents in the Life of a Slave Girl* helps prepare the way for reading the contemporary view of that time period explored by Toni Morrison in *Beloved*. When students begin to understand the particular horrors of female slaves in this country, they can approach *Beloved*. Frances Watkins Harper's moving poem "Bury Me in a Free Land" also helps students understand these "particular horrors." Mari Evans's poem "I Am a Black Woman" shows students that mothers actually did kill their babies rather than have them grow up to be raped by white masters, smothering them in the cane fields by cupping their "lifebreath." However, as always with Morrison, except perhaps for *The Bluest Eye*, students have to be prepared for the use of myth, magical realism, and the supernatural.

Another contemporary black woman writer is Alice Walker. We use *Meridian* in American Studies as one of two choices of novels for the 1960s. It focuses on three activists in the civil rights movement of the 1960s. Meridian is a strong and appealing protagonist, and the characters of her friends Lynne and Truman are complex.

The Third Life of Grange Copeland is also highly suitable; it carries us through the three lives of a southern black man. Grange Copeland's tale, a harrowing one, ends with redemption in his granddaughter Ruth. Angered and drained by the futility of his life as a tenant farmer, he flees his farm, his wife, and his son, heading North where his second life wastes away in one debauch after another. Flattened and stilled by his ugly life in the North, he returns home to find his son, enraged himself by his father's desertion and weakened by his own failures, imprisoned for murdering his wife. As Grange raises his granddaughter, he works out his freedom from his old selves at great cost, while Ruth inherits his strength and turns it to creating her own freedom. This, Walker's first novel, stands as eloquent testament to her ability to create believable, fully realized male characters. She has been unfairly criticized by black males for her depiction of black men in *The Color Purple*.

The Color Purple is used by many high schools throughout the country (though some schools are put off by the lesbian relationship between Celie and Shug). This novel is important for many reasons: it is an excellent example of the epistolary novel; it shows the evolution of a strong black woman that is ultimately positive and affirming; it documents the lives of some black people in the early part of this century; it is an endearing tale of friendship betwen Celie and Shug (the lesbianism is only a small part of that friendship and is tastefully handled); and (as Alice Walker herself has pointed out) the black men are ultimately redeemed. Mister evolves and grows into a caring person: he asks Celie to marry him in the spirit as well as in the flesh; he designs a shirt for people to wear with the pants she designs; and he sews alongside her. Harpo, his son and Sofia's husband, grows also: he doesn't mind if Sofia wants to work, and he comes to comfort and love his father. It is a sad comment on the contemporary definition of masculinity that, as Walker says, when men change into nurturing and kind persons, they are no longer seen as masculine in our culture; hence the rush to negative judgments about her depiction of black males in this novel.

A relatively new novel that well might be paired with *The Color Purple* is *Fair and Tender Ladies* by Lee Smith, the story of Ivy Rowe Fox, a strong, backwoods mountain woman from Virginia's Appalachia. The novel tells the story of a woman who, as a girl, dreamed of becoming a writer; but life and love overtook her and she settled for letter writing. Again, this is an epistolary novel, which comes quickly alive under the talented writing of Lee Smith. Ivy writes her life: the murder of Babe, twin brother to Ivy's favorite sister Silvaney; her involvement with a boy going off to war, leaving her pregnant; her sister, who tries to marry her off to Franklin Ransom, the wealthy son of a manager in the coal business; her marriage to Oakley Fox and the births of their several children; her brief but electrifying affair with Honey Breeding. These are but a few of the incidents in Ivy's hardscrabble but full life. In her late thirties Ivy writes to her hospitalized, mentally disturbed sister, Silvaney, who is in many ways Ivy's alter ego:

> For all of a sudden when I saw those lights [electricity had recently come to Sugar Fork], I said to myself, *Ivy, this is your life, this is your real life, and you are living it. Your life is not going to start later. This is it, now.* It's funny how a person can be so busy living that they forget *this is it. This is my life.*

Later, in the same letter, she writes:

> The statue of Oakley [her husband] is always working. Its back is always bent, its face is always turned away. For it aint no way to make a living from a farm. And you know, I must of *knowed* that somehow . . . from childhood, from watching it kill Daddy first, then Momma. But that is the thing about being young—you never think that what happened to anybody else might happen to you, too. Your life is your own life, that's how you think, and you are always so different. You never listen to anybody else, nor learn from what befalls them. And the years go so fast. . . . It seems like yesterday that me and Oakley planted those taters in the dark of the moon. Well, we still plant them that time of the month. And Oakley still gets a deal of pleasure from this land, more so than me, for when his work is done of an evening then it is *done,* for he don't have to mend the clothes or can the corn or feed the baby.

Seven or eight years later Ivy writes to her oldest child, her daughter Joli, who has become a writer, encouraging her not to forget who she is and where she came from. She advises Joli to remember even if the remembering is painful.

We should also mention Gloria Naylor's *The Women of Brewster Place*, a book with a chapter on a lesbian couple—two of the residents of Brewster Place, a dead end where women have settled when their lives seem to have become hopeless. But "Brewster Place became especially fond of its colored daughters as they milled like determined spirits among its decay, trying to make it a home. Nutmeg arms leaned over windowsills, gnarled ebony legs carried groceries up double flights of steps, and saffron hands strung out wet laundry on back-yard lines." In a series of interlocking vignettes, Mattie Michael, the strong central figure who had lived for her no-good son, tries valiantly with some success to strengthen these various women. Students reading this novel individually have enjoyed the emerging power of these women to control their lives, symbolized by the dream to tear down the brick wall at the end of the settlement, which blocks them off from the rest of the world. Death comes to Ciel's child, but she recovers and even prevails; Cora Lee, exhausted by too many children and too many men, finds some self-esteem when Kiswana energizes her by taking them all to a Shakespearean play, and she discovers that the babies she loves are lovable as older children as well. Even though horror still haunts their lives and at least two women break under its blows, Brewster Place doesn't die. A street doesn't die because it is condemned by aldermen or because its inhabitants move out; it dies "when the odors of hope, despair, lust, and caring are wiped out by the seasonal winds; when dust has settled into the cracks and scars, leveling their depths and discolorations—their reasons for being; when the spirit is trapped and fading in someone's memory." So Brewster Place is not dead because:

> the colored daughters of Brewster, spread over the canvas of time, still wake up with their dreams misted on the edge of a yawn. They get up and pin those dreams to wet laundry hung out to dry, they're mixed with a pinch of salt and thrown into pots of soup, and they're diapered around babies. They ebb and flow, ebb and flow, but never disappear.

Margaret Atwood, the Canadian author, and Marge Piercy, the American poet and novelist now living in Wellfleet, Massachusetts, bear discussing together. Both are poets and novelists; Atwood also writes short stories. Two of their novels that high school students can read are Atwood's *The Handmaid's Tale* and Piercy's *Woman on the Edge of Time.* Either or both could be used in a unit on feminist utopias or dystopias. The movie of *The Handmaid's Tale* is now available in video; it might be worthwhile to examine the story in both mediums. The novel details grimly what might happen in this country if the far right takes over. In this dystopia some women have been made infertile while others can give birth only to stillborn or deformed babies, all because of toxic waste seepage. While old women work unprotected at hazardous jobs and lower-class women procreate at will if they can, attractive, possibly fertile young women are drafted and trained to be "handmaidens." They, prisoners in the homes of the elite men and women in power, must submit to sex with the husbands once a month when the time is optimal for conception and while the wives look on. Those who resist or fail to conceive or give birth to defective babies usually are killed or committed to cleaning up the toxic waste sites, where sooner or later they will surely die. The tale is told by one of the handmaidens who survived, who was somehow smuggled out by a member of the resistance.

A book describing a utopia, *Woman on the Edge of Time,* is about Connie, a Chicana woman living in utter poverty who is incarcerated when she attacks the pimp who has seized control of her niece's life. We learn of the horrors inflicted on patients in a New York state mental hospital, her place of imprisonment. But, as an escape, Connie is propelled into the twenty-first century to a feminist utopia called Mattapoisett. Here, living is simple, clothes are practical, girls are as strong as boys and have as much opportunity for careers. Babies are gestated in big tanks and when born have three mothers each; men can nurse as well as women (yes, physically nurse!). The idea is that being a mother for eight hours a day is sufficient—who could do it every day for twenty-four hours? You sign up to be a mother; you choose to be one. Piercy offers a glimpse of a life of equality between men and women, and has many suggestions for improvements over contemporary culture, from settling political conflicts to relegating the tedious, necessary, and unpleasant work to either everyone equally or to mechanical devices. At one point Connie gets called into the wrong future and here we see a mechanized, overly technological future where people are brain dead, living on artificial food in a world run by machines and robots. Horrifying! Piercy's warning echoes Atwood's admonition in *The Handmaid's Tale*.

Another feminist utopia, from earlier this century, is Charlotte Perkins Gilman's more humorous *Herland*. Herland is an isolated country inhabited only by women who over time have learned to reproduce (female babies only) parthenogenetically. Three men crash their plane in this place, and as the women educate the men about their society, we, the readers, learn, too. Cooperation, sharing, development of each individual's talents and interests, and gracious respect for one another mark this community of women, whose practical solutions for organizing, feeding, and clothing themselves while maintaining a strong economy foreshadow the practices of Piercy's Mattapoisett.

We'll end this chapter by discussing two more contemporary novels.

We've used Bobbie Ann Mason's *In Country* in several courses, and most of the students have responded very favorably. For one thing, many of them know very little about the Vietnam War. *In Country* is told from the perspective of an inquisitive, bright, rebellious eighteen-year-old, Sam. Sam wants to find out about her father, whom she never knew; he went off to Vietnam before she was born. But her Uncle Emmett, a Vietnam veteran, lives with Sam and Sam's mother until the mother takes off for Louisville. Sam sees herself as her uncle's protector. He is reluctant to talk about the war, but ultimately he does for Sam's sake. She is given letters her father wrote to his parents and is stunned to uncover the man he was: human, limited, not the hero she had envisioned. The novel reaches its climax in the final pages when Sam, Emmett, and her paternal grandmother journey to Washington, D.C., to find Sam's father's name on the Wall. Students find much to identify with; Sam is a full and complex character, as is her uncle.

Finally, we turn to Anne Tyler's brilliant and complex novel *Dinner at the Homesick Restaurant*, which gives us Pearl Tull, an agitated, tough, difficult, and complicated woman (on her deathbed). Much of the novel is a series of flashbacks. We see Pearl's early life, when she was married to Beck Tull; and what happened to her and her three children, Cody, Jenny, and Ezra, when Beck one day left home for good. The book, like many contemporary novels, tells its story from multiple points of view: by the various members of the Tull family, including the grandson Luke, Cody's son. It is too easy simply to call this novel the story of a dysfunctional family. After all, what family isn't, to some degree, dysfunctional? What is normal? Students are quick to see connections between themselves and Tyler's fictional characters. All students can find someone in the Tull family to write about in their final paper: some choose Cody with his obsession with time and how to outwit and control it. He has become a time management consultant—an efficiency expert—in his career. Here is Cody talking to Luke:

> Time is my obsession: not to waste it, not to lose it. It's like . . . I don't know, an object to me; something you can almost take hold of. If I could just collect enough of it in one clump, I always think. If I could pass it back and forth and sideways, you know? If only Einstein were right and time were a kind of river you could choose to step into at any place along the shore.

And here is Ezra talking about the restaurant to Jenny:

> A restaurant is not all food, you know. Sometimes it seems that food is the least of it. I feel the place is falling apart on me, but Mrs. Scarlatti says not to worry. It always looks like that, she says. Life is a continual shoring up, she says, against one thing and another just eroding and crumbling away. I'm beginning to think she's right.

As often with an Anne Tyler novel, what at first seems bizarre and far from the reality of normal people's lives soon comes to seem very familiar and much the story of all of us at some point in our lives. Cody comes through at the end with a better understanding of his mother and of his family. He actually feels drawn to his family when he sees them while he's talking with his father, who has shown up, after all these years, for Pearl's funeral at Ezra's invitation:

The drab colors of their funeral clothes turned their faces bright. The children's arms and legs flew out and the baby bounced on Joe's shoulders. Cody felt surprised and touched. He felt that they were pulling him toward them—that it wasn't they who were traveling but Cody himself.

Then he invites his father to return to the restaurant to finish their dinner. Finally the Tulls will actually finish a dinner at the Homesick Restaurant. Ezra has long wished they would—Ezra, the peace-maker and nurturer. The ending provides an epiphany and a redemption, for Cody also makes his peace with his mother in the novel's final paragraph.

Many other appropriate novels exist, ones that raise the issue of the treatment of women in our society and that give young women a chance to see themselves, to feel validated, to be empowered. In this chapter, we have described ones we have used successfully in our classrooms. We're sure you could add many other titles. The point is to use some, to choose good ones, to have a balance between novels written by men and ones by women, and to have female protagonists in a number equal to that of male protagonists. As this happens, boys and girls begin to identify with both genders, to find role models that aren't always the same sex. At the least, boys will not sigh when a book or story centering on a girl or woman is introduced. And girls will be glad and excited to find their own lives, thoughts, aspirations, feelings more honestly portrayed in fiction about women. Truly, as Morrison said, they will be able to read the "kind of book that [they] had never read before"—varied, rich, diverse, yearning, sad, funny, tragic, deep, compassionate—the full range of human experience, thought, and feeling. These kinds of novels help students become their fullest selves.

Works Cited

ARNOW, HARRIETTE. 1954. *The Dollmaker.* New York: Avon.

ATWOOD, MARGARET. 1985. *The Handmaid's Tale.* New York: Fawcett.

Brontë, Charlotte. 1988. *Jane Eyre*. New York: Signet.

Cather, Willa. 1972. *A Lost Lady*. New York: Vintage.

———. 1988a. *My Ántonia*. Boston: Houghton Mifflin.

———. 1988b. *O Pioneers!* Boston: Houghton Mifflin. All Cather works are available in several editions.

Dickens, Charles. 1980. *Great Expectations*. New York: Signet.

———. 1981. *David Copperfield*. New York: Bantam.

Eliot, George. 1987. *The Mill on the Floss*. New York: Bantam. Available in several editions.

Evans, Mari. 1970. "I Am a Black Woman." In *I Am a Black Woman*. New York: Morrow.

Faulkner, William. 1990a. *Light in August*. New York: Vintage.

———. 1990b. *The Sound and the Fury*. New York: Vintage International.

Fitzgerald, F. Scott. 1953. *The Great Gatsby*. New York: Scribner.

———. 1962. *Tender Is the Night*. New York: Scribner.

Giardina, Denise. 1987. *Storming Heaven*. New York: Ivy Books.

Gilman, Charlotte Perkins. 1992. *Herland and Selected Stories*. Ed. Barbara Solomon. New York: Signet. A good introduction to Gilman and the works included in this volume. A selected bibliography of biographical and critical sources for Gilman. Includes twenty short stories, one of which is "The Yellow Wallpaper."

Harper, Frances Watkins. 1992. "Bury Me in a Free Land." In Margaret Busby, ed., *Daughters of Africa: An International Anthology of Words and Writings by Women of African Descent: From the Ancient Egyptian to the Present*. New York: Pantheon.

Hemingway, Ernest. 1983. *A Farewell to Arms*. New York: Scribner.

Hurston, Zora Neale. 1978. *Their Eyes Were Watching God*. Urbana: University of Illinois Press.

Jacobs, Harriet (Linda Brent). 1973. *Incidents in the Life of a Slave Girl*. Ed. Walter Teller. New York: Harcourt Brace Jovanovich.

JEWETT, SARAH ORNE. 1986. *A Country Doctor.* New York: Meridian.

MASON, BOBBIE ANN. 1985. *In Country.* New York: Perennial.

MORRISON, TONI. 1970. *The Bluest Eye.* New York: Washington Square.

———. 1973. *Sula.* New York: Bantam. (Annotated in Chapter 7.)

———. 1977. *Song of Solomon.* New York: Signet.

———. 1979. Quoted in "Complexity: Toni Morrison's Women—An Interview Essay." In Roseann P. Bell, Bettye J. Parker, and Beverly Guy-Sheftall, eds., *Sturdy Black Bridges: Visions of Black Women in Literature.* New York: Anchor. Book has three parts: analytical essays about black women writers; conversational interviews with these women; and creative works by these women.

———. 1987. *Beloved.* New York: New American Library.

NAYLOR, GLORIA. 1980. *The Women of Brewster Place.* New York: Penguin.

PETRY, ANN. 1946. *The Street.* Boston: Beacon.

PHELPS, ELIZABETH STUART. 1985. *The Story of Avis.* New Brunswick, NJ: Rutgers University Press.

PIERCY, MARGE. 1976. *Woman on the Edge of Time.* New York: Fawcett.

ROSE, PHYLLIS. 1983. *Parallel Lives: Five Victorian Marriages.* New York: Vintage. Besides the Dickens marriage, other relationships explored are Jane Welsh and Thomas Carlyle; Effie Gray and John Ruskin; Harriet Taylor and John Stuart Mill; and George Eliot and George Henry Lewes.

SMITH, LEE. 1988. *Fair and Tender Ladies.* New York: Putnam.

STEINBECK, JOHN. 1986. *The Grapes of Wrath.* New York: Penguin.

TYLER, ANNE. 1982. *Dinner at the Homesick Restaurant.* New York: Berkley.

WALKER, ALICE. 1970. *The Third Life of Grange Copeland.* San Diego: Harvest/Harcourt Brace Jovanovich.

———. 1976. *Meridian.* New York: Pocket Books.

———. 1982. *The Color Purple.* New York: Washington Square.

WHARTON, EDITH. 1981. *The House of Mirth.* New York: Berkley.

————. 1983. *The Age of Innocence*. New York: Scribner.

————. 1987. *Ethan Frome*. New York: Penguin.

WRIGHT, RICHARD. 1992. *Black Boy*. New York: Perennial.

YEZIERSKA, ANZIA. 1975. *Bread Givers*. New York: Persea.

Suggested Books for Students

ALLENDE, ISABEL, 1985. *The House of the Spirits*. New York: Bantam. A powerful and vivid portrayal of three strong and colorful women in the Trueba family of an unnamed South American country. Has adventure, love, magical realism, politics, and redemption.

ATWOOD, MARGARET. 1969. *The Edible Woman*. New York: Popular Library. In this, Atwood's first novel, she traces the consciousness-raising of Marion from woman as something to be consumed by her fiancé, Peter, to woman who understands what it means to be liberated from the undervaluing that society places on women.

————. 1972. *Surfacing*. New York: Warner Books. The nameless heroine journeys toward her childhood home in Northern Canada, ostensibly looking for her scientist father, who has mysteriously disappeared. At the same time, the journey becomes a quest for her own identity and a determination at the end of the novel to be her own person.

————. 1988. *Cat's Eye*. New York: Doubleday. An accomplished painter, Elaine Risley, fifty, returns to Toronto from Vancouver for an exhibit of her work. She revisits her past and comes to terms with some of the demons of her childhood and a particular girlhood "tormentor," Cordelia.

CATHER, WILLA. 1975. *Sapphira and the Slave Girl*. New York: Vintage. A late novel of Cather's in which she returns to her Virginia roots to tell the story of the relationship between a nineteenth-century Virginia lady and the slave woman, Nancy.

————. 1983. *The Song of the Lark*. Boston: Houghton Mifflin. A young girl with great singing talent struggles to break away from the conventions and restrictions of a small town. The book explores the conflicts a woman who wants to be an artist encounters between her personal relationships and her artistic ambition. Very long—almost 600 pages.

GIARDINA, DENISE. 1992. *The Unquiet Earth.* New York: Norton. A follow-up to *Storming Heaven,* set in the coal fields of Blackberry Creek, West Virginia, it spans the period from the 1930s through the 1980s and concerns the lives of Dillon Freeman and Rachel Honaker. Dillon is a union organizer; and in the next generation Jackie, Rachel's daughter, as a journalist, exposes American Coal's community-destroying tactics.

LAURENCE, MARGARET. 1964. *The Stone Angel.* New York: Bantam. A gripping account of the last day in the life of an elderly woman, Hagar, with a long flashback into her life and why she has grown into a woman who has trouble expressing her feelings.

———. 1974. *The Diviners.* New York: Bantam. A Canadian woman's coming to grips with her essential self through a series of experiences. Well-developed minor characters; the conflicts between mother and daughter are well handled.

MATTHEE, DALENE. 1986. *Fiela's Child.* New York: Ballantine. Nineteenth-century South Africa; a story in which two families, one white and one black, both claim a young white boy. A wonderful story of a young boy searching for his identity; great parts on ostriches and elephants too.

NAYLOR, GLORIA. 1985. *Linden Hills.* New York: Ticknor & Fields. Beyond the cul-de-sac of Brewster Place in Naylor's first novel lies the upper-middle-class black residential area of Linden Hills. With parallels to Dante's *Inferno,* Naylor reveals the lives, hopes, dreams, frustrations, and scandals of this upscale black community.

———. 1989. *Mama Day.* New York: Vintage. In her inimitable and luminous prose, Naylor builds a tale of beauty and darkness set on the Georgia sea island of Willow Springs. Mama Day, the island's matriarch and powerful practitioner of herbal medicine, battles to save the soul of her liberated great-niece, Cocoa, who comes to the island from New York.

PETRY, ANN. 1988. *The Narrows.* Boston: Beacon. Racial conflict in a Connecticut town in the 1950s. An Ivy League black graduate falls in love with a rich white married woman.

PIERCY, MARGE. 1972. *Small Changes.* New York: Fawcett. This early Piercy novel traces the contrasting lives of two different women, Miriam and Beth. The novel convincingly portrays the lifestyles that the women have adopted in order to bring meaning to their lives, in the personal as well as the political arena.

———. 1979. *Vida.* New York: Fawcett. An excellent novel of the underground during the Vietnam era and afterwards. Vida is a strong and passionate woman who rebelled in the 1960s, protested the war, and had to remain underground for years after that. A little long for students (472 pages), but still highly accessible.

———. 1982. *Braided Lives.* New York: Summit. A novel of the 1950s that tells the story of two strong young women, Jill and Donna. Deals with important social issues of the time, including the McCarthy hearings and illegal abortion. Has strong, fully realized women—and men—characters.

———. 1984. *Fly Away Home.* New York: Summit. Daria Walker is a cookbook writer living in an affluent Boston suburb at the start of the novel. During its course she learns the truth about her husband and is galvanized into social activism.

———. 1987. *Gone to Soldiers.* New York: Summit. Although this novel is very long (703 pages), it is a wonderful, wide-ranging, inclusive, vivid account of the lives of ten people during World War II—on the home front and at war. The lives of these people interlock, and Piercy recreates a full and complex picture of life at that crucial time in history. Despite its length, it is very accessible to students. Available in paperback.

SMITH, LEE. 1983. *Oral History.* New York: Ballantine. Jennifer arrives at Hoot Owl Holler from the city to do some taping for her Oral History class. She learns of the dark history of her family, including stories of murder, love, and a long-standing witch's curse. Rich in dialect and suspense.

TYLER, ANNE. 1965. *The Tin Can Tree.* New York: Berkley. A poignant, vivid, and compelling look at a family that endures the loss of a child. Tyler makes the survivors real people.

———. 1970. *A Slipping-Down Life.* New York: Popular Library. A motherless, unpopular high school girl falls for Drumstrings Casey, a rock star whose singing is more like talking, marries him, has his baby, and grows into a woman with self worth. (Casey is the "slipping-down" one.)

———. 1974. *Celestial Navigation.* New York: Warner Books. Jeremy Pauling, an uncommon artist who suffers from agoraphobia, comes alive in this moving novel in which Tyler makes the eccentric true to life.

———. 1985. *The Accidental Tourist.* New York: Knopf. Macon, the travel writer who hates to travel, and Muriel, who works at the kennel where he boards his dog, come together in another of Tyler's keenly observed, witty, humorous, poignant novels.

Useful Works for Teachers

ATWOOD, MARGARET. 1982. *Second Words: Selected Critical Prose.* Boston: Beacon. A marvelously eclectic collection of fifty essays spanning twenty years. Atwood discusses other writers such as Adrienne Rich and Marge Piercy; also has pieces on the art of writing, human rights, and being a Canadian, a woman, and a writer.

———. 1990. *Conversations.* Ed. Earl G. Ingersoll. Princeton, NJ: Ontario Review Press. Twenty-one interviews with Atwood, beginning with one by Graeme Gibson, "Dissecting the Way a Writer Works" (1972). In the course of this book Atwood discusses Canadian cultural nationalism and feminism, among other topics; she addresses the problem of readers who insist on seeing fiction as autobiography. Atwood in conversation can be alternately biting, witty, trenchant, humorous, and wise.

GELFANT, BLANCHE H. 1984. *Women Writing in America: Voices in Collage.* Hanover, NH: New England Press. Includes essays on older and newer writers, among them Grace Paley, Ann Beattie, Jean Stafford, Tillie Olsen, Meridel Le Sueur, Willa Cather.

GILBERT, SANDRA M., and SUSAN GUBAR. 1988–1989. *No Man's Land: The Place of the Woman Writer in the Twentieth Century.* 2 vols. New Haven: Yale University Press. Vol. 1: *The War of the Words.* Survey of social, literary, and linguistic conflicts between men and women traced back to their sources in the late nineteenth century. Vol. 2: *Sex Changes.*

Continues the investigation of the influences on the roles of men and women in the early twentieth century.

HENRIKSEN, LOUISE LEVITAS. 1988. *Anzia Yezierska.* New Brunswick, NJ: Rutgers University Press. Yezierska's daughter writes of her mother's life in a New York ghetto tenement, her work in sweatshops, her two failed marriages, her relationship with John Dewey, and her writing about the poor people of the Lower East Side. Good reference supplement to *Bread Givers.*

PEARLMAN, MICKEY, ed. 1989. *American Women Writing Fiction: Memory, Identity, Family, Space.* Lexington: University of Kentucky Press. Ten original essays on ten diverse American women writers. Each essay is followed by a bibliography of the writer's works and critical works about her. Writers discussed are Toni Cade Bambara, Joan Didion, Louise Erdrich, Gail Godwin, Mary Gordon, Alison Lurie, Joyce Carol Oates, Jayne Anne Phillips, Susan Fromberg Schaeffer, and Mary Lee Settle.

RAINWATER, CATHERINE, and WILLIAM J. SCHEICK, eds. 1985. *Contemporary American Women Writers: Narrative Strategies*. Lexington: University of Kentucky Press. Various writers analyze the work of ten contemporary American women writers and show how they transform and revise literary tradition to be more inclusive of women's lives, experiences, and visions. Writers discussed are Ann Beattie, Annie Dillard, Maxine Hong Kingston, Toni Morrison, Cynthia Ozick, Grace Paley, Marge Piercy, Anne Redmon, Anne Tyler, and Alice Walker.

SHOWALTER, ELAINE. 1991. *Sister's Choice: Tradition and Change in American Women's Writing*. New York: Oxford University Press. Traces the relationships between early and contemporary American writings, and between women's rights and women's writing. Looks closely at *Little Women, The Awakening,* and *The House of Mirth,* and "traces the transformations in such major themes, images, and genres of American women's writing as the American Miranda, the Female Gothic, and the patchwork quilt."

ELEVEN

A Women's Literature Course

I myself have never been able to find out precisely what feminism is: I only know that people call me a feminist whenever I express sentiments that differentiate me from a doormat.

REBECCA WEST

Her development, her freedom, her independence must come from and through herself.

EMMA GOLDMAN

In 1978 the principal of our school told us that if we received a sufficient subscription, we could teach a women's literature course. He added that women's literature was in, and that in five years it wouldn't be! We've had a steady subscription for the past fourteen years for this one-semester elective; some years we've had two sections. The administration often asks us to consider offering it every other year, but we insist on teaching it as often as we can because we continue to see a need for it. We also need to continue our efforts to raise the consciousness of our colleagues about the importance of women's studies and women's literature at the high school level.

Changing the world to include women as equals is a tremendous, Sisyphean task. You take two steps forward and three backward all the time, or so it seems. As we write this, in July of 1992, we are in the midst of a systemic backlash against what rights women have won. In the past twelve months we have had the Clarence Thomas/Anita Hill Senate hearings, the William Kennedy Smith rape trial, and the Desirée Washington/Mike Tyson rape trial. And most recently the Supreme Court narrowly upheld *Roe* v. *Wade* five to four even as they lowered the standard to say that a woman has a right to an abortion, but that states may place restrictions on that right so long as they don't put an undue burden on the woman.

Women and men who refuse to see the above as civil rights cases have much to learn. Deeply embedded attitudes toward women in which women are seen as less important and less valuable than men are reflected in contemporary issues. The habit of putting women on pedestals and worshiping them is just the flip side of degrading and dehumanizing them. People—men and women, boys and girls—have to begin ultimately to change these attitudes, but in the meantime, they have to change their behavior.

We think that a women's literature course in high school is a good place to begin the change. In some ways our women's literature course is women's studies in disguise. At first we frequently heard questions such as these two: "Why are all these stories so sad?" and "What's —————— complaining about? She has plenty of money and a nice house and a husband who looks after her." Also memorable was the reaction of the brightest girl in the very first class to Margaret Drabble's *Thank You All Very Much* (originally entitled *The Millstone*) about a young unwed woman in England who gets pregnant and decides to have the baby but not to get married: "We don't want to read about pregnancy; none of us wants to think about that now." Of course, now (as then) we're apt to have a pregnant young woman in the class.

We realized quickly that we would have to teach students about women's actual situations and problems. Guest lecturers came to talk about such issues as two-career marriages, with and without children. Students learned about assertiveness training in miniworkshops. We

216

showed films like "Killing Us Softly: Advertising's Image of Women" and "Violence Behind Closed Doors." An outreach person came from a shelter for battered women to do a two-day presentation about the problems of violence against women. Finally, by circulating five copies of A History of Women in America by Carol Hymowitz and Michaele Weissman, each student gave an oral report, passing out photocopied notes for the rest of the class so that by the end of the reports, each student had a sheaf of notes tracing chronologically the history of women in America.

The following statements come from a handout students receive at the outset of our course.

Purpose: To provide participants with models of women from a wide spectrum of society who have struggled to free themselves from traditional roles and who have come to recognize that the modern woman must merge her inner and outer selves in order to become wholly human.

General Objectives: The course will examine a variety of genres of the best women writers from the 1840s through the 1990s and their depiction of changing life-styles and values that women have experimented with, successfully and unsuccessfully. The course will also serve as a consciousness-raising experience with assignments from time to time in feminist political and historical writings, weekly discussion of current media treatment of women's issues, guest speakers, and films.

Rationale:
1. Women's literature courses do not seek to promote the superiority of women over men, but to claim for women their equal place in the world and to retrieve their accomplishments throughout history so that people can study and evaluate them. Our ultimate goal is to eliminate the need for women's literature and/or women's studies courses; that day will come when the contributions of women to history and literature are given the attention they deserve in all our schools. And this includes contributions in art, science, math, foreign languages, business—all the disciplines.

2. Jean-Jacques Rousseau, the renowned eighteenth-century French philosopher, said, "Women in general have no love of art; they have no proper knowledge of any; they have no genius." Robert Southey, a minor English Romantic poet of the nineteenth century, wrote in response to Charlotte Brontë, who had sent him some of her poems: "Literature cannot be the business of a woman's life, and it ought not to be. The more she is engaged in her proper duties, the less leisure she will have for it, even as an accomplishment and a recreation." Such pronouncements need to be disproved in courses such as women's literature.

3. Women's literature courses should contribute to the emancipation not only of women but of men too—emancipation from the rigid roles to which they have been socialized.

The rationale concludes with a quote from Adrienne Rich's "Claiming an Education" (1977) to be kept in mind by the young women and young men as they become actively engaged in the course. Indeed, its admonition is one we advocate for all students in all courses: "Responsibility to yourself means refusing to let others do your thinking, talking, and naming for you; it means learning to respect and use your own brains and instincts; hence, grappling with hard work. It means that you do not treat your body as a commodity" (p. 233). Rich then quotes Charlotte Brontë's Jane Eyre: "I have an inward treasure born with me, which can keep me alive if all the extraneous delights should be withheld or offered only at a price I cannot afford to give."

We have encountered periodically the criticism that we don't have a men's literature course, so why women's literature? Isn't that just another form of discrimination? When you realize that it has taken two thousand years to skew things so that men predominate in every area, in all disciplines, and have control and power of all the institutions of the world, you begin to realize, as Peggy McIntosh told us in the Dodge Seminar back in 1983–84, that it will take at least one hundred years to unskew it. We need to work on many fronts. Certainly women should be integrated into all the disciplines, as we have been doing and advocating for many years. But having a women's literature course is especially important now. Our students have gone to the legislature in Concord and spoken in favor of reproductive rights for women. Students write about women and women's issues for research papers in their U.S. history classes now and nudge their teachers in all disciplines to get them to offer more material on women.

True, no great numbers of males have enrolled in this elective over the years. The largest was thirty percent one year. But we do not see these numbers as quite the failure some others do. Young women need their consciousness raised. And it is a difficult thing for young women to become feminists or to begin to think in feminist ways in high school, a time when many of them seek attention from boys, yearn for relationships, cry out for acceptance from their peers. They may be very strong receptors of feminist teaching on an intellectual level, but emotionally and viscerally it may be much harder for them to act on what they learn. However, when they get to college, or when they are a little bit older and have more experience, things change. Time and again students have returned or written to say that they are taking women's studies, that they value what they learned in our class, that they are Women's Studies majors or minors—that they really understand now what we were talking about. If it's difficult for young women to learn about sexism, it's even harder for most young men.

What does the course entail? The syllabus describes three required outside projects:

1. Everyone must read a biography or autobiography of a woman and write a paper on it during the first quarter. Autobiographies are preferable because they provide more opportunity for the women to describe their own thoughts, feelings, ideas, changes in attitude, epiphanies. The hope is to get to know a woman's mind and emotions, not just her public persona. (A list of some of the more popular choices for this project is given at the end of this chapter.)
2. Everyone keeps a scrapbook, journal, or notebook of current material on women, taken from newspapers and magazines. Summaries of personal experiences and/or items

heard on the radio or seen on television are also encouraged. Cartoons and ads from newspapers and magazines are excellent. The entries should be on women's issues—a broad topic covering everything from abortion and rape to women rock stars and women winners of the Nobel Prize in Literature (Nadine Gordimer from Johannesburg, South Africa, won in the fall of 1991, only the seventh woman to win in literature since the awards began almost a hundred years ago). These scrapbooks are collected early in the second quarter for grading. Students need to find a way to organize their material, which should have some range in topic and kind of entry (article, ad, cartoon, comic strip). They should comment briefly on most entries, and the scrapbook should reflect a serious accumulation of material over time from the beginning of the course.

3. Everyone interviews her or his mother and hands in a paper based on the interview. The paper should take the form of a profile or character study, not just the writing of answers to interview questions. Students over the years have generated a list of over a hundred questions, photocopied for the students each year. Students choose whatever questions they wish from this list. Divided into categories like "Childhood," "Adolescence," "Work/Career," and "Marriage," the questions are wide ranging. "Were you treated any differently from your brother(s) when you were a child?" "How important is sex in marriage?" "If you had it to do over again, would you still marry your husband?" "What do you hope to be doing ten years from now?" "Has your divorce been essentially a positive or negative factor in your life?" Some students claim they already know all the answers to the questions, but as it turns out, nearly every student will admit to learning something new about her or his mother in the process of doing the interview. (One favorite anecdote is about the girl who found out in the interview that the four men her mother had dated before selecting her husband had all become priests!) The

reason for this assignment is our belief in the need for mothers and daughters and sons to talk honestly with each other, and for daughters and sons to know more about where they come from. One of the problems uncovered in the reemergence of the women's movement in the late 1960s was that mothers had not communicated honestly with daughters about their lives.

The course proceeds in different ways in different semesters, but some activities remain fairly constant. We begin with three, four or five feminist articles, such as Mary Donovan's "Why Study Women?" or Linda Ellerbee's "The Feminist Mistake" from *Seventeen,* in which she speaks out loudly and clearly on the need for young women to be willing to call themselves feminists; she states that they *are* feminists if they believe in such things as equal pay for equal work. Other articles include some feminist essays or speeches from the nineteenth century, such as Lucy Stone's "Disappointment Is the Lot of Women"; "The Bonds of Womanhood" by Sarah Grimké; "Keeping the Thing Going While Things are Stirring," a speech by Sojourner Truth; and, of course, the "Declaration of Sentiments and Resolutions" by Elizabeth Cady Stanton et al., from the 1848 Seneca Falls Women's Rights Convention.

We have little mini-units along the way on such topics as domestic violence, acquaintance rape, sexual harassment, and reproductive rights. For instance, for domestic violence we use "Trifles," Susan Glaspell's one-act play set in the midwest early this century. It's about an isolated farm wife driven by her loneliness and overly silent husband to kill him. Men come to collect clues, but the women uncover in the "trifles" (the unsteady stitching in a quilt, a dead canary with its neck twisted, stuffed in a sewing box) the real clues to this tragedy. Students see many parallels to present-day domestic violence. We work in fiction, nonfiction, and current media treatment of these topics. We have guest speakers and films. Last semester one of our guest speakers was an enlightened male friend who explained his conversion over time in a talk called "From Male Chauvinist Pig to Feminist-Minded Man." Recent films or videos we've watched are "She's

Nobody's Baby," "Warning: The Media May Be Hazardous to Your Health," "True Light: The Life of Marilla Ricker" (the first woman lawyer in New Hampshire; she also tried to run for governor); a video on date/acquaintance rape; and a tape of the Barbara Walters interview with Desirée Washington after Mike Tyson was convicted of raping her.

Another integral part of the course is media day. Once a week or once every two weeks students come to class with an article from a newspaper or magazine having to do with women's issues. These articles can and should become a part of their scrapbooks. They should know the article well enough to summarize it succinctly and clearly for the class; they might read a small section or two. They may bring in ads or cartoons to discuss, but not for every media day. They must mix up their contributions so that some of them are longer, more substantial magazine articles.

As a means of making students accountable for either a guest lecturer or the media day presentations, when they don't write reaction papers, they sometimes write a PMI—PMI for the *pluses*, the *minuses*, and what's *interesting*. When students write these about media day presentations they keep a little chart, writing the name of each presenter followed by a *P*, *M*, and *I* for each one. Sometimes they can't come up with all three for each; sometimes we discuss these later; sometimes PMI's are collected. We often take two days for media day presentations for a class of sixteen or more. These presentations count for oral work, and they provide a viable forum in which the shyer students can participate.

Now for a look in some detail at a few of the works we use consistently in this course. We realize that few teachers have the luxury of a semester course every year exclusively devoted to women's literature. But you can certainly use many of these units, activities, books, films, and ideas in the courses that you do teach.

We'll begin with *Jane Eyre* by Charlotte Brontë, admittedly a challenge in this age of short attention spans and TV addiction. However, it's an important feminist novel, and it is as timely today as it was in the 1840s, maybe more so, for in it we have a strong young woman who develops morally, sticks to her principles, and maintains her integrity in the face of overwhelming pressure to loosen them. Starting out as a rebellious and unhappy orphan in the Reed household, Jane grows under her friendship with Helen Burns at Lowood to see the need for understanding and humility. From Helen she learns: "If all the world hated you, and believed you wicked, while your own conscience approved you, and absolved you from guilt, you would not be without friends." From Miss Temple, her teacher, she learns to value her intellect. She moves on to Thornfield as Adele's governess and meets the rough, brooding, enigmatic, but ultimately compelling Edward Rochester who, despite his many humiliations of her, truly appreciates her intellectual acumen and emotional strength.

Brontë buries an absolutely amazing feminist passage in Chapter 12:

> Women are supposed to be very calm generally: but women feel just as men feel; they need exercise for their faculties and a field for their efforts as much as their brothers do; they suffer from too rigid a constraint, too absolute a stagnation, precisely as men would suffer; and it is narrow-minded in their more privileged fellow-creatures to say that they ought to confine themselves to making puddings and knitting stockings, to playing on the piano and embroidering bags.

The above passage is all the more amazing when placed beside a passage in a letter of Charlotte Brontë's in the Brontë Parsonage Museum in Haworth, Yorkshire, England. In it Brontë said that she didn't think women should aspire to careers men had traditionally pursued because it was hard enough for men to find work and women shouldn't take those positions from them. She must have had to wrestle with her conflicts, but in *Jane Eyre* she was free to put her more feminist thoughts into the mind of the enlightened protagonist.

Adrienne Rich's provocative essay, "*Jane Eyre*: The Temptations of a Motherless Woman" (1973) in *On Lies, Secrets, and Silence*, reminds us of the feminist perspective that teachers should offer present-day students of this novel. Rich says that one of the most impressive qualities of Charlotte Brontë's heroines is that they refuse to be romantic. They are sorely tempted by the romantic, much more so than Jane Austen's heroines, but they don't yield. Rich points out that in *Jane Eyre* marriage is not an end in itself; "it is not patriarchal marriage in the sense of a marriage that stunts and diminishes the woman" (p. 106), but it is one that enables Jane to continue to grow as a woman and a person. Furthermore, the novel offers a second break with tradition in that the women, rather than being rivals, nurture and strengthen each other and do so "not simply as points on a triangle or as temporary substitutes for men" (p. 106).

Students are caught up in the romance between Rochester and Jane, but they are critical of Rochester and his teasing and baiting of Jane. When they look closely at the conversations the two have, they come to see how Jane is Rochester's intellectual match at every turn. Their verbal sparring is noteworthy. For example, one time Rochester sends for Jane and invites her to speak so that he may draw her out. When she asks what she is to speak about, he says the choice is hers. She remains dumb. He accuses her of being stubborn:

> He had deigned an explanation; almost an apology: I did not feel insensible to his condescension, and would not seem so.
>
> "I am willing to amuse you if I can, sir: quite willing; but I cannot introduce a topic, because how do I know what will interest you? Ask me questions, and I will do my best to answer them."
>
> "Then, in the first place, do you agree with me that I have a right to be a little masterful, abrupt; perhaps exacting, sometimes, on the grounds I stated; namely, that I am old enough to be your father, and that I have battled through a varied experience with many men of many nations, and roamed over half the globe, while you have lived quietly with one set of people in one house?"
>
> "Do as you please, sir."
>
> "That is no answer; or rather it is a very irritating, because a very evasive one; reply clearly."
>
> "I don't think, sir, you have a right to command me, merely because you are older than I, or because you have seen more of the world than I have; your claim to superiority depends on the use you have made of your time and experience."

Turning to another aspect of the novel, we encourage students to contrast Eliza and Georgiana Reed from the book's beginning with the

Rivers sisters, Diana and Mary, in the Ferndale section. Scholars tell us these latter two are patterned after the Brontë sisters. We can see true friendship here; girls are not jealous of each other or vying for the same prospective husband. By way of contrast, in Blanche Ingram Charlotte Brontë satirizes that artificial and superficial segment of society she had encountered herself as a governess.

Occasionally a student wants to read Jean Rhys's novel *Wide Sargasso Sea*, in which Rhys imagines the earlier life of Bertha Mason, Rochester's mad wife imprisoned in the attic at Thornfield Hall. The book can stand on its own merits but takes on an extra dimension, of course, if one has read *Jane Eyre*. Part I of *Sea* is told in the heroine's words; in Part II Mr. Rochester describes his arrival in the West Indies, his marriage, and the subsequent horrifying result; Part III has the heroine picking up the tale from her attic room in Thornfield Hall.

Above all, *Jane Eyre* inspires students, especially young women. Their papers attest to their admiration for her, and they wonder if they could be as stalwart and unwavering as she.

Another novel is *The Awakening* by Kate Chopin. A young woman, Edna Pontellier, seeks to define herself after Robert LeBrun awakens her sensuality in the summer of her twenty-ninth year on Grand Isle off the coast of Louisiana in the late nineteenth century. Students are fascinated to learn what a stir this novel caused when it was published in 1899, some accounts going so far as to say it was banned in the author's home town of St. Louis. At the time it was daring: a depiction of a woman unhappy in her marriage, awakened to sensual desires and artistic possibilities; her abandonment of her husband; and ultimately her suicide. Early in the novel Edna says to her friend Adele Ratignolle, "I would give up the unessential; I would give my money, I would give my life for my children; but I wouldn't give myself. I can't make it more clear; it's only something which I am beginning to comprehend, which is revealing itself to me." Adele cannot understand what Edna is talking about, for Adele is one of the mother-women vacationing on the island:

In short, Mrs. Pontellier was not a mother-woman. The mother-women seemed to prevail that summer at Grand Isle. It was easy to know them, fluttering about with extended, protecting wings when any harm, real or imaginary, threatened their precious brood. They were women who idolized their children, worshiped their husbands, and esteemed it a holy privilege to efface themselves as individuals and grow wings as ministering angels.

It becomes increasingly clear to the reader that Edna has married because that was what one did if one was a young woman in that time period and needed financial security because a professional career was out of the question. Edna discovers after having two children with Léonce Pontellier that much is missing from her life, namely her essential self. The novel charts the emergence of that self in language that is simple but beautiful in its images, particularly in the sustained metaphors of birds and of the sea:

> The voice of the sea is seductive; never ceasing, whispering, clamoring, murmuring, inviting the soul to wander for a spell in abysses of solitude; to lose itself in mazes of inward contemplation.
>   The voice of the sea speaks to the soul. The touch of the sea is sensuous, enfolding the body in its soft, close embrace.

Robert teaches Edna to swim that summer, and that becomes important symbolically, for, while the sea is liberating for Edna, it is ultimately the place of her suicide. Suicide seems her only way out when Robert leaves, because he can't accept her on her terms, and when she realizes that she cannot drag her children into the unconventional life of an artist, one who, perhaps, might practice free love.

Provocative for young people, this novel offers many topics for discussion and writing: Léonce as a man who sees his wife as a piece of property; the mother-women who sew even their children's underwear; Mademoiselle Reisz as foil to Edna, but who is asexual and cold; the letter that someone might write trying to explain Edna's suicide to a friend. Sometimes students, reading this novel so soon after *Jane Eyre*, see Edna as weak. Many, however, come to understand how isolated Edna is in a society not yet ready for her, and one in which she has no role models. What if Edna had lived today?

The final full-length work we often use is Maya Angelou's *I Know Why the Caged Bird Sings,* often saved until the very end of the course, when students read it on their own for the final exam. (We may have one discussion day.) The final exam usually has two essay questions. The first involves the quote from Adrienne Rich used in the rationale for the course. Students must choose five or six women they've encountered in the course and discuss how they have chosen to live responsibly according to Rich's definition and how well they've succeeded or failed. The other question is on *Caged Bird.* Almost every student I've ever had responds well to this autobiography; it has an effect similar to that of Richard Wright's *Black Boy.* (For those who like such aids, the book is available in PermaBound, complete with a twelve-page teacher's guide.) Two strong statements used on the exam come near the very end of the book. Angelou says, at the end of Chapter 34, that the black female, in her youth, is caught up against "masculine prejudice, white illogical hate, and Black lack of power," and she claims that her survival deserves respect, if nothing else. We ask students to support this statement as it is illustrated in the book and in what students know of Angelou's life. Angelou makes the other statement a few paragraphs earlier:

> Without willing it, I had gone from being ignorant of being ignorant to being aware of being aware. And the worst part of my awareness was that I didn't know what I was aware of. I knew I knew very little, but I was certain that the things I had yet to learn wouldn't be taught to me at George Washington High School.

Students explain how these words are a direct commentary on Maya's growing up as it happens in this book from age six to sixteen. Maya Angelou's is a powerful, affirmative survival story, rich in detail, anecdote, reflection, and colorful language.

We plan to use *Lakota Woman* by Mary Crow Dog (with Richard Erdoes). A strong, no-holds-barred autobiography, this book has been praised by many students who have read it for the required autobiography early in the course. Here's a taste from the opening chapter:

They put me in jail at Pine Ridge and took my baby away. I could not nurse. . . . It's hard being an Indian woman.

My best friend was Annie Mae Aquash, a young, strong-hearted woman from the Micmac Tribe with beautiful children. It is not always wise for an Indian woman to come on too strong. Annie Mae was found dead in the snow at the bottom of a ravine on the Pine Ridge Reservation. The police said that she had died of exposure, but there was a .38-caliber slug in her head. The FBI cut off her hands and sent them to Washington for fingerprint identification, hands that had helped my baby come into the world.

My sister-in-law, Delphine, a good woman who had lived a hard life, was also found dead in the snow, the tears frozen on her face. A drunken man had beaten her, breaking one of her arms and legs, leaving her helpless in a blizzard to die. . . .

When I was a small girl at the St. Francis Boarding School, the Catholic sisters would take a buggy whip to us for what they called "disobedience." At age ten I could drink and hold a pint of whiskey. At age twelve the nuns beat me for "being too free with my body." All I had been doing was holding hands with a boy. At age fifteen I was raped. If you plan to be born, make sure you are born white and male.

Now that we've discussed some full-length works, we will high-light a few stories and videos from a typical semester.

The text we've used over the years, *By Women: an Anthology of Literature* edited by Marcia McClintock Folsom and Linda Heinlein Kirschner, has sections arranged sometimes by genre and sometimes by theme, such as "Search for Self" or "In a Role." (Another recom-mended text is *Women in Literature: Life Stages Through Stories, Poems, and Plays* edited by Sandra Eagleton. This book is divided into sec-tions, such as "Childhood," "Adulthood, Women and Work," "Adult-hood, Women and Family," and "Old Age"; each section has fiction, poetry, and usually drama. Discussion questions appear after each group of poems or each story.) From our text, *By Women*, we use a series of short stories before we begin a novel. Kate Chopin's brief "The Story of an Hour" prepares students for *The Awakening*. Louise Mallard, a woman not unhappily married, hears that her husband has been killed in a train crash. She grieves immediately, copiously, and briefly; then, looking out the window at the blue sky and the signs of spring, she realizes she is now free and can be in charge of her life, not having to worry about always pleasing someone else and being controlled by him: "There would be no one to live for during those coming years; she would live for herself. There would be no powerful will bending hers in that blind persistence with which men and women believe they have a right to impose a private will upon a fellow-creature. A kind intention or a cruel intention made the act seem no less a crime as she looked upon it in that brief moment of illumination." At the end of the story the husband appears alive and well; there had been a mistake in the report of his death. Louise Mallard drops dead (Chopin had told us in the opening sentence that she had a weak heart): "When the doctors came they said she had died of heart disease—of the joy that kills." The irony, of course, is that she dies of disappointment in her husband's sudden resurrection. When students recover from their initial shock that a woman could actually rejoice at news of her husband's death in this very, very short story in which so much happens so swiftly, they find much to discuss. The story raises the important issue of a woman's identity. How does she define herself? Is it easier for a woman to marry happily today because women are so much freer and have so much more opportunity to make sure they are marrying for true love and commitment that will survive? What about today's high divorce rate? (One student looked around the room during a recent semester and discovered that eleven of the twenty students had parents who were divorced.)

"The Sentimentality of William Tavener" by Willa Cather is a little known Cather story, very short, in which the Taveners experience an epiphany in their marriage. They had become almost business partners, with wife Hester always intervening on behalf of their two sons, making sure they were indulged a bit. But one night she and William sit up late talking and recover the tenderness and passion of their early years, so much so that at the end of the story the sons feel their mother's loyalties have shifted a bit when Hester admonishes them not to spend too much money at the circus, showing a concern for her husband and a concurrence with his frugality: "The boys looked at each other in astonishment and felt that they had lost a powerful ally."

In "A New England Nun" by Mary Wilkins Freeman, Louisa Ellis welcomes home Joe Dagget, her fiancé, who has been away establishing himself financially for fourteen years, only to discover that she has become too comfortable in her single state to allow any intruder, however eagerly anticipated. When she secretly discovers that Joe has a new sweetheart whom he plans on rejecting out of a misplaced honor toward his commitment to Louisa, she finds a way to break the engagement. Students debate earnestly the appropriateness of Louisa's choice: Is she a rigid old maid or a confident single woman choosing what is decidedly the best path for her? "[Louisa] gazed ahead through a long reach of future days strung together like pearls in a rosary, every one like the others, and all smooth and flawless and innocent, and her heart went up in thankfulness."

Emily Prager's "A Visit from the Footbinder" and Isak Dinesen's "The Ring," both fairy tales set far back in time, have decided applications to the lives of present-day women in American society. In "The Ring," set in Denmark, Lise marries beneath her, a young man who had been secretly courting her since she was nine years old. The reality of marriage hits her and when her husband, Sigismund, is tending his sheep, Lise wanders off on her own and accidentally meets a known thief who is hiding in the neighborhood; she offers her wedding ring to him as ransom for his not hurting her. He does not take it, but she does not retrieve it, and he vanishes without harming her. This, Lise's first encounter with the pain and ugliness in the world, awakens her to the knowledge that she can't return to the innocence of her previous life. She elects not to tell her husband about how she lost her ring, the first of many facts she will withhold from him—not out of slyness or deviousness but in an effort to preserve her own individuality. She, who at the beginning of the story had looked forward to a picture-perfect marriage in which "she moved and breathed in perfect freedom because she could never have any secret from her husband," now realizes her loss of innocence: "With this lost ring she had wedded herself to something. To what? To poverty, persecution, total loneliness. To the sorrows and sinfulness of this earth."

In "A Visit from the Footbinder," six-year-old Pleasure Mouse in thirteenth-century China eagerly awaits the ceremony that will allow her to wear beautiful tiny shoes similar to the "one thousand pairs of tiny satin shoes" of her thirteen-year-old sister, Tiger Mouse. Prager builds suspense by alternating scenes of Pleasure Mouse's joyful anticipation with incidents foretelling the actual misery awaiting her. When she wanders far from her courtyard to the Meadow of One Hundred Orchids, she talks eagerly to the master painter, Fen Wen, about the upcoming ceremony that will make her a grown-up. Fen Wen says, "Ah, . . . then we won't see you any more." He explains to Pleasure Mouse that she won't be able to walk at all in the beginning; later she may get "as far as the front Moon Gate." But, he tells her, she'll never get "as far as this Meadow." When Pleasure Mouse understands that Fen Wen is telling her she won't be able to walk, she insists that Lady GuoGuo and Tiger Mouse both walk, even though she concedes they cannot run as she can. Later Pleasure Mouse runs into her father's older sister, Lao Bing. When she asks her aunt if the procedure hurts, Lao Bing replies: "Beauty is the stillbirth of suffering, every woman knows that. Now scamper away, little mouse, and dream your girlish dreams, for tomorrow you will learn some secret things that will make you feel old."

We prepare students for this story with some factual information on the now-outlawed practice of footbinding. Since we are always looking for comparisons with women in present-day society, students cite the discomfort of high heels and girdles women wore in the 1950s, and then go on to more serious health and medical problems, such as unnecessary hysterectomies and mastectomies and forced sterilization. Footbinding was ostensibly practiced so men of the upper class could marry women with beautiful, tiny, dainty feet; if women didn't have their feet bound, they couldn't capture a husband of means. The harsh result was that women were actually crippled, literally confined to their homes to hobble around, virtually imprisoned by men.

Students puzzle interminably over Charlotte Perkins Gilman's "The Yellow Wallpaper," a perennial favorite. They usually read part of an essay by S. Weir Mitchell, the real doctor from the early

231

twentieth century to whom Gilman was sent for a cure for her depression. His essay, entitled "Rest," describes a "cure" requiring such complete passivity that one would die from inactivity and boredom were one to undertake it, but it was a regimen actually prescribed. "The Yellow Wallpaper" has an interesting history. It was rejected when it was first written as too morbid; later it was anthologized with horror stories. The story documents the mental deterioration of a woman suffering from what today would probably be diagnosed as post-partum depression. Her doctor-husband moves with her to a country home and puts them upstairs in what was once apparently a nursery with bars on the windows and bilious yellow wallpaper. The unnamed protagonist is not allowed to write, which is her avocation and her talent, nor can she visit with people. The husband feels sure he knows best, and there is reference to the infamous Weir Mitchell. At the end, having become increasingly obsessed by the wallpaper and by the woman she sees trapped behind it, the isolated protagonist goes mad. She has tried along the way to speak up to her husband, but to little avail: "I sometimes fancy that in my condition if I had less opposition and more society and stimulus—but John says the very worst thing I can do is to think about my condition, and I confess it always makes me feel bad." As for the wallpaper: "The outside pattern is a florid arabesque, reminding one of a fungus. If you can imagine a toadstool in joints, an interminable string of toadstools, budding and sprouting in endless convolutions—why, that is something like it." The story is an excellent portrayal of a woman feeling totally isolated and identifying with the woman she sees trapped behind the wallpaper. By the end she has peeled it all off. When her husband finally finds the key to the room and enters, he finds her creeping on the floor: " 'I've got out at last,' said I, 'in spite of you and Jane. And I've pulled off most of the paper, so you can't put me back!' " The story allows us to focus not only on the entrapment of women in constricted roles in the early twentieth century but on the ways in which women are still trapped today.

Three stories for a mini-unit on women and aging are Doris Lessing's "An Old Woman and Her Cat," Eudora Welty's "A Worn Path," and Alice Munro's "Spelling." They present decidedly different aspects of the older woman. Hetty in the Lessing story is a step beyond eccentric as she insists on being on her own with her rag-tail cat, Tibby, living on pigeons the cat brings them and moving into abandoned houses rather than being taken to a nursing home, where she would not be allowed to keep Tibby. Phoenix Jackson in the Welty story is an old black woman who makes a challenging and obstacle-strewn journey to town to get medicine for her chronically sick grandson—it is a journey of love from which she never swerves, and Phoenix is surely one who rises from the ashes. Flo in the challenging Munro story has reached senility. Her stepdaughter, Rose, arrives at Flo's home, hoping to be able to stay and care for her there. However, when she realizes how much Flo has deteriorated, she and her stepbrother arrange for her to move to a nearby nursing home. Munro weaves in the stories of the rather stormy relationship between Flo and Rose and the uncomfortable one between the stepbrother, Brian, and Rose. In the final scene Rose and Flo reach a reconciliation. Students are reminded of their grandparents, of their visits to nursing homes; we discuss the problems of caring for the elderly and how this care often falls to women in their forties and fifties just when they've got children in college. Hetty evokes the problem of the homeless; Phoenix inspires with her unswerving journey along the "worn path" of love.

Now for some videos.

For anyone who has never heard of Jean Kilbourne's thirty-minute video "Still Killing Us Softly: Advertising's Image of Women" (an update of her earlier video of the late 1970s, "Killing Us Softly: Advertising's Image of Women"), we definitely recommend it. The accumulation of ads and their copy, plus Kilbourne's low-key, almost good-humored commentary, reach a climax when we get to the ads subliminally allowing violence toward women. Students are overwhelmed by this video the first time they see it. A similar one, perhaps more appropriate for today's high school students, is "Warning: The Media May Be Hazardous to Your Health." Some statistics from the video: six thousand cosmetic surgery operations are performed annually; pornography is an eight-billion-dollar-a-year business; fifty percent of all women will be beaten more than once in their lives.

The filmmakers of "The Life and Times of Rosie the Riveter," made in the late 1970s, interviewed five women who had worked in defense plants in the 1940s; they have interspersed news films and clips from propaganda films of that time with the women's comments to show graphically how women were wooed into the plants when they were needed and summarily fired when the men came home. These women had always worked, had to work, and they had trained to become first-rate welders in two cases and a burner in another, only to have to go back to low-paying jobs like dishwashing in restaurants and domestic work after the war.

One more excellent film, on video, to show young people is *A World Apart.* This film was written by Shawn Slovo, daughter of anti-apartheid activists in South Africa, Ruth First and Joe Slovo. Ruth First's book *117 Days* recounts her months in prison in the early 1960s when she was one of the first to be arrested and jailed without being charged under the then new Ninety-Day Law. She fights back fear, anger, and mental weakness, only to be re-arrested at the end of her ninety-day term. Her husband, his life in danger as a Communist member of the African National Congress, had previously fled the country. She has three young daughters. The film is told from the point of view of the oldest one, Molly, a thirteen-year-old fictional version of the screenwriter. The film shows the complexity of Molly's life with her alternating pride in her mother for her work and hatred of her for abandoning her. This riveting film raises this question: Why is a mother who pursues her political cause relentlessly seen somehow as a more cruel parent than a father who does the same thing? The three women actors in the movie are excellent: the mother, the daughter, and the black maid, the surrogate mother for Molly and her sisters.

One other appropriate film, also in video, is *The Long Walk Home* about the Montgomery, Alabama, bus boycott of 1956, starring Sissie Spacek and Whoopi Goldberg. We see clearly how the white Southern woman character evolves from a bridge-playing, apolitical, gracious hostess into an active civil rights worker as she comes to realize what the events of the time mean to her black maid.

We'll close this chapter with a description of some possible mini-units, projects, and problems.

Some years students engage in individual projects, such as conducting surveys within the school to compile statistics on attitudes toward sexism. Other projects have involved visiting elementary schools and observing the treatment of boys and girls, the variety of textbooks and materials used, and whether or not teachers are sensitive to issues of sex discrimination. Also, we take advantage, when we can, of events on women's issues going on at the nearby University of New Hampshire. When we study poems, after an initial mini-unit or two of looking at the same poems as a whole class, students choose an individual woman poet to study in some depth. Selections from the Folsom and Kirschner anthology comprise the initial mini-unit; students then choose collections by individual women poets for in-depth study. Each student presents her or his poet according to certain guidelines; presenters must photocopy one or two of the poems by their poet for their classmates to read and consider as they explicate. A good oral component of the course, these presentations also expose students to a number of women poets.

In another project students bring in one or two songs having to do with women and music. They must provide a typed copy of the lyrics for photocopying. We introduce this unit by playing a selection of music from Holly Near, Ronnie Gilbert, Tracy Chapman, and the Australian songwriter/singer Judy Small. These songs are political and deal also with social and cultural issues in this country and around the world. The class brainstorms what we mean by the terms "women's music" or "women and music." We look at treatment of women in lyrics written by men and differences in styles of singing by men and women. Students become more aware of women's issues by analyzing the lyrics of the songs.

Ultimately all of the materials—the books we read, the stories, poems, articles, plays, and videos we study—heighten students' consciousness and expose them to many women writers they never encountered before. Students, both male and female, are grateful for the exposure, the experience, the discussions. Sometimes girls wish there were more boys in the class. Sometimes boys feel personally attacked, as if we're conducting an anti-male or male-bashing course, an impression that's sometimes hard to dislodge. We tell the male students repeatedly not to take remarks personally, that we are talking about the patriarchal system and what institutionalized sexism has done to make women second-class citizens, not about the boys themselves.

Adrienne Rich, in her poem "Integrity" (1981), refers to "a wild patience." This oxymoron names exactly the particular strength we need to carry on the work of weaving in the women. Patience becomes "wild" indeed when women continue to be accused of being too demanding, too shrill, too militant in simply asking to be treated equally with men.

The Rebecca West epigraph that opened this chapter reminds us that "precisely what feminism is" may become much clearer by the end of our course. We hope that no student will expect women to be doormats, and that young women will feel comfortable refusing to be doormats.

And as Emma Goldman reminds us in the second epigraph, women can achieve true freedom, development, and independence only through themselves. We must "name ourselves," as Adrienne Rich says in our rationale for the course; and, having named ourselves, we must accept ourselves and move forward. As teachers we must encourage all our students, male and female, to know themselves, accept those selves, and develop them to their fullest potential.

Works Cited

ANGELOU, MAYA. 1970. *I Know Why the Caged Bird Sings.* New York: Bantam.

BRONTË, CHARLOTTE. 1988. *Jane Eyre.* New York: Signet. Other editions available.

CATHER, WILLA. 1976. "The Sentimentality of William Tavener." In Folsom and Kirschner.

CHOPIN, KATE. 1972. *The Awakening.* New York: Bard/Avon. Various editions available, many of which have selected short stories, too.

———. 1976. "The Story of an Hour." In Folsom and Kirschner.

CROW DOG, MARY, with RICHARD ERDOES. 1990. *Lakota Woman.* New York: Grove Weidenfeld.

DINESEN, ISAK. 1976. "The Ring." In Folsom and Kirschner.

DONOVAN, MARY. 1982. "Why Study Women?" *Darmouth Alumni Magazine* (October).

DRABBLE, MARGARET. 1965. *Thank You All Very Much* (originally published as *The Millstone*). New York: Signet.

EAGLETON, SANDRA. 1988. *Women in Literature: Life Stages Through Stories, Poems, and Plays.* Englewood Cliffs, NJ: Prentice-Hall.

ELLERBEE, LINDA. 1990. "The Feminist Mistake." *Seventeen* 49 (March): 274–75.

FIRST, RUTH. 1989. *117 Days.* New York: Monthly Review Press.

FOLSOM, MARCIA MCCLINTOCK, and LINDA HEINLEIN KIRSCHNER, eds. 1976. *By Women: An Anthology of Literature.* Boston: Houghton Mifflin.

FREEMAN, MARY WILKINS. 1976. "A New England Nun." In Folsom and Kirschner.

GILMAN, CHARLOTTE PERKINS. 1976. "The Yellow Wallpaper." In Folsom and Kirschner. Also 1973. New York: Feminist Press.

GLASPELL, SUSAN. 1976. "Trifles." In Folsom and Kirschner (and in a number of anthologies).

GOLDMAN, EMMA. 1984. Quoted in Candace Falk, *Love, Anarchy, and Emma Goldman: A Biography,* p. 125. New York: Holt, Rinehart and Winston.

GRIMKÉ, SARAH. 1983. "The Bonds of Womanhood." In Zak and Moots.

HYMOWITZ, CAROL, and MICHAELE WEISSMAN. 1978. *A History of Women in America.* New York: Bantam.

LESSING, DORIS. 1976. "An Old Woman and Her Cat." In Folsom and Kirschner.

MITCHELL, S. WEIR. 1985. "Rest." From *Fat and Blood: And How to Make Them.* In Angela G. Dorenkamp, John F. McClymer, Mary M. Moynihan, and Arlene C. Vadum, eds., *Images of Women in American Popular Culture.* New York: Harcourt Brace Jovanovich.

MUNRO, ALICE. 1977. "Spelling." In *The Beggar Maid: Stories of Flo and Rose.* New York: Bantam.

PRAGER, EMILY. 1982. "A Visit from the Footbinder." In *A Visit from the Footbinder and Other Stories.* New York: Vintage.

RHYS, JEAN. 1982. *Wide Sargasso Sea.* New York: Norton.

RICH, ADRIENNE. 1979. "Claiming an Education." In *On Lies, Secrets, and Silence: Selected Prose, 1966–1978.* New York: Norton.

———. 1979. "*Jane Eyre*: The Temptations of a Motherless Woman." In *On Lies, Secrets, and Silence: Selected Prose, 1966–1978.* New York: Norton.

———. 1981. "Integrity." In *A Wild Patience Has Taken Me This Far.* New York: Norton.

STANTON, ELIZABETH CADY et al. 1983. "Declaration of Sentiments and Resolutions" (Seneca Falls Woman's Rights Convention, July 20, 1848). In Zak and Moots.

STONE, LUCY. 1983. "Disappointment Is the Lot of Women." Speech delivered by Lucy Stone extemporaneously before a national women's rights convention in 1855 when most colleges were not open to women. In Zak and Moots.

TRUTH, SOJOURNER. 1983. "Keeping the Thing Going While Things Are Stirring." In Zak and Moots.

WELTY, EUDORA. 1975. "A Worn Path." In Susan Cahill, ed., *Women and Fiction: Short Stories by and About Women.* New York: New American Library.

WEST, REBECCA. 1985. Quoted in Cheris Kramare, and Paula A. Treichler, *A Feminist Dictionary.* London: Pandora.

ZAK, MICHELE WENDER, and PATRICIA A. MOOTS. 1983. *Women and the Politics of Culture.* New York: Longman.

Videos Cited

"Killing Us Softly: Advertising's Image of Women." 1978. Cambridge Documentary Films. 30 minutes (color). Narrated by Jean Kilbourne.

The Long Walk Home (film)

"The Life and Times of Rosie the Riveter." 1980. Directed by Connie Field. 60 minutes.

"She's Nobody's Baby." 1982. Susan Dworkin. Deerfield, IL: MTI Teleproduction, Inc. 56 minutes. A look at how far women have come since the nineteenth century. Documentary footage.

"Still Killing Us Softly: Advertising's Image of Women." c.1988. Cambridge Documentary Films. 32 minutes (color). Jean Kilbourne with an update of "Killing Us Softly."

"True Light: The Life of Marilla Ricker." 1991. Hampton Falls, NH: Presto! Productions.

"Warning: The Media May Be Hazardous to Your Health." 1990. By Jenai Lane. Santa Cruz, CA: Media Watch.

A World Apart (film)

Suggested Books for Students

Novels and Plays

BROWN, RITA MAE. 1973. *Rubyfruit Jungle*. New York: Bantam. A coming-of-age novel about Molly Holt, lesbian. Affirming, humor-filled, positive image of gay life. Many individual students over the years have asked for this book.

HELLMAN, LILLIAN. 1974. *The Children's Hour*. In Victoria Sullivan and James Hatch, eds., *Plays by and About Women*. New York: Vintage.

HENLEY, BETH. 1982. *Crimes of the Heart*. New York: Dramatists Play Service. Pulitzer-Prize-winning play suitable for in-class oral reading to study the personalities, experiences, values, and dreams of three very different sisters. Three male roles also provide a range.

HOFFMAN, ALICE. 1979. *The Drowning Season.* New York: Fawcett.

———. 1982. *White Horses.* New York: Putnam.

———. 1985. *Fortune's Daughter.* New York: Ballantine.

———. 1987. *Illumination Night.* New York: Putnam.

KELLEY, EDITH SUMMERS. 1982. *Weeds.* New York: Feminist Press. A bleak but honest portrayal of a rural Kentucky woman married to a tenant farmer.

KONECKY, EDITH. 1987. *Allegra Maud Goldman.* New York: Feminist Press. A wonderfully perceptive, wise, feisty, funny novel about a young Jewish girl growing up in Depression-era Brooklyn—not poor but decidedly misunderstood. Resurrected from undeserved obscurity.

LE GUIN, URSULA. 1969. *The Left Hand of Darkness.* New York: Grosset & Dunlap. Science fiction at its best.

MERRIAM, EVE, PAULA WAGNER, and JACK HOFSISS. 1989. "Out of Our Fathers' House." In Sylvan Barnet et al., eds., *Types of Drama: Plays and Essays.* Glenview, IL: Scott, Foresman. A hypothetical conversation between six of the women from Eve Merriam's anthology of journals and letters, *Growing Up Female* (1971). The women are Eliza Southgate, Elizabeth Cady Stanton, Maria Mitchell, Mother Jones, Dr. Anna Howard Shaw, and Elizabeth Gertrude Stern. A marvelous vehicle for having students learn about these important women in history and about the issues they raised. Personal and conversational, the women "live" their lives in the conversations, and, since the words are taken from their actual writings, this drama reinforces our belief in the importance and necessity of honoring women's journals and letters as viable forms of literature.

OATES, JOYCE CAROL. 1966. *A Garden of Earthly Delights.* New York: Fawcett.

PIELMEIER, JOHN. 1978. *Agnes of God.* New York: Plume. Provocative play that raises issues of psychology and religion in women's lives; features a psychiatrist and two nuns.

RICE, ANNE. 1976. *Interview with the Vampire.* New York: Ballantine. This is Book One of *The Vampire Chronicles.* Forceful and compelling confessions of a vampire that students love.

————. 1985. *The Vampire Lestat.* New York: Ballantine. Book Two of *The Vampire Chronicles.* Lestat, the vampire hero, has evolved from an aristocrat of prerevolutionary France to a 1980s rock star. He searches through the centuries for others of his ilk; complex and hypnotizing.

SHANGE, NTOZAKE. 1975–77. *For Colored Girls Who Have Considered Suicide When the Rainbow Is Enuf.* New York: Bantam. A choreopoem. Series of vignettes of women showing their anger at poor treatment by men.

SMEDLEY, AGNES. 1987. *Daughter of Earth.* New York: Feminist Press. A harsh, bleak book about the struggle of a working-class person to survive in poverty and deprivation. Anticipates the contemporary feminist movement's concerns about class.

WASSERSTEIN, WENDY. 1991. *The Heidi Chronicles and Other Plays.* New York: Vintage. Also contains *Uncommon Women and Others* and *Isn't It Romantic.*

WINTERSON, JEANETTE. 1985. *Oranges Are Not the Only Fruit.* New York: Atlantic Monthly Press. The trials and tribulations of a young lesbian growing up in a dour and repressed Evangelical religious household in England. Funny!

Autobiography and Biography

BAEZ, JOAN. 1987. *And a Voice to Sing With.* New York: Summit.

CARY, LORENE. 1991. *Black Ice.* New York: Knopf. One of the first females—and also black—at St. Paul's School looks back on her years at the prestigious preparatory school, recalling her ambivalent feelings.

CHOPIN, KATE. 1990. *Kate Chopin* by Emily Toth. New York: Morrow. A biography that makes an admirable effort to connect the people in Chopin's life with some of her characters.

COLLINS, JUDY. 1987. *Trust Your Heart: An Autobiography.* Boston: Houghton Mifflin.

CONWAY, JILL KER, ed. 1992. *Written by Herself: Autobiographies of American Women, An Anthology.* New York: Vintage. Selections from twenty-five writings, spanning 150 years with sections, such as "My Story Ends with Freedom," "Research Is a Passion with Me: Women Scientists and Physicians," "Arts and Letters," and "Pioneers and Reformers."

DINESEN, ISAK. 1987. *Out of Africa.* New York: Crown. Similar to Beryl Markham, Dinesen, a strong, independent, passionate woman, confronts adventure, sacrifice, illness, love, and work in early twentieth-century Nairobi.

EARHART, AMELIA. 1970. *Winged Legend: The Life of Amelia Earhart* by John Burke. New York: Berkley.

FRENCH, EMILY. 1987. *Emily: The Diary of a Hard-Worked Woman.* Lincoln: University of Nebraska Press. Writing in her diary in 1890, Emily French recorded her austere life and the difficulties she experienced as a divorced woman trying to survive without alimony or child support.

HURSTON, ZORA NEALE. 1979. *A Zora Neale Hurston Reader: I Love Myself When I Am Laughing . . . and Then Again When I Am Looking Mean and Impressive.* Ed. Alice Walker. New York: Feminist Press. A little bit of everything by Hurston. A wonderful introduction to her.

KINGSTON, MAXINE HONG. 1975. *The Woman Warrior: Memoirs of a Girlhood Among Ghosts.* New York: Vintage. Combines myth, tradition, nonfiction, and poetry. Chapters can be read separately; recommended for mature readers. Shows the double displacement of the Chinese American girl/woman.

KUSZ, NATALIE. 1990. *Road Song: A Memoir.* New York: Farrar, Straus & Giroux. Contemporary story of California family resettling in Alaska. Natalie suffers severe facial damage from an attack by a husky when she is six during their first winter. But the book attests to the family's enduring courage, sensitivity, and wisdom in dealing with the tragedy, and how ultimately they transcend it.

MOODY, ANNE. 1968. *Coming of Age in Mississipi.* New York: Dell. One of the early civil rights memoirs by a black woman; written without sentimentality and with honesty; a good companion piece to Maya Angelou's *I Know Why the Caged Bird Sings.*

MORGAN, SALLY. 1987. *My Place.* New York: Little, Brown. Sally Morgan's search for her own aboriginal people in Australia reads like a mystery novel.

NISA. 1981. *Nisa: The Life and Words of a !Kung Woman* by Marjorie Shostak. New York: Vintage. Nisa is a member of the !Kung tribe of hunters and gatherers from southern Africa's Kalahari desert. Excellent collaboration between the woman and the author; extraordinarily strong woman whose life included adventure and tragedy but who showed an indomitable spirit.

PLATH, SYLVIA. 1977. *Letters Home by Sylvia Plath: Correspondence 1950–1963.* Ed. Aurelia Schober Plath. New York: Bantam. Interesting to try to figure out what Mrs. Plath may have excised from her daughter's letters.

PRETTY-SHIELD. 1974. *Pretty-shield: Medicine Woman of the Crows* by Frank B. Linderman. Lincoln: University of Nebraska Press. Pretty-shield told her story of what it was like before the white people came and the buffalo went away.

RICH, LOUISE DICKINSON. 1970. *We Took to the Woods.* Camden, ME: Down East. Inspirational account of the author's life in the woods in Maine in the 1930s.

SARTON, MAY. 1968. *Plant Dreaming Deep.* New York: Norton. Honest, tough, provocative. Another of her journals.

———. 1973. *Journal of a Solitude.* New York: Norton. Continues Sarton's honest journals of daily life and philosophical thinking; shows her closeness to nature, books, music.

SIMON, KATE. 1982. *Bronx Primitive: Portraits in Childhood.* New York: Harper & Row. Coming-of-age story of an immigrant in the years after World War I. Takes Kate up to the age of thirteen; strong feminist undercurrent. Book has been followed by two more volumes covering later years in the author's life (see below).

———. 1986. *A Wider World: Portraits in an Adolescence.* New York: Harper & Row.

———. 1990. *Etchings in an Hourglass.* New York: Harper & Row.

SMEDLEY, AGNES. 1988. *Agnes Smedley: The Life and Times of an American Radical* by Janice R. MacKinnon and Stephen R. MacKinnon. Berkeley: University of California Press. An inspiring account of a passionate American radical. Shows her time spent in China and her understanding of Chinese history.

STONE, LUCY. 1981. *Loving Warriors: Selected Letters of Lucy Stone and Henry B. Blackwell, 1853–1893.* Ed. Leslie Wheeler. New York: Dial. Reveals strong woman who entered into a marriage of equality and kept her own birth name. Henry emerges as very sympathetic male.

TALLCHIEF, MARIA. 1973. *Maria Tallchief* by Marion E. Gridley. Minneapolis, MN: Dillon Press. Vivid descriptions of Tallchief's hard work in her career as a ballerina.

TARBELL, IDA M. 1985. *All in the Day's Work: An Autobiography*. Boston: G. K. Hall. The life story of the most important muckraker of her time. First published in 1939.

TRUITT, ANNE. 1986. *Turn: The Journal of an Artist*. New York: Viking. A continuation (begun in her earlier *Daybook*) of her exploration of her life as woman, artist, and mother.

WAUNEKA, ANNIE. 1972. *Annie Wauneka* by Mary Carroll Nelson. Minneapolis, MN: Dillon Press. A biography of the woman who made her life's work health improvement for her Navajo people.

Women Poets: Collections

AKHMATOVA, ANNA. 1973. *Poems of Akhmatova*. Ed. Stanley Kunitz. Boston: Little, Brown.

FORCHÉ, CAROLYN. 1981. *The Country Between Us*. New York: Harper & Row.

GIOVANNI, NIKKI. 1975. *The Women and the Men*. New York: Morrow.

GLÜCK, LOUISE. 1968. *Firstborn*. New York: Ecco.

———. 1975. *The House on Marshland*. New York: Ecco.

———. 1980. *Descending Figure*. New York: Ecco.

———. 1985. *The Triumph of Achilles*. New York: Ecco.

HARJO, JOY. 1983. *She Had Some Horses*. New York: Thunder's Mouth Press.

KENDRICK, DOLORES. 1984. *Now Is the Thing to Praise*. Detroit: Lotus Press.

———. 1989. *The Women of Plums: Poems in the Voices of Slave Women*. New York: Morrow.

KENYON, JANE. 1986. *The Boat of Quiet Hours*. St. Paul, MN: Greywolf Press.

———. 1990. *Let Evening Come.* St. Paul, MN: Greywolf Press.

KUMIN, MAXINE. 1982. *Our Ground Time Here Will Be Brief: New and Selected Poems.* New York: Penguin.

———. 1985. *The Long Approach.* New York: Viking.

———. 1989. *Nurture.* New York: Viking.

———. 1992. *Looking for Luck.* New York: Norton.

LORDE, AUDRE. 1978. *The Black Unicorn.* New York: Norton.

———. 1982. *Chosen Poems—Old and New.* New York: Norton.

———. 1986. *Our Dead Behind Us.* New York: Norton.

PIERCY, MARGE. 1982. *Circles on the Water: Selected Poems.* New York: Knopf.

———. 1983. *Stone, Paper, Knife.* New York: Knopf.

———. 1985. *My Mother's Body.* New York: Knopf.

———. 1988. *Available Light.* New York: Knopf.

RICH, ADRIENNE. 1993. *Collected Early Poems, 1950–1970.* New York: Norton.

RUKEYSER, MURIEL. 1978. *The Collected Poems.* New York: McGraw Hill.

SAPPHO. 1958. *Sappho.* Ed. and trans. Mary Barnard. Berkeley: University of California Press. A new translation.

SARTON, MAY. 1974. *Collected Poems; 1930–1973.* New York: Norton. Other, later collections also available.

SEXTON, ANNE. 1981. *The Complete Poems.* Boston: Houghton Mifflin.

SHANGE, NTOZAKE. 1978. *Nappy Edges.* New York: Bantam.

WAKOSKI, DIANE. 1974. *Trilogy.* New York: Doubleday.

———. 1988. *Emerald Ice: Selected Poems, 1962–1987.* Santa Rosa, CA: Black Sparrow Press.

Women Poets: Anthologies

BARAKA, AMIRI (LeRoi Jones) and AMINA BARAKA, eds. 1983. *Confirmation: An Anthology of African American Women.* New York: Quill. Biographical material at end of book. Has a table of contents but no index.

BARNSTONE, ALIKI, and WILLIS BARNSTONE, eds. 1992. *A Book of Women Poets from Antiquity to Now.* New York: Schocken. Revised and with an expanded section of American poets. Selections from all over the world. Biographical information with the poems, many of which are, of course, translations. Well indexed.

BERNIKOW, LOUISE, ed. 1974. *The World Split Open: Four Centuries of Women Poets in England and America, 1552–1990.* New York: Vintage. Includes an excellent forty-five page introduction by Bernikow and brief biographical entries on all the poets.

KONEK, CAROL, and DOROTHY WALTERS, eds. 1976. *I Hear My Sisters Saying: Poems by Twentieth-Century Women.* New York: Crowell. Divided into sections with headings such as "I am trying to think how a woman can be a rock," "Sister, let the rain come down," and "Now you are my literary ghost," this anthology includes many poets, both well known and little known. Has good indexes for titles, first lines, and poets; contains biographical material on poets in back of book.

PIERCY, MARGE, ed. 1987. *Early Ripening: American Women's Poetry Now.* New York: Pandora. Good range of contemporary women poets. Biographical material at end of book. Table of contents but no index.

SEWELL, MARILYN, ed. 1991. *Cries of the Spirit: A Celebration of Women's Spirituality.* Boston: Beacon. Over three hundred poems and a few prose pieces by contemporary writers like Angelou, Dillard, Piercy, and Walker, and earlier writers such as Hildegard of Bingen and Margaret Fuller. Organized by themes such as "Owning Self," "Generations," "Death and Lesser Losses." Index by topics and allusions; another index of contributors.

Useful Works for Teachers

ABEL, ELIZABETH, MARIANNE HIRSCH, and ELIZABETH LANGLAND. 1983. *The Voyage In: Fictions of Female Development.* Hanover, NH: University Press of New England. Challenges the *Bildungsroman* novel, traditionally male-centered, by analyzing novels of female development from nineteenth-century through modern novels. Shows that in many cases women's development comes after marriage and children. Includes study of such novels as *Villette, Little Women, The Mountain Lion,* and *Maud Martha.*

ASHER, CAROL, LOUISE DeSALVO, and SARA RUDDICK, eds. 1984. *Between Women: Biographers, Novelists, Critics, Teachers, and Artists Write About Their Work on Women.* Boston: Beacon. Women artists in a variety of fields talk about the women who have inspired them and helped to shape their work. Samples: Alice Walker on Zora Neale Hurston; Martha Wheelock on May Sarton; Leah Blatt Glasser on Mary Wilkins Freeman; Jane Lazarre on Charlotte Brontë.

BEER, PATRICIA. 1974. *Reader, I Married Him. A Study of the Women Characters of Jane Austen, Charlotte Brontë, Elizabeth Gaskell, and George Eliot.* New York: Barnes & Noble. The first chapter discusses the novelists themselves as their own lives related to women's position in society. The other chapters concentrate on the novels and in particular on the variety of experiences in which not only the main characters but also the minor women characters engage.

BELL-SCOTT, PATRICIA, et al., eds. 1993. *Double Stitch: Black Women Write About Mothers and Daughters.* New York: Perennial. Nonfiction, fiction, and poetry, tracing bonds between mothers and daughters. Excellent bibliography.

BERNIKOW, LOUISE. 1981. *Among Women.* New York: Harper Colophon. Hard to categorize this book in which Bernikow, talking with her friends, discusses women and their relationships in life and literature. Has chapters such as "Cinderella: Saturday Afternoon at the Movies," "Mothers and Daughters: Blood, Blood and Love," and "The Light and the Dark: White Women Are Never Lonely; Black Women Always Smile." The book's introduction gets us off to a great start with Bernikow reading the passage from Woolf's *A Room of One's Own,* "Chloe Liked Olivia." Then Bernikow ruminates on the fact that women are too often seen in literature only in relation to men; while men are *not* seen only as lovers of women but in terms of their friendships, careers, adventures, and battles. Then she moves into a study of women's lives and all that they include besides men.

CAHILL, SUSAN, ed. 1978. *Women and Fiction 2: Short Stories by and About Women.* New York: Mentor. This collection, her *Women and Fiction,* and *New Women and New Fiction* are useful supplementary texts.

CLINE, SALLY, and DALE SPENDER. 1987. *Reflecting Men at Twice Their Natural Size.* New York: Henry Holt. The authors talked with over 280 women and learned that women are still trained to be second-class citizens. Sample chapters are "Schooling for Subordination," "The Mandatory Smile and the Obligatory Orgasm," and "Harmony in the Home." Witty, informative, incisive, insightful.

DAVIDSON, CATHY N., and E. M. BRONER, eds. 1980. *The Lost Tradition: Mothers and Daughters in Literature.* New York: Ungar. Various writers from different disciplines, and from several countries, examine connections between mothers and daughters from 2300 B.C. into the twentieth century. How have the daughters accepted or rejected the traditions of the mothers? Examines various genres from myths and novels to diaries and oral tradition. Some topics explored include mother as loving role model in the works of Willa Cather, Colette, and Virginia Woolf; motherless Victorian heroines as seen in the works of George Eliot, Jane Austen, and their contemporaries; and reconciliation and healing in the contemporary literature of Toni Morrison, Adrienne Rich, Simone de Beauvoir, and Maya Angelou.

DONOVAN, JOSEPHINE. 1983. *New England Local Color Literature: A Woman's Tradition.* New York: Ungar. Studies of Harriet Beecher Stowe, Sarah Orne Jewett, Rose Terry Cooke, Elizabeth Stuart Phelps, and Mary E. Wilkins Freeman, showing how each writer rejected romantic stereotypes and portrayed strong women in their realistic local settings.

DUBOIS, ELLEN CAROL, ed. 1981. *Elizabeth Cady Stanton, Susan B. Anthony: Correspondence, Writings, Speeches.* New York: Schocken. DuBois's informative introduction places the material in context. It is invaluable to have these important documents together in one place so that students can appreciate the great contribution to women's rights made by these two extraordinary women. Both students and teachers can read this.

FRIEDAN, BETTY. 1963. "The Problem That Has No Name." In *The Feminine Mystique.* New York: Norton. We often use this as a consciousness-raising article at the beginning of our women's literature course along with the Ellerbee, Stone, and Donovan pieces.

GILBERT, SANDRA M., and SUSAN GUBAR. 1979. *The Madwoman in the Attic: The Woman Writer and the Nineteenth-Century Literary Imagination.* New Haven: Yale University Press. Feminist readings of the great English women novelists of the nineteenth century and the American poet Emily Dickinson. Dip into it and take what you like. Jane Austen, the Brontës, George Eliot are all introduced in Part One, which points out the limitations of an "explicitly patriarchal theory of literature" so far as women writers are concerned.

HEILBRUN, CAROLYN G. 1988. *Writing a Woman's Life.* New York: Norton. Heilbrun makes the point that, for the most part, until recently, biographies of women have had to downplay their assertive and powerful sides; the more bold and adventurous spirits of women have been revealed in their diaries and correspondence. Heilbrun calls for a synthesis of the two so that we can get a picture of the whole woman.

———. 1990. *Hamlet's Mother and Other Women.* New York: Ballantine. A collection of essays written between 1972 and 1988 (except for "The Character of Hamlet's Mother," which was written in 1957 before Heilbrun became a feminist). The range is exciting: from Margaret Mead to Harriet Vane in Dorothy Sayers's detective novels; from May Sarton to Virginia Woolf; from Louisa May Alcott to Vera Brittain.

HUNGRY WOLF, BEVERLY. 1980. *The Ways of My Grandmothers.* New York: Quill. Oral histories of the women of the Blackfoot Nation. The title is explained by the fact that, in keeping with tribal custom, all the old women of the past are the author's grandmothers.

MOERS, ELLEN. 1976. *Literary Women: The Great Writers.* New York: Doubleday. One of the early feminist literary books that investigated writers from Fanny Burney to Erica Jong to show that the word "feminine" is a much more inclusive adjective than historicaly or generally accepted. Moers shows how new genres and new insights came about as women became more assertive and more aware. Particularly good chapters are "Money, the Job, and Little Women: Female Realism" and "Metaphors: A Postlude."

MOGLEN, HELEN. 1976. *Charlotte Brontë: The Self Conceived.* New York: Norton. An important and accessible biography of Charlotte Brontë, which charts the interaction of Brontë's life and her novels and in so doing presents a feminist reading of both the life and the work. Excellent discussion of *Jane Eyre.*

OLSEN, TILLIE. 1978. *Silences.* New York: Delacorte. A potpourri of facts, essays, statistics, musings, and quotations showing the silences in the careers of famous writers and ones that never got started. Shows the relationship between the circumstances of one's life, such as gender, race, class, and the creation of written literature. A delightful book that one can read straight through or root around in.

SALMONSON, JESSICA AMANDA, ISABELLE D. WAUGH, and CHARLES G. WAUGH, eds. 1991. *Wife or Spinster: Stories by Nineteenth-Century Women*. Camden, ME: Yankee Books.

STEINEM, GLORIA. 1992. "Romance Versus Love." Chapter 6 of *Revolution from Within: A Book of Self-Esteem*. Boston: Little, Brown. Steinem makes an interesting case for the love between Jane Eyre and Edward Rochester being more enduring than the romance between Catherine Earnshaw and Heathcliff in *Wuthering Heights*, beginning with dictionary definitions of "romance" and "love."

TURKEL, KATHLEEN DOHERTY. 1986. "Teaching About Women to Male-Identified Students." *Teaching Sociology*. 14 (July):188–190.

WHITE, BARBARA A. 1985. *Growing Up Female: Adolescent Girlhood in American Fiction*. Westport, CT: Greenwood. This engaging study begins with girl protagonists before 1920 and continues right up through modern times with Jean Stafford's *The Mountain Lion* and Carson McCullers's *The Member of the Wedding*, and on into contemporary literature with Claudia in Toni Morrison's *The Bluest Eye* and a discussion of Beth Gutcheon's *The New Girls*.

TWELVE

Evaluation

The people I love the best
jump into work head first
without dallying in the shallows
and swim off with sure strokes almost out of sight.

MARGE PIERCY
"To Be of Use"

We're not the only teachers who rejoice when our students outgrow us, when they fly off, no longer imping on our wings, but stretching out on their own, when they become restive and impatient with high school, when they write their best on end-of-unit papers and final exams. We're not the only teachers who dread grading because, for one thing, some of the most important things we want students to learn can't be tested or measured easily. And we're not the only teachers who look high and low for ways for students to show us what they know.

When we have given workshops on bringing women and student-centered pedagogy into English programs, one of the first questions asked is about how to test. If we don't give lectures and set the topics to be studied or discussed, if students lead discussion, and if we don't reach closure, what kinds of things can we put on a test? Good question. Like you, we've experimented, talking out our goals for units and courses. Generally, what we want is for students to figure out what a piece of writing means to them and why: how it makes them feel and why, what they learned, and what in the text taught them. We want them to be more skillful readers, picking up all the clues in the content and seeing the artistry in the presentation. And we want them to see ways different works relate to each other. Tests, then, become opportunities for students to review what they know and capture it in some form for others to understand and enjoy.

This chapter describes evaluation techniques not suggested in the earlier chapters.

When we give reading check quizzes, we usually pick a number of quotes for students to identify for speaker, situation, and why they think the quote is important to the story or novel so far. The idea is not to trip up students, but to inspire them to think about the story. The quotes are selected to be instructive and memorable, the sort to hang your hat on as it were. At the end of a unit on short stories, we sometimes take such a quote from each story, asking students to identify the author and title and then discuss how any three of the quotes connect to their stories as a whole (they reread the stories to prepare, and in the process rethink them). Very few students miss the authors and titles, and very few fail to connect the quotes in interesting ways, though some may be less able writers.

Instead of having tests on novels, we ask students to write papers. We used to type lists of possible topics, but now we brainstorm with the students, putting ideas on the board and asking if everyone has some ideas for a paper when we've finished. Students think of other topics at home and often combine topics. Whatever they do, they've decided; it's their choice; they're responsible. Because they have a stake in the topic, they usually write their best and work hard to make their thinking and writing clear, knowing that we have no conclusions in mind. We have, of course, been telling them all along that they need to support their conclusions with details from the text, that we cannot read their minds, that they are not to wallow around in generalities, and that their grade depends upon how well they present their ideas, not on how much we agree with them.

To help students work their way through a difficult reading assignment, a Shakespearean play for ninth graders for instance, try assigning each student (or two or three students together, depending on your class) a word, a motif, a theme, or a concept. Students look for the item as they read, noting pages and events and even writing out appropriate passages. At the end of the reading and other activities, students share their discoveries. One way a colleague managed it was to have the class sit on the floor in a circle and invite one student to say something about his or her topic. She handed the student a large ball of string. Then another student was invited to make a connection between the previous student's comments and her or his topic. The ball of string passes to the second student while the first holds on to the end. The second speaker passes the ball to the third, holding on to a loop of the string, and so on until everyone has had something to tie in and each holds a place on the string. The result is a visible web. Afterwards, students write on their word, motif, theme, or concept, explaining the places it comes up in the text and how it relates to the work as a whole. (Of course, sharing without using the string works also.) The resulting paper replaces a test.

Another colleague found a delightful way to have students write on a final exam about some of the works and characters encountered during the course. This works well with short story units or even a longish play, when some complex people or villains have played major roles. Students pick three or four characters from a list and write in the characters' voices, accounting for their behavior. What an opportunity for students to write about Jack in *Lord of the Flies*, Lady Macbeth, Ma Blackie in *The Bride Price*, or Daisy in *The Great Gatsby*.

Chapter 6 included some ideas about using projects. Since we find these can be difficult to grade in and of themselves, we insist that students provide written explanations of any projects. These rationales reveal the student's process, thinking, and command of his or her focus and information. Also, the quality of the writing influences the grade. That way, effort alone is not the sole basis for the grade; besides, we don't feel comfortable judging the artistic merit of a project. In writing the rationale, students show their thinking about what they know. For students with little artistic ability, providing a rationale equalizes the assignment. In one course after finishing a unit on identity, students created some sort of visual to represent something of themselves. Some did collages, one brought in a bag of items associated in her mind with important aspects of herself, a young man created a sculpture of personal items, another represented himself as he would like to be. Sharing these—passing them around the class, listening to students talk about them—perks us all up. In an American literature class one year, we talked about the viability of having a senior project as a graduation requirement, with students given at least one semester to work on it. (Projects could be anything from building a dinghy or testing a hypothesis on sources and solutions for local pollution problems to holding a recital or reporting on the expanding desert in sub-Sahara Africa.)

If students have been working collaboratively, evaluation should include some group paper, project, or task as well as something from individuals. If the collaborative task has been complex enough, the group activity will most likely draw upon a variety of skills for students to complete it, so that computer, artistic, verbal, and organizing skills will be as necessary as writing skills. In such group work, homework should be shared with group members rather than collected and graded; classroom activities should provide chances to experiment rather than items to be evaluated. Group members could take some responsibility for reviewing individual papers both before and after revision.

We've puzzled over ways to meet the different learning styles of students in testing situations. One way is to have choices, to offer more than one question, topic, or task to meet a variety of learning styles. We want all students to be successful in testing situations if they have done the work up to testing time. So we think about having something factual and structured, something personal and interpretive, something conceptual and issue-oriented, and something of an exploratory nature for students to do.

We like to have students use what they know in discussing a new situation when they take a test. Sometimes that means ranking some main characters from a group of short stories from, say, most to least courageous or lonely. Students' rankings differ widely. That's fine. What we're interested in are their reasons for their rankings, their criteria, their ability to compare and contrast the characters and use

254

the facts from the stories. When ninth graders read *Julius Caesar*, for example, they may have to rank the four main characters from most to least responsible for the chaos in Rome following Caesar's death or to rank these men according to how ambitious they were.

We believe that people prove what they can do by doing, not by remembering what they've done. Therefore, after studying a group of poets, we present students with unfamiliar poems by each of the authors we've been studying and invite students to pick two and write a response/analysis of each, also showing how each connects to other poems by that author. The best papers reflect students' knowledge of some hallmarks of the poets and include some specific images and details from the earlier poems.

If we've been reading a variety of works from several genres on a theme, we might assign a test paper based on one of several topics we've devised. Such a paper might be written at home. It would certainly be open book. For example, for a unit on diversity, a topic might be like the following:

> During this unit we have listened to many voices. What three voices do you think should be heard and why? What did you hear each voice saying?

For a unit on personal values we might ask:

> One purpose of this unit has been to explore our values, what we think is important or fair. Choose the three works that most success-fully helped you think about your values. What values did each raise? How exactly did the work raise the question of values? (Refer to specifics here—who did what, when, where.) What effect did the work have on you and your thinking?

Or for a unit on identity:

> Often it is difficult to be an individual in the midst of tradition, convention, and peer pressure. Discuss how three people we've read about in this unit defy the norm to become themselves.

Since no right answers exist for such questions, students' grades depend upon the strength of their thinking, the clarity of their writing, their ability to organize their material, and their use of information from the works read. We enjoy reading such papers, for they introduce us to new ways to think and feel about the works.

Sometimes as part of a final exam in a literature course, we ask students to memorize a short poem or a stanza or a passage from a prose piece from among all they have read during the course and, after writing it out, explain why they found it worth remembering. Most students get an A because they write with such passion and eloquence.

In survey courses such as American or English literature, we do not expect students to reread everything for the final exam. Rather, we ask them to read whatever moved them, interested them, delighted them, puzzled them, or irked them, and then check to see that they have selected from each unit or period studied and that they have been inclusive: prose and poetry, white and nonwhite authors, male and female authors. We also explain approximately how many authors and works they will be expected to write about. With this preparation, they not only strengthen their acquaintance with some authors and works, probably revisiting those they have written about before, but also bring the whole scope and sequence of the literature into focus. Exam questions, then, invite students to discuss in some depth works that matter to them. Actually, these questions could be used for any course with substantial reading. Some sample questions follow.

One term often used in connection with twentieth-century American literature is "slice of life." In such literature the author takes a slice of the real world and examines it. Select at least ———— works that you think deal with significant and vivid slices of life. Explain what each slice is about, how it is significant, and why it is significant and vivid.

In his famous "I Have a Dream" speech, Martin Luther King, Jr., said: "I say to you today, my friends, that in spite of the difficulties and frustrations of the moment I still have a dream. It is a dream deeply rooted in the American dream." Discuss some of the dreams and/or nightmares found in the literature of this course by examining at least ——— works.

Sometimes when you read, you encounter a character you get to care about so that when the work is over, you feel cheated somehow—as if you'd like to know more about this person. Select ——— characters from your reading this semester [or year] and make me understand by the eloquence and specificity of your writing why these people matter to you. (You could, if you wish, include people whom you would *not* like to know, but who impressed you.)

Pick ——— poems that compel you because of their stunning imagery. Describe each in some detail and then explain how these images, and consequently the poems, affect you.

Great literature should lift us out of ourselves, should take us on a journey away from our concerns with just ourselves. If this great literature cannot galvanize us into some new awareness, appreciation, or insight, it should at least provide what Robert Frost called "a momentary stay against confusion," a little breathing space between the urgencies and necessities of everyday life. Choose ——— works and show how they have influenced your thinking, broadened your horizons, or in some way added to your knowledge.

America's people comprise a delightful stew at a full boil, its various ingredients swirling together, bumping, nudging, rising to the top, and sinking. Discuss ——— works, each a different voice but each an American voice. What does each have to say? Not all white voices are the same, not all black voices are the same. If the ingredients could speak, what would they say about this stew, about their place in it or contribution to it?

Study the following quotation from the comic strip *Pogo*: "We have met the enemy and he [she] is us." Pick ——— characters from the reading this semester and discuss how their stories show to what extent the statement is true or false. What does the statement imply about human beings? How much do you agree with its implications, and why?

Annie Dillard wrote: "Why are we reading, if not in hope of beauty laid bare, life heightened and its deepest mystery probed? . . . Why are we reading, if not in hope that the writer will magnify and dramatize our days, will illuminate and inspire us with wisdom, courage and the hope of meaningfulness, and press upon our minds the deepest mysteries, so we may feel again their majesty and power? . . . Why does death so catch us by surprise, and why love? We still and always want waking." Discuss ———— works that awakened you, explaining how you were awakened and what you were awakened to in each case.

We hope that long before the end of a course students understand we have no required interpretations or a short list of important authors or works they should adopt as their own. When we request papers on topics such as those above, we have the pleasure of reading pages of interesting, often new, interpretations of and connections between works; some are even written with passion.

And so, at the end of courses, even at the end of units, students strike out on their own, at our invitation and with our blessing, swimming away. Some flounder, out of shape or lazy, when the going gets a little deep; others paddle around shallows, not yet ready or willing to move out; and some "swim off with sure strokes almost out of sight." Part of the great fun of watching the strong swimmers is knowing what they sometimes do not yet know: they're using their own power, power they've accumulated for themselves because they've welcomed opportunity just about every time it has come along.

Works Cited

PIERCY, MARGE. 1973. "To Be of Use." In *Circles on the Water: Selected Poems of Marge Piercy.* New York: Knopf.

Epilogue
What's Gained? What's Lost?

The function of freedom is to free somebody else.

TONI MORRISON

In the end, what is gained from weaving in the women is the empowerment of students, female and male, the quiet as well as the louder ones. Students get excited about learning and want to know more. They want to make more and more connections to what they've read previously and to their own lives. After they've read enough, they can begin to appreciate a culture totally different from theirs so that they can have some idea of what life actually was like for Edna Pontellier in *The Awakening* or for the reluctant bride in Alice Walker's "Roselily." Their minds begin to wander in preferred directions; they won't stay rigidly on the questions-after-the-story page in the textbook. They want to read more. Students have increased self-esteem because they're taken seriously. They are more willing to take risks, to be vulnerable.

Girls and boys see with Louisa May Alcott that women have not been given a fair shake through history—that they were forced to lead diminished lives, but that those lives and accomplishments, experiences, and perspectives were nevertheless important. We hope students will continue to value the study of women and that it will inform their lives—their thinking, their work, and their relationships.

As teachers, we spend less time reading critics and less time becoming experts. We start with what students know. Writing problems decrease because students write about what they like and what they know. The concept of an expert reading of a text vanishes. But we do not allow off-the-wall reading of a text, not at all; we must be grounded in the words of the author, but from there we are free to soar and dip and cruise, guided initially by the author's language.

Here is a student response to Section II of Adrienne Rich's poem "North American Time," read in American Literature II:

> Adrienne Rich is discussing the "terms" of being a poet. You must know, when you start, that anything you write down on paper, no matter how slight or large your intentions, "will be used against [you]." I suppose what it comes down to is that you have a choice in whether you are willing to give people your words, knowing full well that they may later twist them, use them to "be blazed on a wall in spraypaint." The poet decides to "take" the terms, in the hopes of showing people a new way of seeing, in the hopes that their intentions will be somewhat apparent, but also knowing that "[their] words stand / become responsible / for more than [they] intended." Rich's poem pointed out to me, more clearly than I had ever seen before, the tragedy and strength of being a poet, using "verbal privilege," which seems such a contradiction. By discussing and trying to interpret poems too much we can do more harm than good, and twist the meaning. But what Rich says is that, as a poet, you must know this when you write even the smallest thing because "poetry never stood a chance / of standing outside history." Realize the responsibility of your words.

Another student, after reading Alice Walker's poem "On Stripping Bark from Myself," concentrated on the lines in the first stanza about not being willing to keep silent while others label her a "nice" woman. She wrote, among other things:

> I'm never sure what to think when someone says "you don't *look* like a feminist," or "but you aren't one of *those* feminists" ("how *nice* she is!"). I'm inclined to be angered by those comments because they

show both a too narrow perception of me and a generalization about what feminists are like. Sometimes, though, it pleases me to hear that, pleases me to know that there *is* more to me than what they can see. There is also the satisfaction of knowing that I do not conform to any stereotypical image of the feminist. Nor do I conform to their assumptions about a well-groomed, middle class young woman. Hearing comments like those, I am also confirmed in my conviction that it is ignorance and narrow-mindedness which creates negative assumptions about feminists. My identity is, to them, an exception to the rule, though in fact I am only one person among many who proves their rule incorrect. We refuse to accept the "adoration of the retouched image," and must strip bark from ourselves, as Walker says. . . . This poem is specifically affirming to women, who "are expected to keep silent." Walker emphatically and sensitively applauds the struggle of women to live as *themselves,* and *for* themselves, standing strong in a conformity-oriented world. It is this in the poem that touches me deeply.

We free students from their fear of the authority figure in the classroom, the one who has the power, who figures the grade, who helps decide whether they get into the college of their choice or not. We begin to engage in a true dialogue of learners. We as teachers may know more than our students about many literary and academic subjects, but none of us can take to any work of literature the particular perspective of any of our young charges. They show us new angles from which to consider literature. At the very least they own their responses, as we can see from the two papers just quoted.

What are some drawbacks? Students have much to adjust to; they're often used to doing what they are told. Student-centered pedagogy puts a big responsibility on them. Some aren't ever able to make connections or tie the various strands of the course together. Some never learn to direct their contributions in class to their peers rather than to the teacher. Some students find this approach too unstructured and essay questions too amorphous: not enough questions on specifics, details, dates, authors' names, characters' names. Some students are much more comfortable memorizing information about authors and works, and they look in vain in their notes for the teacher's pronouncement of a story's theme. This pedagogy can breed discomfort, but discomfort leads to change and growth.

Girls may become overprotective of boys in a women's literature unit or course. Other girls, strong young women, become uneasy with the frequent laments in women's literature, and they snap out denials and reminders that, after all, women have come a long way, men are oppressed too, and this isn't just an issue for women.

In group work shy and lazy students can hide. In structured discussion some students can opt to pass and avoid having to speak up. Students can come to class unprepared and jump into discussion after it gets going and they find an opening, especially if no writing has been assigned.

What's lost? First of all, we lose some content; we can't teach *all* the men and *all* the women, too. We must make some hard choices. We lose our own agendas, what we used to think were *the* important outcomes in studying any work of literature. We must respect a student's analysis if she or he has considered a work thoroughly and honestly and has paid attention to the total story, to all of its details, to its language, and includes all of these in his or her paper.

Something else lost in student-centered classrooms is closure. Little or no closure frustrates those students wanting things tied up neatly. We have had students, very conscientious ones, raise their hands and say, "I've looked over my notes and I can't find what decision we reached about that story yesterday. Did it have a point, or is it just telling us about a slice of time in the lives of the characters?" or "What lesson is this story supposed to be teaching us?" Indeed, we may simply have generated more questions than answers. Ultimately students have to accept some ambiguity in literature as in life and learn to live with it. The solid blacks and whites of childhood give way to an increasing gray in adolescence, in books as well as in life.

And further, some colleagues will scoff openly or behind your back about your too-loose approach to learning and to academics. They may imply that you do not have high enough standards. They may suggest that students should pay more attention to learning names and dates, to analyzing traditional aspects of literature, to studying the classics. Of course, we disagree.

What we have been promoting in this book is worth the struggle because we as teachers are freed from the burden of false notions of ourselves as experts, pouring the truth into student vessels. Having achieved the freedom to teach honestly and inductively, and to start where the students are, we free students to ask their own questions, fulfilling Toni Morrison's admonition in this chapter's epigraph. Students frame the debate and the discussion, and they hone their skills; they learn to use their own tools. They keep asking questions of us, of other teachers, of their peers, of their parents. They see connections between life and literature and between different works of literature. They build bridges to the literary islands they particularly like, as mentioned in Chapter 2, so that "over time a webwork of bridges begins to bind the islands together until a whole land/seascape evolves."

We think the jury is in, and that the research is clear on the need for all of us to study about all of us in order to have a fuller understanding of humankind. We can't help being opened and broadened and deepened from learning about women and their literature. In the next hundred or so years, perhaps we can sort it all out somehow and decide what are the best works by writers of both sexes and from all the various cultures, races, and ethnicities to put into the ideal high school literature anthology. In the meantime, we must keep reading, selecting, balancing, and offering the best that we have retrieved thus far. We must keep these works before our students, our colleagues and administrators, parents, school board members, our communities, and the world at large so that Dale Spender will not have to do a new edition of *Women of Ideas and What Men Have Done to Them.* In "Each One, Pull One," Alice Walker speaks for all the dissenters, all the different ones, buried by people in power. We must heed her rallying cry and apply it to women writers: we must pull them all "back into the sun."

Those of us who treasure words and books and who deal with them on a daily basis must continue to demand that women's writing everywhere be recorded, published, valued, shared, and taught so that everyone can know the truth of those experiences. We must seek to uncover women's words about their experiences, and not accept only the male views, the male versions, and the historical trivialization or obfuscation or demeaning and ultimate erasing of women's writing. Images of diving, exploration, water, and wrecks wind through Adrienne Rich's poetry to suggest women's search for the truths of their own experiences, as opposed to men's interpretations of those experiences. In "Diving into the Wreck" the speaker goes over the side of the boat, alone, to explore what is down there in the water, to see for herself what the wreck is all about. Like Adrienne Rich we must search for the "wreck" and "not the story of the wreck." Those of us who insist on the truth and "not the myth" cannot unknow what we have come to know. We have seen the "wreck," women's experience, as it has been rediscovered and retrieved in the words of women's writing and not in the "story" that men have told about women's writing. We are everywhere, and we invite others to join us in seeing that our students also use words as "purposes" and "maps" to discover and appreciate the enriched tapestry of their English curriculum when we weave in the women.

Works Cited

MORRISON, TONI. 1981. Quoted in Amy Shapiro, ed., *A Woman's Notebook II.* Philadelphia: Running Press.

RICH, ADRIENNE. 1984. "Diving into the Wreck" and "North American Time." In *The Fact of a Doorframe: Poems Selected and New, 1950–1984.* New York: Norton.

SPENDER, DALE. 1982. *Women of Ideas and What Men Have Done to Them: From Aphra Behn to Adrienne Rich.* London: Routledge.

WALKER, ALICE. 1972. "Roselily." In *In Love and Trouble: Stories of Black Women.* San Diego: Harvest/Harcourt Brace Jovanovich.

———. 1984. "On Stripping Bark from Myself." In *Good Night, Willie Lee, I'll See You in the Morning.* San Diego: Harvest/Harcourt Brace Jovanovich.

———. 1986. "Each One, Pull One." In *Horses Make a Landscape Look More Beautiful.* San Diego: Harvest/Harcourt Brace Jovanovich.

Further Works for Teachers
Anthologies

ALEXANDER, JO, DEBI BERROW, LISA DOMITROVICH, MARGARITA DON-
NELLY, CHERYL McLEAN, eds. 1986. *Women and Aging: An Anthology by
Women.* Corvallis, OR: Calyx. A wide-ranging collection including
photography, essays, fiction, poetry, profiles, art, and book reviews. An
extensive bibliography.

ALLEN, PAULA GUNN, ed. 1989. *Spider Woman's Granddaughters: Traditional
Tales and Contemporary Writing by Native American Women.* Boston:
Beacon. Storytellers represented include Louise Erdrich, Linda Hogan,
Pretty-Shield, Vickie Sears, Mary Tall Mountain, and others; they are
varied in lifestyle, age, and attitude.

ANDERSON, LORRAINE, ed. 1991. *Sisters of the Earth: Women's Prose and
Poetry About Nature.* New York: Vintage. Various sections such as "Her
Pleasure: The Delight We Take in Nature," "Her Wildness: What Is
Untamed in Nature and in Us," and "Her Solace: How Nature Heals
Us." Writers include Emily Dickinson, Opal Whiteley, Marjorie Kin-
nan Rawlings, Sarah Orne Jewett, Joy Harjo, and Maxine Kumin.

ANTLER, JOYCE, ed. 1980. *America and I: Short Stories by American Jewish
Women Writers.* Boston: Beacon. Chronologically arranged from 1900 to
1988, these stories offer a variety of scenes and characters. They exem-
plify the book's epigraph by Marge Piercy: "A woman and a Jew, sometimes more of a contradiciton than I can sweat out, yet finally the
intersection that is both collision and fusion, stone and seed" (from
"The Ram's Horn Sounding" in *Available Light*) .

ANZALDUA, GLORIA, ed. 1990. *Making Face, Making Soul (Haciendo Caras): Creative and Critical Perspectives by Women of Color.* San Francisco: Aunt Lute. A powerful collection of material that is sometimes raw, often eloquent, and always provocative.

ASIAN WOMEN UNITED OF CALIFORNIA, ed. 1989. *Making Waves: An Anthology of Writings by and About Asian American Women.* Boston: Beacon. Autobiographical writings, short stories, poetry, essays, and photographs by and about women in America who trace their roots to China, Japan, Korea, the Philippines, India, Pakistan, Vietnam, Cambodia, Burma, and Thailand.

BOSTON, ANNE, ed. 1988. *Wave Me Goodbye: Stories of the Second World War.* New York: Viking. Stories written primarily between 1939 and 1949, mostly by British women (five are American). Includes Elizabeth Bowen, Kay Boyle, Doris Lessing, Barbara Pym, Stevie Smith, Jean Stafford, and Sylvia Townsend Warner, among others.

BROWN, WESLEY, and AMY LING, eds. 1991. *Imagining America: Stories from the Promised Land.* New York: Persea. A multicultural anthology of thirty-seven short stories from 1900 to the present. Follows immigration and migration within the United States. Includes African, Asian, Latino, Native American, Jewish, Middle Eastern, and European writers.

BRUNER, CHARLOTTE H., ed. 1983. *Unwinding Threads: Writing by Women in Africa.* Portsmouth, NH: Heinemann. Short stories and novel excerpts from women writers from all over Africa. Organized by geographical area; includes a map in the front of the book to show where the different contributors come from.

CAHILL, SUSAN, ed. 1989. *Among Sisters: Short Stories by Women Writers.* New York: Mentor. Twenty stories about sisters by American, British, and Irish women writers.

ESTEVES, CARMEN C., and LIZABETH PARAVISINI-GEBERT, eds. 1991. *Green Cane and Jucy Flotsam: Short Stories by Caribbean Women.* New Brunswick, NJ: Rutgers University Press. A rich collection of twenty-seven stories, some written originally in English; others, originally in French, Dutch, and Spanish, have been translated. Writers are from Guadeloupe, Dominica, Jamaica, Trinidad, Puerto Rico, Martinique, Antigua, Haiti, Cuba, the Dominican Republic, and Surinam. Along with tales from the oral tradition and stories that present women's views on the history of Caribbean slavery, the collection conveys the cadences of the language of Caribbean women.

FANNIN, ALICE, REBECCA LUKENS, and CATHERINE HOYSER MANN, eds. 1979. *Woman: An Affirmation.* Lexington, MA: D.C. Heath. An assortment of many genres (short stories, folktales, poems, drama, autobiography) organized around themes such as self-definition, autonomy, and women's life experiences. Mostly contemporary women writers, although there are a couple of male authors, several early-twentieth-century women writers, and a few nineteenth-century women.

FERGUSON, MARY ANNE, ed. 1986. *Images of Women in Literature.* 4th ed. Boston: Houghton Mifflin. Stories and poems by men and women organized around themes. Twenty pages of suggestions for further reading at end, including two excellent annotated lists, one of anthologies of literary criticism and one of anthologies of literature by women.

FRANKLIN, PENELOPE, ed. 1986. *Private Pages: Diaries of American Women, 1830s–1970s.* New York: Ballantine. A fascinating collection of excerpts from previously unpublished diaries and journals of women found in archives around the country. One woman is a Japanese-American writing at age nineteen when she was interned at Tule Lake Relocation Center during World War II. Another is a midwestern farm wife trapped in a loveless marriage in the 1890s. Photographs of many of the women.

GISCILO, HELENA, ed. 1989. *Balancing Acts: Contemporary Stories by Russian Women.* New York: Dell. Nineteen stories (a few authors represented by more than one story) show the conflicts Russian women suffer in having to balance professional and domestic lives.

GREEN, RAYNA, ed. 1984. *That's What She Said: Contemporary Poetry and Fiction by Native American Women.* Bloomington: Indiana University Press. More poetry than fiction. Many pieces by each contributor; also a photo of each contributor. Excellent extended glossary at end and a bibliography of further readings. Louise Erdrich, Joy Harjo, Gladys Cardiff, Linda Hogan, and Wendy Rose, among others.

KILGORE, EMILIE S., ed. 1991. *Contemporary Plays by Women*. New York: Prentice Hall. Outstanding winners and runners-up for The Susan Smith Blackburn Prize (1978–1990). Playwrights included are Marsha Norman, Wendy Kesselman, Lynn Siefert, Tina Howe, Anne Devlin, Caryl Churchill, and Lucy Gannon. Introduction by Wendy Wasserstein.

KOPPELMAN, SUSAN, ed. 1985. *Between Mothers and Daughters: Stories Across a Generation*. New York: Feminist Press. One of several anthologies that Koppelman has published in her determination to return to print women's writing that has not been anthologized because books historically have overwhelmingly overrepresented male writers. An informative introduction and informational biographical sketches about the women writers. Dates of stories range from 1848 (Caroline W. Healey Dall) to 1980 (Ann Allen Shockley).

———. 1988. *"May Your Days Be Merry and Bright" and Other Christmas Stories by Women*. Detroit: Wayne State University Press. Fifteen stories from the past 120 years. Louisa May Alcott, Elizabeth Stuart Phelps, Sarah Orne Jewett, Mary Wilkins Freeman, Willa Cather, Dorthy Canfield Fisher, Grace Paley, and Ntozake Shange are some of the writers included.

———. 1991. *Women's Friendships: A Collection of Short Stories*. Norman: University of Oklahoma Press. Collection shows the many roles of friendship, and also the conditions and concerns, in women's lives throughout American history. Good bibliography of articles and books on women's friendships.

LIM, SHIRLEY GEOK-LIN, and MAYUMI TSUTAKAWA, eds. 1989. *The Forbidden Stitch: An Asian American Women's Anthology*. Corvallis, OR: Calyx. A collection of writers and artists, many of whom are young and being published for the first time. Includes poetry, fiction, artwork, and reviews. Extensive bibliographies (not annotated).

MARTIN, MOLLY, ed. 1988. *Hard-Hatted Women: Stories of Struggle and Success in the Trades*. Seattle, WA: Seal. A collection of twenty-six articles in which women in nontraditional blue-collar work talk about their experiences. Phone repair technician, fisher, steelworker, sprinkler fitter, police officer—these are just some of the occupations covered. Funny, inspirational, and powerful.

MARTIN, WENDY, ed. 1990. *We Are the Stories We Tell: The Best Short Stories by North American Women Since 1945*. New York: Pantheon. Includes classic writers such as Eudora Welty, Joyce Carol Oates, and Flannery O'Connor right up through contemporary women writers like Bobbie Ann Mason, Sandra Cisneros, Francine Prose, Toni Cade Bambara, and Leslie Marmon Silko. Good biographical information on contributors.

MARTZ, SANDRA, ed. 1987. *When I Am an Old Woman I Shall Wear Purple: An Anthology of Short Stories and Poetry*. Manhattan Beach, CA: Papier-Mache Press. An anthology devoted to the theme of women and aging. Illustrated with photographs of real elderly women, but not the women in the stories.

————. 1990. *If I Had a Hammer: Women's Work in Poetry, Fiction, and Photographs*. Watsonville, CA: Papier-Mache Press. A wide-ranging, multicultural collection in which women describe and celebrate their work, in traditional and nontraditional jobs, at home and in the workplace, with humor, wit, power, and eloquence.

MERRIAM, EVE, ed. 1987. *Growing Up Female in America: Ten Lives*. Boston: Beacon. Excerpts from the writings of Eliza Southgate, Elizabeth Cady Stanton, Maria Mitchell, Mary Ann Webster Loughborough, Arvazine Angeline Cooper, Dr. Anna Howard Shaw, Susie King Taylor, "Mother" Mary Jones, Elizabeth Gertrude Stern, and Mountain Wolf Woman. There is also a wonderful section at the end called "Attic," a potpourri of documents that didn't fit into the framework of the book proper. Examples: "A Young Girl's Day Work, 1775" and "Investigation of the Ku Klux Klan 1871—Testimony Taken by the Joint Select Committee to Inquire into the Condition of Affairs in the Late Insurrectionary States. Examination of the colored woman, Hannah Tutson. Testimony taken from her."

MOFFAT, MARY JANE, and CHARLOTTE PAINTER, eds. 1975. *Revelations: Diaries of Women*. New York: Vintage. Samples of the diaries from thirty-two women from the early nineteenth century to the recent past.

Presented under three themes: love, work, power. Some women included: Louisa May Alcott, Anne Frank, George Sand, Anaïs Nin, Ruth Benedict, Alice James, George Eliot, Käthe Kollwitz, Selma Lagerlof, Katherine Mansfield, and Emily Carr.

MORAGA, CHERRIE, and GLORIA ANZALDUA, eds. *This Bridge Called My Back: Writings by Radical Women of Color.* Watertown, MA: Persephone. A strong and powerful feminist collection of prose, poetry, personal narrative, and analysis by African American, Asian American, Latina, and Native American women.

MORGAN, ROBIN, ed. 1970. *Sisterhood Is Powerful: An Anthology of Writings from the Women's Liberation Movement.* New York: Vintage. First comprehensive collection from the Women's Movement of the 1960s and 1970s; includes articles, poems, photographs, and manifestoes. Captures the range of problems considered by feminists at the time. Interesting now as both a historical document and a comparison with women's issues today.

MORRIS, HOLLY, ed. 1991. *Uncommon Waters: Women Write About Fishing.* Seattle, WA: Seal. Stories, poems, memoirs, and essays. Includes "The Treatise of Fishing with an Angle," circa 1421, by Dame Juliana Berns, supposedly the first published essay on sport fishing by man or woman. Contemporary writers include Margaret Atwood, Audre Lorde, Linda Hogan, Tess Gallagher, and many others.

PARK, CHRISTINE, and CAROLINE HEATON, eds. 1989. *Close Company: Stories of Mothers and Daughters.* New York: Ticknor & Fields. The wide range of feelings and emotions in the mother-daughter relationship is reflected in a compilation of diverse writers from around the world. From Ama Ata Aidoo of Kenya ("The Late Bud") to Fay Zwicky from Australia ("Hostages") to Zhang Jie from Beijing ("Love Must Not Be Forgotten"), this is an eclectic delight. The more familiar American and English writers are also included: Sue Miller, Margaret Atwood, Fay Weldon, Alice Munro, Jamaica Kincaid.

PAYNE, KAREN, ed. 1983. *Between Ourselves: Letters Between Mothers and Daughters, 1790–1982.* Boston: Houghton Mifflin. A wide range; includes Lady Mary Wortley Montagu to her daughter Mary Bute

(1751–53); Lucy Stone to her mother Hannah (1846); Amelia Earhart to her mother Amy (1928); and three Indian women: Mira, her mother (Protima), and her daughter (Rita).

PHELPS, ETHEL JOHNSON. 1981. *The Maid of the North: Feminist Folktales from Around the World.* New York: Holt, Rinehart and Winston. Twenty-one traditional tales, chosen for their spunky, nontraditional heroines.

PORTER, ANDREW J., JR., HENRY L. TERRIE, JR., and ROBERT A. BENNETT, eds. 1984. *American Literature.* Lexington, MA: Ginn and Company.

ST. AUBIN DE TERAN, LISA, ed. 1990. *Indiscreet Journeys: Stories of Women on the Road.* Boston: Faber and Faber. An interesting collection of twenty-six stories of women who took to the road or some other form of escape, for a short time or for a lifetime. The stories range over two centuries and six continents. In a few cases, the fiction is excerpted from novels, but most of the entries are bona fide short stories. A few of the authors: Toni Cade Bambara, Isabella Bird, Colette, Beryl Markham, Dorothy Parker, Sylvia Townsend Warner, and Malachi Whitaker.

SENNETT, DOROTHY, ed. 1988. *Full Measure: Modern Short Stories on Aging.* St. Paul, MN: Greywolf Press. Stories by both men and women. The women include Carol Bly, Joyce Carol Oates, Grace Paley, Hortense Calisher, Nadine Gordimer, Jean Rhys, and Arthenia J. Bates.

———. 1991. *Vital Signs: International Stories on Aging.* St. Paul, MN: Greywolf Press. Many women from around the world represented: Tatyana Tolstaya from Russia, Elizabeth Jolley from Australia, Zhang Jie from China, Leslie Marmon Silko from the United States, to name a few. Reflects the different perspectives on aging in various cultures.

SMITH, BARBARA, ed. 1983. *Home Girls: A Black Feminist Anthology.* New York: Kitchen Table/Women of Color Press. A collection of short stories, poems, photographs, essays, and literary criticism by contemporary black women, including Toi Derricotte, Alexis de Veaux, Michelle Cliff, Audre Lorde, Cheryl Clarke, Donna Kate Rushin, Luisah Teish, and Bernice Johnson Reagon.

271

SOLOMON, BARBARA, 1986. *American Wives: Thirty Short Stories by Women.* New York: Mentor.

———. 1989. *American Families: Twenty-Eight Short Stories.* New York: Mentor. Fourteen stories by men and fourteen by women cover the diversity of American families.

WASHINGTON, MARY HELEN, ed. 1987. *Invented Lives: Narratives of Black Women, 1860–1960.* New York: Anchor. Novel excerpts and short stories from Harriet Jacobs, Zora Neale Hurston, Gwendolyn Brooks, Frances Harper, Pauline Hopkins, Nella Larsen, and Dorothy West.

———. 1991. *Memory of Kin: Stories About Family by Black Writers.* New York: Anchor. Stories from 1899 to 1989. Valuable commentaries sprinkled throughout.

WILKERSON, MARGARET B., ed. 1986. *Nine Plays by Black Women.* New York: Mentor. Includes a fragment from Lorraine Hansberry's unfinished historical drama *Toussaint* and Aishah Rahman's *Unfinished Women Cry in No Man's Land While a Bird Dies in a Gilded Cage,* an underground classic of teenage pregnancy. Also Ntozake Shange's "spell #7."

ZAHAVA, IRENE, ed. 1991. *My Mother's Daughter: Stories by Women.* Freedom, CA: Crossing Press. Decidedly multicultural.

ZIPES, JACK, ed. 1986. *Don't Bet on the Prince: Contemporary Feminist Fairy Tales in North America and England.* New York: Methuen. The women writers assembled here, whether they identify themselves as feminist or not, have written innovative stories (sometimes in the form of poems) that break with the traditional fairy tale. Also includes a section on feminist literary criticism, with four essays on how fairy tales play an important role in early socialization.

Resource Books

BANK, MIRRA. 1979. *Anonymous Was a Woman.* New York: St. Martin's. Invaluable collection of materials from the eighteenth and nineteenth centuries; reproductions of samplers, paintings, quilts, and needle-pictures are grouped with etiquette books, ladies' magazines, and excerpts from diaries and letters of women of all ages.

BROWNMILLER, SUSAN. 1975. *Against Our Will: Men, Women, and Rape.* New York: Bantam. An early, important book on this subject, it paved the way for the many studies that have succeeded it.

BROWNSTEIN, RACHEL M. 1982. *Becoming a Heroine: Reading About Women in Novels.* New York: Viking. Witty and wise, this book shows how women define themselves and their lives in terms of novels. Several great novels by women or with women as protagonists are analyzed, including *Mrs. Dalloway, Daniel Deronda,* and *The Portrait of a Lady.*

COTT, NANCY F. 1972. *Root of Bitterness: Documents of the Social History of American Women.* Boston: Northeastern University Press. Invaluable primary source material, from the church trial of Ann Hibbens to an excerpt from Charlotte Perkins Gilman's *Women and Economics.*

———. 1987. *The Grounding of Modern Feminism.* New Haven: Yale University Press. For those who want more historical background on feminism, this well-written study of post–1920s feminism documents problems, such as racism and class prejudice. Inclusive of black women and working-class women's activities.

DAVIS, ANGELA Y. 1981. *Women, Race and Class.* New York: Vintage. An investigation of how the three themes of the title converged in the growth of American society, and how all this ties in with the women's movement of the 1970s.

———. 1989. *Women, Culture, and Politics.* New York: Random House. Provocative continuation of her earlier book; activist Davis asks the tough questions as she points up the inequities in our culture. She also makes comparisons and contrasts between our culture and that of other countries, for example, Egypt.

DOUGLAS, ANN. 1988. *The Feminization of American Culture.* New York: Anchor. Argues that Victorian America fostered "a sentimental society and the beginnings of modern mass culture." Shows how the popular literature of the time exploited feminine images of powerlessness, piety, and timidity. A little long-winded in places, but worth exploring.

EHRENREICH, BARBARA, and DEIRDRE ENGLISH. 1978. *For Her Own Good: 150 Years of the Experts' Advice to Women.* New York: Anchor.

273

EISENSTEIN, SARAH. 1983. *Give Us Bread But Give Us Roses: Working Women's Consciousness in the United States, 1890 to the First World War.* Boston: Routledge.

ELLMANN, MARY. 1968. *Thinking About Women.* New York: Harcourt Brace Jovanovich. A literary and feminist meditation on women's writing and male criticism. Ahead of its time. Brilliant, witty, hilarious.

EVANS, MARI, ed. 1984. *Black Women Writers (1950–1980): A Critical Evaluation.* New York: Anchor. Organized by authors, each section begins with the author's reflections on her own writing, then is followed by two critical essays, and then biographical and bibliographical information.

FADERMAN, LILLIAN. 1981. *Surpassing the Love of Men: Romantic Friendship and Love Between Women from the Renaissance to the Present.* New York: Morrow. A provocative study in which Faderman constructs a cultural history of women's passionate friendships. A revolutionary book when it was published, it opened the way for subsequent studies of the subject.

FALUDI, SUSAN. 1991. *Backlash: The Undeclared War Against American Women.* New York: Crown. Extensively researched and documented, this book shows that whenever in history women have succeeded in making a few gains in equality, patriarchal forces combine to undermine them and make it seem as if "too much" feminism is a dangerous achievement. Focus, however, is the present.

FAUST, LANGDONE LYNNE, ed. 1983. *American Women Writers: A Critical Reference Guide from Colonial Times to the Present.* 2 vols. New York: Ungar. Contains entries on 400 women.

FAUSTO-STERLING, ANNE. 1985. *Myths of Gender: Biological Theories About Women and Men.* New York: Basic Books. Thorough and objective study of data on the biological basis for gender differences.

FRIEDAN, BETTY. 1963. *The Feminine Mystique.* New York: Norton. The book that had such an influence on women in the 1960s. The chapter entitled "The Problem That Has No Name" has been anthologized many times; it asserts that women in suburbia in the late 1950s weren't happy but didn't know why. The book has been criticized because it focuses primarily on white, middle-class women, but it's still important feminist background reading.

FRYE, JOANNE S. 1986. *Living Stories, Telling Lives: Women and the Novel in Contemporary Experience.* Ann Arbor: University of Michigan Press. In traditional female-centered novels, marriage and death have been the most common plot resolutions. This study shows how a female first-person narrator can shape other lives for herself.

GANNETT, CINTHIA. 1992. *Gender and the Journal: Diaries and Academic Discourse.* Albany: State University of New York Press. Explores the connections between gender studies and psychology of women as they inform writing; sensitive and sophisticated. Gannett uses her own experience as well as research.

GILBERT, SANDRA M., and SUSAN GUBAR, eds. 1979. *Shakespeare's Sisters: Feminist Essays on Women Poets.* Bloomington: Indiana University Press. Nineteen strong essays on women poets, ranging from the seventeenth century to the late twentieth. Title comes form Virginia Woolf's speculation on what would have happened if Shakespeare had had an equally brilliant sister: her work would have been stifled. These essays show the conflicts many of these women had between their art and their society, with its limited expectations for women.

GOODMAN, ELLEN. 1979. *Close to Home.* New York: Fawcett. Collection of her columns from *The Boston Globe.* Insightful, entertaining, informative, and clever.

The Heath Anthology of American Literature. 1990. 2 vols. Lexington, MA: D.C. Heath. Intended for college, but high schools could use. Very inclusive: 2900+ and 2600+ pages of tissue-thin paper; but worth the cost.

JAMES, EDWARD T., ed. *Notable American Women, 1607–1976: A Biographical Dictionary.* 4 vols. Cambridge, MA: Harvard University Press. Entries for 1,359 women!

JELINEK, ESTELLE C., ed. 1980. *Women's Autobiography: Essays in Criticism.* Bloomington: Indiana University Press. After analyzing autobiographies written by women from the seventeenth through the twentieth centuries, the essayists determined that these autobiographies differ from those written by men in form, content, and intention. Women's autobiographies reflect the dailiness of their lives and focus on family, friends, and feelings.

275

KERBER, LINDA K., and JANE DeHART-MATHEWS, eds. 1987. *Women's America: Refocusing the Past.* New York: Oxford University Press. Combines new scholarship on women with primary source documents from 1600 through Betty Friedan's *The Feminine Mystique.* A companion piece to *Root of Bitterness* (Cott 1972).

KIM, ELAINE H. 1982. *Asian American Literature: An Introduction to the Writings and Their Social Context.* Philadelphia: Temple University Press. The title speaks for itself.

OSTRIKER, ALICIA SUSKIN. 1986. *Stealing the Language: The Emergence of Women's Poetry in America.* Boston: Beacon. Surveys women's poetry from the seventeenth century to the present: forms, styles, and criticism. Considering whether there exists an especially female language, a "mother tongue," Ostriker argues that what distinguishes this poetry is not a specific, shared, exclusive female language but "a vigorous and varied invasion of the sanctuaries of existing language." She suggests that revisionist mythmaking in women's poetry is a way to redefine both women and culture.

PRYSE, MARJORIE, and HORTENSE J. SPILLERS, eds. 1985. *Conjuring: Black Women, Fiction, and Literary Tradition.* Bloomington: Indiana University Press. Sixteen perceptive analyses of black women's writing from slave narratives through the fiction of Toni Morrison and Toni Cade Bambara.

RICH, ADRIENNE. 1976. *Of Woman Born: Motherhood as Experience and Institution.* New York: Norton. Deals with the "power and powerlessness embodied in motherhood in patriarchal culture." Rich uses her own personal experience along with research, history, and literature.

ROSSI, ALICE S., ed. 1973. *The Feminist Papers: From Adams to De Beauvoir.* Boston: Northeastern University Press. The "essential works of feminism" published over a period of two hundred years. Another companion piece to *Root of Bitterness* (Cott 1972), but larger and more comprehensive.

SEAGER, JONI, and ANN OLSON. 1986. *Women in the World: An International Atlas.* New York: Simon and Schuster. A complete guide to the global status of women in a very attractive presentation.

SHREVE, ANITA. 1989. *Women Together, Women Alone: The Legacy of the Consciousness-Raising Movement.* New York: Viking. In 1987 seven women gathered for a reunion of their consciousness-raising group from the 1970s. Shreve interviewed them and almost a hundred more women to find out what has happened to women in the intervening time, and to offer a blueprint for new consciousness-raising groups for the 1990s.

SMITH-ROSENBERG, CARROLL. 1985. *Disorderly Conduct: Visions of Gender in Victorian America.* New York: Knopf. Shows how, particularly in New England, the freewheeling Jacksonian society was replaced by the rigidities of class and gender we think of as Victorian; also reveals how women escaped from these constrictions and threatened the new bourgeois social order through a spectrum of "disorderly conduct."

SPACKS, PATRICIA MEYER, ed. 1977. *Contemporary Women Novelists: A Collection of Critical Essays.* Englewood Cliffs, NJ: Prentice Hall. A leading feminist scholar offers an insightful introduction to eleven lively essays on a mix of contemporary British and American writers. Margaret Drabble, Doris Lessing, Mary McCarthy, Iris Murdoch, Ann Petry, Jean Rhys, Muriel Spark, and Eudora Welty are the subjects. Three of the essays are by men (one of whom, you should be warned, is Norman Mailer on Mary McCarthy).

STEINEM, GLORIA. 1987. *Outrageous Acts and Everyday Rebellions.* New York: Signet. A wonderful, wide-ranging collection of Steinem articles, including a tender one about her mother, "Ruth's Song," and a hilarious one, "If Men Could Menstruate."

STERNBURG, JANET, ed. 1980. *The Writer on Her Work: Contemporary Women Writers Reflect on Their Art and Situation.* New York: Norton. Interesting and lively interviews with selected women writers.

———. 1991. *The Writer on Her Work.* Vol. II: *New Essays in New Territory.* New York: Norton. Commissioned essays on what it means to be a woman who writes. Some of the twenty women included in this multicultural collection are Bharati Mukherjee, Harriet Doerr, Elene Poniatowska, Anita Desai, Elizabeth Jolley, Rita Dove, Luisa Valenzuela, and Ursula LeGuin.

TATE, CLAUDIA, ed. 1983. *Black Women Writers at Work.* New York: Continuum. Conversations with fourteen contemporary black women writers. Foreword by Tillie Olsen.

TOTH, EMILY, ed. 1985. *Regionalism and the Female Imagination: A Collection of Essays.* New York: Human Sciences Press. Eleven essays that belie the notion that the greatest works are about war and whale hunting. These essays show that the greatest emotions can be expressed in writings about home and region. Examples of essay titles: "Harriette Arnow's Kentucky Novels: Beyond Local Color" and "Geography as Psychology in the Writings of Margaret Laurence."

WADE-GAYLES, GLORIA. 1984. *No Crystal Stair: Visions of Race and Sex in Black Women's Fiction.* New York: Pilgrim Press. Focuses on black women who have been doubly oppressed because of race and gender. Shows how black women have had to live in relation to white women (as mammies and maids), black men, and their own children. Focuses on the writings of Alice Walker, Toni Morrison, Gwendolyn Brooks, and Ann Petry.

WHITE, BARBARA. 1991. *Edith Wharton: A Study of the Short Fiction.* New York: Twayne. White examines Wharton's short stories from a feminist perspective and from the particular view that Wharton was probably a victim of incest. White also examines Wharton's criticism of the institution of marriage and other social conventions.

WOLF, NAOMI. 1991. *The Beauty Myth: How Images of Beauty Are Used Against Women.* New York: Morrow. Wolf examines the tyranny of the beauty myth on many fronts: work, home, literature, media, relationships.

WOOLF, VIRGINIA. 1928. *A Room of One's Own.* New York: Harcourt Brace Jovanovich. This book should begin and end everyone's list!

Reading for Pleasure

An alphabetical list of authors and titles for your enjoyment. Books are novels unless otherwise indicated.

ATWOOD, MARGARET. *Bodily Harm.*

———. *Lady Oracle.*

BALLANTYNE, SHEILA. *Imaginary Crimes.*

BARRECA, REGINA. *They Used to Call Me Snow White . . . But I Drifted: Women's Strategic Use of Humor* (nonfiction).

BEATTIE, ANN. *Picturing Will.*

BLY, CAROL. *Letters from the Country* (nonfiction).

BRONTË, CHARLOTTE. *Villette.*

BROWN, RITA MAE. *Bingo.*

———. *Six of One.*

———. *Southern Discomfort.*

BUMILLER, ELISABETH. *May You Be the Mother of a Hundred Sons* (nonfiction).

CATHER, WILLA. *My Mortal Enemy.*

———. *Shadows on the Rock.*

CHASE, JOAN. *During the Reign of the Queen of Persia.*

CHERNIN, KIM. *In My Mother's House* (autobiography).

COLETTE. *My Mother's House.*

———. *Sido.*

———. *The Vagabond.*

DAVIDSON, ROBYN. *Tracks* (nonfiction).

DESAI, ANITA. *Clear Light of Day.*

DILLARD, ANNIE. *Pilgrim at Tinker Creek* (nonfiction).

DOERR, HARRIET. *Stones for Ibarra.*

DRABBLE, MARGARET. *The Ice Age.*

———. *The Middle Ground.*

———. *A Natural Curiosity.*

———. *The Needle's Eye.*

———. *The Radiant Way.*

———. *The Realms of Gold.*

———. *The Waterfall.*

ELIOT, GEORGE. *Middlemarch.*

EL SAADAWI, NAWAL. *Two Women in One.*

ERDRICH, LOUISE. *The Beet Queen.*

———. *The Crown of Columbus* (with Michael Dorris).

———. *Tracks.*

FLAGG, FANNIE. *Coming Attractions* (now called *Daisy Fay and the Miracle Man*).

———. *Fried Green Tomatoes at the Whistle Stop Cafe.*

GODWIN, GAIL. *A Mother and Two Daughters.*

———. *The Odd Woman.*

GORDON, MARY. *The Company of Women.*

———. *Final Payments.*

———. *Good Boys and Dead Girls and Other Essays* (nonfiction).

———. *Men and Angels.*

GRAFTON, SUE (mystery writer par excellence). *A Is for Alibi.*

———. *B Is for Burglar.*

———. *C Is for Corpse* (and so on down the alphabet).

GREENE, MELISSA FAY. *Praying for Sheetrock* (nonfiction).

HAIEN, JEANNETTE. *The All of It.*

HEIMEL, CYNTHIA. *If You Can't Live Without Me, Why Aren't You Dead?* (humorous nonfiction).

HOFFMAN, ALICE. *Seventh Heaven.*

———. *Turtle Moon.*

HOLLANDER, NICOLE (humorist; author of the following feminist cartoon books). *I'm in Training to Be Tall and Blonde.*

———. *Ma, Can I Be a Feminist and Still Like Men?*

———. *Never Take Your Cat to a Salad Bar.*

———. *You Can't Take It with You, So Eat It Now!*

HUBBELL, SUE. *A Book of Bees* (nonfiction).

———. *A Country Year* (nonfiction).

HUGGAN, ISABEL. *The Elizabeth Stories.*

JEN, GISH. *Typical American.*

KADOHATA, CYNTHIA. *The Floating World.*

KINCAID, JAMAICA. *At the Bottom of the River.*

———. *Lucy.*

———. *A Small Place* (nonfiction).

KINGSOLVER, BARBARA. *Animal Dreams.*

———. *Another America* (poetry).

———. *Holding the Line: Women in the Great Arizona Mine Strike of 1983.* (nonfiction).

KUMIN, MAXINE. *In Deep: Country Essays* (nonfiction).

LEBOWITZ, FRAN. *Metropolitan Life* (humorous nonfiction).

———. *Social Studies* (humorous nonfiction).

LEGUIN, URSULA. *Dancing at the Edge of the World: Thoughts on Words, Women, Places* (nonfiction).

———. *The Dispossessed* (utopian/feminist vision).

LIGHTFOOT, SARA LAWRENCE. *Balm in Gilead: Journey of a Healer* (biography of the author's mother).

MARKOE, MERRILL. *What the Dogs Have Taught Me and Other Amazing Things I've Learned* (humorous nonfiction).

MARSHALL, PAULE. *Daughters.*

———. *Praisesong for the Widow.*

MASON, BOBBIE ANN. *Love Life* (short stories).

———. *Shiloh and Other Stories.*

MILLER, SUE. *Family Pictures.*

———. *The Good Mother.*

MUKHERJEE, BHARATI. *Jasmine.*

———. *The Middleman and Other Stories.*

MUNRO, ALICE. *Friend of My Youth* (short stories).

———. *The Progress of Love* (short stories).

OATES, JOYCE CAROL. *Because It Is Bitter and Because It Is My Heart.*

———. *Them.*

———. *The Wheel of Love* (short stories).

———. *You Must Remember This.*

PARETSKY, SARA. (mystery writer par excellence—books were written in the following order). *Indemnity Only.*

———. *Deadlock.*

———. *Killing Orders.*

———. *Bitter Medicine.*

———. *Blood Shot.*

———. *Burn Marks.*

———. *Guardian Angel.*

PYM, BARBARA. *Quartet in Autumn.*

QUINDLEN, ANNA. *Object Lessons.*

ROBINSON, MARILYNNE. *Housekeeping.*

RUSS, JOANNA. *The Female Man* (utopian/feminist vision).

SANDEL, CORA. *Alberta and Jacob.*

————. *Selected Short Stories.*

SARTON, MAY. *As We Are Now.*

————. *At Seventy* (journal).

————. *I Knew a Phoenix* (journal).

————. *Kinds of Love.*

————. *The Magnificent Spinster.*

————. *Mrs. Stevens Hears the Mermaids Singing.*

————. *Plant Dreaming Deep* (journal).

————. *A Reckoning.*

————. *Recovering* (journal).

————. *The Small Room.*

SHIELDS, CAROL. *The Republic of Love.*

————. *Swann.*

SIMPSON, MONA. *Anywhere But Here.*

SMILEY, JANE. *The Greenlanders.*

————. *Ordinary Love and Good Will* (two novellas published together).

————. *A Thousand Acres.*

STAFFORD, JEAN. *Boston Adventure.*

TRUITT, ANNE. *Daybook: The Journal of an Artist* (journal).

TYLER, ANNE. *Breathing Lessons.*

————. *Saint Maybe.*

ULLMANN, LIV. *Changing* (autobiography).

WELTY, EUDORA. *Losing Battles.*

————. *The Optimist's Daughter.*

WITZLING, MARA A., ed. *Voicing Our Visions: Writings by Women Artists* (nonfiction).

WOOLF, VIRGINIA. *Moments of Being* (nonfiction).

———. *The Voyage Out.*

ZAROULIS, NANCY. *Call the Darkness Light.*

Index

285

Index

Index

Index

Index

Index